Tales Out Of School

Tales Out of School

*Why 200 teachers say,
"My students are
my best teachers!"*

real-life classroom events in
short story form, seen
through an understanding
of personality styles

PERSONALITY
INSIGHTS

compiled by Robert A. Rohm, Ph.D.

Published by Personality Insights, Inc.
PO Box 28592, Atlanta, GA 30358-0592

Printed in the United States of America

Compiled and edited by Robert A. Rohm, Ph.D.
Cover concept and design, editing and typography by E. Chris Carey
Copyright © 1995, Robert A. Rohm, Ph.D. — All Rights Reserved.

First Edition, October 1995

Library of Congress Cataloging-in-Publication Data

Rohm, Robert A., 1949–
  Tales Out of School
    Why 200 teachers say, "My students are my best teachers!"

    1. Education 2. Classroom discipline

    ISBN Number 0-9641080-2-X

Contents

Dedication

This book is dedicated to

School Teachers and Parents

everywhere — who have all experienced

"one of those stories" with a student

they wish others could have known.

"Children do not make up 100% of our population...
but they do make up 100% of our future!" – *Zig Ziglar*

Introduction

As we begin this study (or better yet... adventure!) together, it might be a good idea to lay out a few ground rules along with a quick review.

Everyone loves stories. Hollywood uses this medium to make billions of dollars each year. Jesus, the greatest teacher who ever lived, used stories as his main method of instruction. Probably no one has opportunity to experience more stories each day than a school teacher. Their environment "gushes" with interaction, excitement, and growth. All of this makes an excellent "spawning ground" for good stories.

The stories you are about to read are the result of a summer training program for approximately 200 teachers, from kindergarten through senior high school. After learning all about the DISC system of personality behavior traits, the teachers were given an assignment. They were to write their best "case study" from their own classroom experiences, applying the principles taught. In reading through their stories, I realized the information had not only been well received by the teachers... it was *caught* by them. And when something is actually caught, then it can really be *taught*.

As the stories were reviewed, several things became evident:

1) Some teachers wrote some of the funniest stories I have ever read. You are in for a real treat! *2)* Some stories revealed teachers as "real people," too. They are still in process, learning how to be good teachers. *3)* A few stories will disappoint you because you will see that the teacher just didn't "get it!" We included these to spur you on to do better. You don't want to be a disappointment to your students who need your help and instruction. *4)* A few teachers were willing to explore their lack of wisdom by revealing how in the past they created some of their own problems. *5)* And a few... well, let's be kind and say, "Some people can show you how *not* to handle a situation!" (By the way, this can prove to be a good teaching tool for seasoned administrators to help newer, less experienced teachers. After reading certain stories, you can see why some teachers have problems... they create them or bring them upon themselves!) *6)* You will get some great classroom ideas you can implement, regardless of the grade level or subject you teach. We did not want to "polish" these stories and make them unbelievable. They are very relatable, understandable and true-to-life. You will relive some past experiences in your own life as you read along. 7) These classroom scenarios will help you to see things that you sometimes overlook. Seeing things in the extreme often helps us to see better in the narrow. Thus, you gain good teaching ideas and methodology.

We designed this book to be very readable. You may want to share some stories with your class in order to reveal the wisdom (or lack of it) in other students... and teachers. They lend themselves to good case study discussions. Of course, all of the teachers and their stories are real — but we have changed or omitted names and places to prevent any writer or character from being too easily identified.

My special thanks goes to my good friend David Derrick, Executive Director of the Mississippi Private Schools Association, and his staff. David has invited me on several occasions to speak at conventions and seminars for a variety of teachers and professional staff. He planted ideas in my mind which ultimately led to this book.

The stories are not always presented in D-I-S-C order. The teachers focused on making the interaction in the stories to communicate, rather than simply to fit a certain formula. This will prove to be of benefit to you, the reader. As you read along, you will find yourself anticipating the students' personality styles before the stories reveal them. In this manner, you read as you grow... and grow as you read!

Lastly, if you are unfamiliar with the D-I-S-C system we refer to in this book, we recommend your purchasing *Positive Personality Profiles* (Robert A. Rohm. Atlanta, Georgia: Personality Insights, Inc., 1994) and *Different Children Different Needs* (Charles F. Boyd, with Robert A. Rohm. Sisters, Oregon: Multnomah Books, 1994). These titles are also available from Personality Insights — see the order form in the back of this book. Learning to understand yourself and others puts all of us in a position to have a better relationship.

Happy reading!

Robert A. Rohm

Robert A. Rohm, Ph.D.

A Brief Review of DISC

It should be stated at the very outset that we are basing this book on the DISC Model of Human Behavior. We have introduced this material to thousands of educators, hoping it will increase their effectiveness in their classrooms. Without understanding the Model of Human Behavior, this book will be meaningless.

Get the Picture

Most people have predictable patterns of behavior — specific personalities. There are four basic types, also known as temperaments. They blend together to determine your unique personality. To help you understand why you often feel, think and act the way you do, the following is a graphic overview of the Four Temperament Model of Human Behavior.

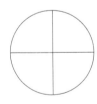

The four types are like four parts of a pie. Before seeing the four parts as they stand alone, let's look at the pie in two parts. These two types are different from each other. Think of it this way: some people are more *outgoing,* while others are more *reserved.*

Outgoing people are more active and optimistic. Reserved types are more passive and pessimistic. One type is not better than the other. Both types of behavior are important. Reserved types need to learn how to be more **d**ominant and **i**nspirational. Outgoing people need to learn how to be more **s**teady and **c**autious.

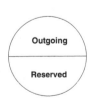

Also, there are two other parts of the pie — two other types of personalities. These are also different from each

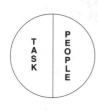

other. Some people are more task-oriented, while others are more people-oriented. Task-oriented types need to learn to relate better with others (*interacting and sharing*). People-oriented individuals need to learn to be more focused on doing "things" (*directing and correcting*).

When you look at the four parts of the pie together, you can visualize the four temperament types. *Everyone is a unique blend of these four parts.* This is a key concept to remember.

You will read how teachers refer to personality "blends." That is, no one is purely a "D" or an "I" or an "S" or a "C." Everyone is a unique blend of these four types. When a teacher refers to a student as an "I with D," you can know she means the student is "**I**nspirational" with some "**D**ominance." A student who is "S with C" means "**S**upportive" with "**C**autious" traits.

If you need to refer to this page or remember these four words, you will have it:

D	=	Dominant
I	=	Inspirational
S	=	Supportive
C	=	Cautious

You will pick up other adjectives describing these personality styles as you read the stories.

Also, you will read such expressions as "high D" or "high C" or "low I" or "low S." The phrases "high" or "low" simply mean more predominate or less dominate in that particular set of traits. If a person is a "high I," he or she is strong or more predominate in "**I**nspirational" characteristics. If they are a "low I," they are weaker or less predominate in those attributes. This, of course, is true for the other traits, as well.

Tales

Out

Of

School

A Report by Robert Rohm
Mrs. Bailey's* Class 6A
Third Ward School

*Mrs. Dottie Bailey was my own 6th Grade
teacher, at Third Ward School in Griffin,
GA (1960–1961). I left behind some of my
own tales to be retold! I love school
teachers… "Mrs. Bailey, may we go out to
recess a little early today, pleeeeease?!"

Junior High Study Hall

After teaching 7th and 9th Grade students all day, I have an end-of-the-day study hall! This is a challenge, especially for me… and *this* is a typical hour in the lives of our students:

Grade averages are due, so this is my chance to catch up on some work. Calling the roll is so much fun with this group. As I am calling the names, in skips Steve, late again. He is an "I," wearing his favorite hat and chewing gum — *Why not?,* he thinks, *it's only study hall?* (Within the confines of our private school, neither activity is allowed.)

Ron (another "I") begs to take my absentee report to the office. It is an "adventure trip" for him. On the way, I know he will swing by the cafeteria, visit other students and get to see who's in trouble in the office. Did I mention stopping by the pay phone? Ron has been sent to the office so many times since 7th Grade, they are thinking of giving him his own mailbox!

Of course, he will be having company on this trip, since our latecomer will have to go to the office as well, for a pink slip. Of course, Steve thinks pink slips are different and kinda cute, like him.

Our two major distractions have left the room. I *think* I can get back to my grade averaging… until Jane comes up to my desk to ask, "How are you averaging the grades?" Jane is a "C" who knows a better, faster, and more efficient way of doing everything. I thank her. She returns to her desk to work on an assignment that is due next week.

Several minutes pass quietly. Then Steve and Ron burst back into the room. Steve is laughing good-naturedly about how he now has more pink slips than any other student! He and Ron exchange stories and wonder aloud, *Does the school give an award for the most unexcused pink slips?*

Ten quiet minutes go by. This is wonderful — then, suddenly I look up. Steve has Matt (an "S" if ever there was one!) around the waist in some sort of wrestling hold. I call tell Matt is in pain, but he pretends he is okay. He so wants to be Steve's friend! I tell Steve to stop. The playing around has turned into trouble. Steve insists he was only playing. Matt and Stan (another "S") even support Steve's idea. When he finally lets go, he is on his way to see the principal... while he is gone, Matt says he hopes Steve is not going to be mad at him.

Steve comes bouncing back into the room, all smiles. The principal is gone for the rest of the day, and because of that Steve thinks he is off the hook. Just then, John (our "D") speaks up from the back of the room — it seems he is the reigning champion of this "waist choking" activity and challenges Steve. I send Steve back to the office unwillingly; he has forgotten about the *assistant* principal who can handle discipline, too. As Steve opens the door, John continues his challenge. I suggest that it would be wise for him to calm down and move to another seat. *John cannot be sent to the office unless his parents know about it* — that's what his mother wrote at the first of the year. (Great... a "D" with parental support!) John refuses to move. He doesn't intend to, ever!

The bell rings. Steve and Ron are the first to jump up and run out. They leave all their books behind. John brags to all who will listen that he didn't move when the teacher told him to. Matt and Stan come by my desk to see if I am mad at them. Jane comes by my desk to ask if I my computations have wrought the same average as she has figured. School is over for the day.

...One last thing before I leave: I have to make a phone call to John's mom. The answering machine again — she is at a party. That explains a lot! Oh well, guess I'll check my mailbox before I leave. *Guess what?* Steve has permission to bring a guest to school tomorrow!!!!!

Looking forward to having an extra "I" in study hall tomorrow... or maybe a "D"... or maybe a "C"... or maybe an "S" like me....

Cheerleader Chaos

Being the Junior High Cheerleader sponsor is an "honor" that has been bestowed upon me for two years at my school. In these two wonderful, exciting years, I have been trying to discover the secret of how to develop a fun, congenial group that works well together! There always seems to be come sort of conflict going on between some of the girls at all times. Up to this point, I have rationalized this as typical of any group of silly, giggly, junior high girls. Now, after just a brief introduction to personality profiles, I can easily see the different personalities reacting differently in the same situation. The following is a true account on such an incident:

Cheerleader practice was scheduled for Wednesday morning, from 8:30 to 11:00. This was the first practice session for the newly elected group of cheerleaders. As the girls were gathering at the football field, the headmaster of my school asked me to come to his office to discuss a matter very briefly. I told Kristen (our "D" type, head cheerleader) to begin teaching the cheers and said I would be back in just a few minutes. The conference with the headmaster took longer than expected, and as I walked out of his office, I walked into "cheerleader chaos."

Julie, a new cheerleader, had arrived to practice 15 minutes late. Kristen had told her to run 15 laps around the football field — one lap for each minute she was late! When I asked why she had done this, she replied, "My rule this year is that everyone must be on time for practice. If you are late, you have to run laps. I don't want to waste time going over something twice because someone can't get here on time. We are going to have a good squad this year if everyone comes to practice. They have to go by my rules, since I'm the head cheerleader." These rules had never been explained to anyone, including me, before this practice. Kristen never seemed to understand that "her" rules needed to be discussed in advance.

At the same time that Kristen was explaining her philosophy to me, Julie — an "S" — was clutching me to keep from passing out after only two laps around the field. I told her she did not have to run 15 laps, but being on time was very important. She "wheezed" this reply: "It was my mother's fault that I'm late. I didn't want to be late, but Mom felt bad this morning and I didn't want to rush her. If you really want me to run laps, I will, even though I may pass out. I really will try never to be late again. Do you want me to run?"

As Julie and I were finishing our talk, Lauren approached me, brimming with "C" questions: "Mrs. O, why are all of you standing over here talking? Why was Julie running around the football field? We are supposed to be practicing and we have wasted at least 30 minutes. I am going to take the new cheerleaders over here in a group and start teaching them. I know all the cheers perfectly, so it won't take me very long. Why isn't this practice more organized? I think I'll write out a schedule for practice and give it to Kristen. There's no sense in wasting time!"

During all of this, two cheerleaders were sitting in the stands — Amy and Morgan, both "I's." They had been calling my name and waving at me continually. "Mrs. O, come over here! We have a great idea!" I finally turned to them and asked, "What wonderful idea do you two have?"

"Mrs. O, we want all 10 cheerleaders to spend the night at your house during our cheerleader clinic! After the clinic is over, we'll go to Pizza Inn for supper! After we eat, we can go to the softball field and watch all the cheerleaders who have games! We can see all our friends who are at the games and show off our new cheerleader shirts! Won't that be fun? We can do it, can't we?"

I left practice feeling like I had been through a whirlwind. I now know that these girls are not incompatible; they simply have different personality styles. Now I can look at them as a group and see each girl as an individual. I am hopeful that I can deal with them more effectively, knowing what to expect from each one.

Classroom Twenty-One

This is a true story. The names and places have been changed to protect the parents of the guilty!

Classroom 21 is occupied by 23 varied students, ranging in personalities, sizes, and academic abilities. The desk in the corner is occupied by "Teacher I" — that's my (uhhh, *her)* personality style. We will not look in her desk, however, where the bottom right drawer is crammed full with all the assigned papers for the past six weeks. We will pretend not to notice that paper clips, rubber bands and stubs of chalk are scattered in the top drawer — nor the spilled, evaporated White-Out® from the bottle that was left open, next to the three pairs of glasses lining the drawer "just in case."

Within minutes of entering Classroom 21, we are able to spot a "D" child — actually, he may be spotted in less time. He used to sit directly in front of the teacher's desk. But now she figures it's not where *he* sits that is as important as *those who sit around him.*

On this particular day, the entire class is alive with excitement. The teacher has written the Class Play and is explaining the parts.

One part of the play features dancing. "Student D" decides that he *will* dance in this role. *He is good — perhaps a young Fred Astaire come back to life,* as (his) rumor has it. *He will die if he can't dance. His grandparents are coming just to see him dance. This is his favorite dance. He must dance!*

Actually, he really is a good dancer and he will get his wish — "Teacher I" wants him to be able to succeed at this. She figures there's a large dose of "I" mixed in with that boy's "D"! His chosen partner is an "I," like her teacher, and is extremely animated by now. She has begun to demonstrate to those around her how well she dances... and what she will wear... and whatever else she thinks they will want to know. She really does know how to dance, and together they will make a cute couple...

Because so many students want to dance and good speakers are needed as well, "Teacher I" delivers her inspiring "Sacrifice For The Play" speech. Perhaps someone would rather speak than dance? Quietly, "Student S" raises her hand — she will do whatever the teacher needs. She will speak, although she will need a microphone.

"Student D" again announces to the class, *He has to dance. Did the teacher know his cousins from out of town are coming to see him dance? If he can't dance, he probably can't be in the program.*

After much discussion, parts are announced. The speakers

are shuffled off to one practice room, the singers to another...
and last, the dancing couple *jeté* themselves away to a third.

As "Fred and Ginger" leave the room, "Student C" is asking,
"When is this play? I can't wait for it to be over — they make
a *scary* couple!"

Footnote: The play was a huge success. "Student D" and his
partner "Miss I" danced well. His parents grinned and grinned
to see their son in this new role as a star. "Miss I" also saw
"Student D" in a new light and developed a severe crush on
him! "Student S" said her part perfectly as her "Mother S"
recorded the play and "Grandmother S" cried softly.

"Teacher I" was thrilled at the success of the play, which
may never be repeated since she lost her only script just two
days before the play. She was extremely honored, however,
by a note left on her desk the day after the performance:

> *Dear Mrs. "I,"*
>
> *Thank you for all your hard work on our
> play. You did a really good job.*
>
> > *Sincerely,*
> > *Student "C"*

═ ─ ─ ─ ─ **Personality "Types"** ─ ─ ─ ═

Years ago, before computers, they called this a "typing
class." Today, I am a "keyboarding instructor." I always
wonder if students have a real appreciation for learning the
proper techniques for keying on a computer. At the beginning
of each school year, I ask the students to explain the importance
of keyboarding in their course of study. The variety of responses

I receive has always amazed me. Now, after learning about personality styles, I understand the responses I get.

Here are some of my favorites from each of the styles:

Peter, a "high D" student declared: "You take keyboarding so you can stay up with the times. If you don't know how to use the computer, you will never get a decent job. If you don't know about computers, you are stupid. How long until we know all the keys? Do you have to use certain fingers or certain keys, or can we use the fingers on the keys that are easiest for us?"

Kenneth, a "high I" student was very excited: "You take keyboarding so you can learn how to play all those neat games. Mrs. H, did you know you can do real neat art on the computer? Do we have homework in here? You know we can't have homework because everybody doesn't have a computer at home. What are all the F-keys for? What are we going to do today?"

An "S" personality, Sandi, just sat and said nothing. When I asked her what she thought, she responded: "We take keyboarding so we can learn to do reports by ourselves instead of asking someone else to do it for us. Mrs. W, our counselor, told us we needed to take it."

A "C" type student, Erin, replied: "We take keyboarding because we can learn how to do things for ourselves. In the long run that will save us time in our work. When you use word processing programs, you can use a spell check so you won't have any mistakes on your paper. You can also save all of your work on a disk. When you work in a business, the computer saves you time which saves you money. The other reason is because you have to take it before you can take computer, which is required for graduation."

The Girls' Retreat

This Spring, I had the opportunity to lead a segment of the Sixth Grade girls' retreat. My topic was "Identifying and Understanding Personality Types." After covering information on the four basic styles and pointing out each style's positive traits, I divided our classroom into four sections, classifying them "D," "I," "S" and "C." Then I instructed the girls to identify their own, individual personality style without talking, and then move to their appropriate area in the room.

Immediately, I saw the small "D" group form. Candace, a very high "D," quickly started directing traffic — although I had told the girls clearly to make their own decisions. She pointed to the "C" section, dispatching Natalie with the command, "You belong over there!"

Several obviously "I" girls blurted, "Now what corner did you send us to, Mrs. E?" (They had not been listening.) But before I could respond, they identified their area — where all of the action was: jumping, giggling, braiding hair, high-fiving...

In the meantime, Natalie had stopped to reread my chart descriptions of the four styles and their characteristics. Candace interrupted her, demanding, "Natalie, why don't you just go to your group?" Natalie lashed back, "I need to make sure I've identified my personality style *correctly* — and *then* I'll go where I belong!"

As I glanced around the room, I noticed a quiet corner. You guessed it — the "S" girls. Obediently, they were standing silently, almost motionless (which is something unbelievable for Sixth Grade girls on a retreat). One hand was raised above their heads in a plea for assistance. "Yes, Kristy," I inquired.

"Well, Anna is my good friend and I want to be in her group, but Jennifer is my good friend, too. May I be in Anna's group for a little while after I stand here a few minutes?" Obviously, Kristy did not want Anna left out of the circle of friends. Anna, one of the "I's," had not noticed the separation.

After a quick review of the positive characteristics, I let the girls point out some of the behaviors and attitudes of each type — things they should be alert for. We also mentioned "blends," the varying strengths of the other "D," "I," "S," and "C" characteristics in our own styles. And then, it was time for the next session, "Friendships." How helpful our "Personalities" segment was in forming a foundation for that session!

A "Class" Team

The Sixth Grade teachers at my school are examples of each of the four basic personality types. We get along very well because we have learned how to understand each other. Based on what I have learned about behavioral styles, this is how I would describe them and why I think we work well together:

Our grade chairperson is an "I" type with some helpful "S." She certainly is a friendly, personable inspiration to all of us. Her door is always open, just to visit or to offer compassionate, supportive, dependable advice. She is imaginative both in and out of her classroom. With discipline problems, she remains calm and diplomatic, yet she is always firm and consistent. She is truly an enthusiastic asset to our staff.

We have two "D" type teachers. One of these seems to be primarily "D" while other seems more a blend of "D with I." While she has the predominant "D" characteristics, she is also outgoing, talkative, enthusiastic, and personable. She is more spontaneous and optimistic, whereas our other "D" teacher is more pessimistic and deliberate. The second "D" can "work rings around" the others because she is both goal- and results-oriented, and her competitiveness drives her to want to finish *first*. These two are very interesting to watch because they are both *so* "D"!

Of the two remaining teachers, one is a blend of "I with S," while the other is a "C with S." The "I with S" is quite outgoing, talkative and enthusiastic; however, she is also reliable, cooperative, efficient, and easygoing. Her humor and amiability make her a pleasure to work with. These qualities allow her to get along well with students and parents, as well as other teachers.

The last, our "C with S" teacher, is conscientious in all areas. She is cautious in handling discipline problems; she has "downgraded" herself within the past five years from teaching Twelfth Grade English and Advanced Placement English to teaching Sixth Grade English. She tries to be consistent and sensitive to the needs of this age child and therefore, she confers often with the grade chairperson. She truly loves teaching and children, and for this reason she realizes she may try to "mother" them too much. She attempts to keep her students' parents aware of their children's progress and development. She also realizes that sometimes she may expect these Sixth Graders to learn too much. In the past five years, though, she has come to recognize her students' limitations because her curiosity, her analytical mind, and her critical thinking have encouraged her to study and observe systematically the developmental progress of an 11 or 12 year old child.

It is interesting to study how well and why these five teachers work well together. The qualities and characteristics of these particular styles tend to complement each other. These teachers have unknowingly been "raising" their positive traits and "lowering" their negative traits in times of unrest. The concern and pleasure which is felt among these teachers seems to be like the closeness and understanding which can be found in a family unit.

Weird Science

As the teacher eagerly awaited the arrival of her Fourth Grade Science class, she checked and rechecked to be sure the day's experiment would be a success. During the previous day's class, she had given all the directions, explaining the mechanics of how things *should* work. She had spent the last week teaching according to the students' differing learning styles — and now they would finish their lesson by experiencing the fun and feeling of being a predator, learning how predators must adapt for survival.

As the students arrived, each child was handed a "scientific method" worksheet, was placed in a work group, and began the wonderful adventure that their teacher had laid out, planned, checked and taught... *she thought!*

The group work went well, as expected. Everything was going according to plan, until the time to go outside... to become the "hunter." She was not sure if it was oxygen deprivation, radiation from erupting solar flares, or the exuberant feeling of breaking out of jail — but when The Door opened, the "I's" thought summer vacation had come early, the "D's" began whooping and screaming at the "C's," the "C's" went into shock because they *knew* this was not a part of the lesson plan *(or at least they hoped they knew the teacher hadn't mentioned this during the lessons, or was this part of what she wanted them to learn, and if so, how could this be related to "predator" and "prey"?)* As the teacher stood there, horrified, watching primal instincts surface, the "S" students were asking what they could do to *help*.

Then the teacher's own, instinctual need to "adapt and survive" kicked in. Her "D" rose and she regained control of the situation. The "lab" procedure continued without a hitch. Everyone completed the experiment, breezed through the follow-up test, and could not wait for the next "fun" lesson!

The Homecoming Float

One of my duties as Ninth Grade Class sponsor is to oversee the building of their homecoming float. This is a BIG DEAL, as it is the first time they have "float parties" at night at someone's house. The class president appoints committees to design the float and buy the necessary materials. The rest of the class meets at a designated house and decorates it… the *float!*

My only study of personality styles was a book I had read several years ago. Therefore, I was completely unprepared for what we encountered on our first night. The president turned out to be a high "I," and he had appointed *all* "I's" to his committee. When I arrived, the committee was outside "socializing" and playing football… while the "C's" were in the garage trying to bring order out of chaos… the "D's" were "chewing out" the president and his committees… and the "S's" were wringing their hands because everyone was upset. We worked hard, but when we left Thursday night, all of knew our entry was shoddy.

At five o'clock the next morning, my phone rang. "Oh, Mrs. M, we (four girls — "C's") stole the float last night and worked on it until this morning. Please come and see it!"

After recovering from my initial shock, I knew this was

something I *had* to see! Yes, it was beautifully done... yes, there were hurt committee feelings... and yes, there was one *angry* parent. (When Mrs. B pushed the garage door button to close it for the night, the four girls had placed their purses in the door's path, causing it to open up again. In taking the float, they had left her garage door open all night.)

What a lesson I learned. Even though I still had not taken a course on understanding personality differences, I had learned to make sure I helped future class presidents select their committees!

Kindergarten Picasso's

Even in a Kindergarten Class, personality styles can be spotted. An art activity is a great way to see different personalities in action.

It is mid-October, and I am about to have art with my class of five-year-olds. There are 26 children in the class, and we are going to create Fall pictures. I talk about the season and some things we might draw — Autumn leaves, pumpkins, a full moon, hay stacks, etc. We discuss the differences between a tree in Fall and a tree in Spring and Summer, and how the leaves will be orange, yellow and red — not green.

I show them a picture I have drawn to give them an idea, reminding them that their pictures do not have to look like mine. I want them to make the pictures "theirs," not mine.

Before giving the instructions, I have passed out the supplies, stacking boxes of crayons in the middle of the table. I am reminding the class to leave the crayons in the middle until I say differently when I discover the high "D" at Table 4 has already checked out every box at her table to see which box has the newest and best crayons. Of course, she has already taken *that* box for herself and has passed out the other boxes to the others sitting at *her* table.

A few minutes into the project, I hear weeping sounds coming from Table 5. Checking to see who is "hurt" or in pain, I find a high "C" falling apart because he cannot make his tree "just like" mine. I try to console him and show him how he can take what he has drawn and make it into a grand tree that doesn't need to be "just like mine." But *no,* that will *not* do! "May I have another piece of paper? I want to start over," he sniffles. The weeping turns to wailing at any *"no"* response.

At this point, another high "D" calls out: "Don't worry, Mrs. B. I went to preschool with him last year and he cried every day! There's nothing wrong with him...!"

By now, it seems the whole room is stretching and staring to see what is happening at Table 5 — except for my high "I" at Table 2. He doesn't even know anyone is crying. He is in his usual "out-of-chair" position, leaning horizontally across the table talking to his best buddy: "You wanna use my red? My red's longer than yours — it's okay with me. Hey can I use your blue? Hey let's draw us playing in the picture. You wanna come over to my house today? You can ride my bike. Do you like my tree?" And on and on and on....

While all of this is going on, a high "S" is steadily working on his picture, pausing only to compliment his neighbors on their good pictures or seeking approval for his own. He stops me as I walk by. "Do you like mine, Mrs. B.? Am I doing good? I'm doing my best. I really like yours — look, I drew *five* pumpkins, just like you did! You're a good artist, Mrs. B."

Obviously, my favorite child... sensitive, caring, and a credible judge of great talent!

Life Under The "C"

In a recent follow-up lesson in science, I announced to my Fourth Graders that we were going to do something fun. Having completed our unit of study on oceanography, we were going to construct booklets with pictures of sea animals. The class was instructed to color the aquarians, using their textbooks for reference, and to write two facts about each animal under each picture.

After giving directions, I walked among my students, checking their progress. I was barely down the first aisle when I saw a hand go up. Immediately, I went to Kyle (high "C") to answer his question. It became obvious that his *question* was *questions.* He quickly asked me to note the coloring directions: "It says to color the shark gray and white. Is that *dark* gray or *light* gray? Also, the fin on the shark is somewhat different in our textbook. Why? Also, you asked us to list two facts about each sea animal. Are the facts written in complete sentences or phrases? Do phrases start with capital letters?"

While attempting to deal with his questions *(do I answer them chronologically, or in order of importance... oh no, now he had me doing it!),* I noticed a puzzled look on Anna's face (high "S"). She had raised her hand shoulder-high, hesitantly, and instantly pulled it down, three or four times. When I went to her to ask if she needed help, she replied, "That's okay, Mrs. C — never mind. Are you through with Kyle? I don't want to interrupt." After assuring her that Kyle had been assisted, she reluctantly asked her question.

As I was answering Anna, I heard a "joyful noise" behind me. Yes, it was Taryn (high "I"). She had become bored and "lonely" halfway through he project and had moved next to Courtney so they could share crayons, ideas and most of all, a good time! Of course, nowhere in the directions were they told this would be a group project! After setting down some boundaries with Taryn, I continued my walk up and down the aisles. It did not take long to determine that Justin (high "D") was not working on his booklet.

Stopping at his desk, I asked if he needed help. "You said this was going to be fun," he said, "but it's not fun to me so I've decided not to do it!" Of course, nowhere in the directions had I stated that the booklet would be optional! After having a "reality check" regarding his options, Justine was able to find a motivation to complete his booklet.

During the assigned activity, it did not occur to me that these children were reacting according to their distinct personality styles. Now, after having been involved in the *Personality Insights* workshop, I have been able to re-live this event and understand why my students behaved as they did. The information I have received in this workshop will be invaluable to me in all relationships in the future.

Read Me Like A Book

This incident took place in my classroom this past school year. We were beginning a new reading incentive program in which the sponsor went along with the principal to explain the program and its rewards to all the classes.

Since she was a high "D," the speaker was prepared to say what she had to say and go on to the next class. The principal, on the other hand, wanted things to go smoothly and he wanted all of the students to like the program and feel comfortable with it.

Alex, my highest "D" child, was impatient for the presentation to begin. Like the speaker, he wanted to hear the message and move on. He lives at a fast pace and hates to be delayed. Of course, he wanted the principal to stop being so nice and move on with the speech.

Carlee, my off-the-chart "I," was bouncing around in her desk and raising — no, *signalling* — with her hand. She felt this was going to be a fun, talking time, not a listening time.

Lori, a confirmed "S," was sitting as quietly as she knew how. While trying to concentrate on our guest speaker's words, she was distracted by the principal's presence in the room. *Had she done something wrong?* Fear was bubbling from her cute face.

Adam, a dedicated "C," was ready to charge the speaker with tons of questions. *Will this work? When will we perform this task? Who will help us?* And so on, and on and on....

The differences in these behavior styles was amazing, to say the least! If anything, I have realized the most important role a teacher plays is that of *guide*. When you throw together a group of students with diverse personality traits in a potentially volatile situation, there is a chance that every child will end up being sorely offended, and the situation can quickly get out of hand.

But if a teacher is a guide, she will have the ability to diffuse these bad situations by allowing the differences in her students to be expressed and appreciated. She will be able to navigate her class successfully through the uncharted waters of conflict and lead them to a safe port.

20-20 Hindsight

K enny was in my Kindergarten Class last year and I could not understand him at all. He was very argumentative — he always had to have the last word. I was so tired and frustrated at the end of each day from constantly "butting heads" with him. I thought, "Why is he so obnoxious?" He never raised his hand and he always had some comment to make, usually about how I could do things better.

I used every kind of discipline possible, but I could not get a handle on his behavior. I didn't understand it at all. Now I see that Kenny was a high "D" and didn't like control. If I had him in my class now, I would handle him differently. I would let him help the others with their writing and coloring (he was very neat). Boy, he would have thrived on that! Next time, I will try to nurture, rather than conform, this personality style.

Jordan joined us in the middle of the year. This is usually hard on a child who doesn't know anyone and feels insecure, having a hard time catching up. *Not Jordan!* After his mother left and we had him settled in, he began talking and carrying on — he had everyone laughing and liking him instantly. What a character! He had so much personality and the children took him in immediately. He was sharp and caught on quickly. However, he had trouble finishing his work and staying in his seat. He was always at someone else's table, talking.

Every time he got in trouble and had to sit at recess, he would cry and it would break my heart. I thought, "If you hate this so much, why do you keep doing the things that get you in trouble?" I didn't understand that Jordan had an "I" type personality. If I had, I would have let him get up and do something else that would give him a break from class work.

Erica was the ideal student: smart, sweet, quiet, and loving. She was always willing to help and ready to please. To this day, she and I enjoy a wonderful relationship. Being an "S" type myself, I really relate to her. There were no problems teaching Erica. She was easy!

Karen was the most inquisitive child I have ever known.

She was so intelligent, but she checked and rechecked everything she did and everything she was supposed to do. She seemed so afraid of making a mistake. She had to know the "why" to everything. It was so exasperating at times. She cried if she missed one question or forgot one little detail.

I would often think, "Karen, you are being ridiculous — no one is perfect!" Now that I know that being wrong is rare and hardest on a "C," I will try to help children like Karen to relax and understand that is really is okay to not always be right. They need to enjoy things more.

This course has opened my eyes so much and I am looking forward to starting over with a new outlook on teaching. This information would save so many people from "going gray" and pulling out their hair if every individual were required to learn it early in life — especially school teachers!

A Pig Tale

This story is the truth, the whole truth, and nothing but the truth... as told through the memories of a six-year-old "I" type girl. The setting is Robert E. Lee Elementary School, Port Arthur, Texas, in November, 1951. I was an outgoing First Grader who had a secret and kept it surprisingly well... until I got caught! You see, I wore the same dress to school every day for a month.

It was a green plaid dress with a pink felt pocket shaped like a pig, complete with a yarn tail. How I loved that dress! The class loved it; and my teacher, Miss Nichols, loved it too! Well, at least the *first* time I wore it! You may ask, *Why did your mother let you wear the same dress every day?* Easy answer: she didn't know!

My organized, high "C" mom always laid out my clothes on my bed every morning. I always wore them without a peep of complaint. She always praised me for being so cooperative. Naturally, I always agreed. Then my web of deceit began. It bothered me — for about two seconds.

Once I had arrived at school, I would go to the bathroom, pull out my "pig dress" from my book satchel, and change clothes. I was just like Superman! After school, I would change back into my "mama dress," stuff the pig dress back into my book bag, and head for home. This was my routine for a full month. The only hitch was that a six-year-old's dress doesn't stay clean very long. New stains appeared daily, ranging from streaks of tempera paint to dried-up food eaten who knows when! It looked awful. Meanwhile, other First Graders were trying to decide what was going on and how to handle it, each in his or her own unique style.

On that fateful day, when I walked into the classroom, tactless Donald Billingsley (a strong "D" type) stuck his feet into a vacant desk so I couldn't sit there. He rolled his eyes, pinched his nose and announced *loudly* that I smelled like "last week's spaghetti!" My feelings were crushed as I slid into a seat in front of Kim Kaley.

Sweet Kim (an "S") whispered that she *still* thought my dress was pretty and that the pig looked *much* better with Koolaid® spots on him. She tried to re-tie his bow that had long ago wilted. Kim even slipped a stick of JuicyFruit® gum into my hand like a true friend.

Then Lawrence Schmidt (a classic "C") passed me a note. Actually, it seemed more like a fill-in-the-blanks questionnaire. It read: *You have had that dress on for 31 days. Why don't you wear something else? Don't you have any other clothes?* Lawrence was very observant — and articulate — for his age.

Sensing my sudden embarrassment, Miss Nichols told me I was the Leader and to take the lunch count to the office. That helped my feelings. I always loved wearing the "Leader" button and being first in line. Of course, I later understood that she used my absence to give the rest of the class a "Do unto others as you would have them do unto you" speech.

"And now..." as Paul Harvey says, *"the r-r-r-rest of the story!"*

It was the holiday season. The class had collected used clothing to give to a needy child. Naturally, Miss Nichols thought I should be the recipient. With me standing at her side, she called my mother, tactfully telling her about the clothes box, saying there were some really nice dresses just my size. Since I had worn the same dress for 31 days (those calculations courtesy of Lawrence Schmidt), she thought mama might be interested.

There was a long silence. Finally, I heard Miss Nichols say, "It's a pig dress... yes... a pig dress." More silence. Miss Nichols hung up the phone, turned to me and said, "Dear, your mother wants you to come home now. And by the way, dear, *don't change clothes."*

The jig was up! Mama usually waited with milk and cookies. Today she waited with a switch from a peach tree. The pig dress disappeared, gone wherever well-worn, much loved pig dress go. As for me, I learned two things: dishonesty can get an "I" child in trouble; and peach branches sure do sting!

─ ─ ─ Curriculum Choice Cards ─ ─ ─

The procedure is simple and straightforward: the counselor talks with the students in a group setting, explaining to them what courses will be available for them the following year. She explains that they must take four required academic courses along with three elective courses. She explains the regular college prep program and the recommendation requirements for the honors college prep offerings. Students then consult with their parents and the counselor individually in deciding which courses to take. These responses are from the choice cards of four students with classic behavioral styles:

William (a "D" type personality) — Mrs. L, sign me up for the regular classes! I don't have time to do extra studying after school because I'll be captain of the football and basketball teams next year and I'm going to run track too. I'll just be too busy for advanced classes. Oh yes, I wanted to be sure to tell you that I need study hall last period since it works out better for my schedule. Thanx — see ya!

Mark (an "I" type personality) — Mrs. L, I'm sorry I'm so late seeing you about my schedule but I lost my card two weeks ago. It was in my book bag, but my dog must have eaten it! I want to take regular classes and Spanish because the Spanish teacher takes lots of field trips and she always takes the class to a Mexican restaurant before coming back to school and she lets them have parties in class too! I really want to take sociology and psychology because I think I want to be a psychologist when I grow up and work with people. I talk to people on the phone all the time about their problems. Can you give me study hall first period? I have lots of activities at night and I could get my homework done in the mornings before my classes. I *know* I'll have time to get it all done first period. Thanks. ("Smiley face" next to his flamboyant signature.)

Cindy (an "S" type personality) — Mrs. L, I just can't decide what to do. My teachers recommended me for advanced science and math and honors English. My parents really want me to take these courses and so do my teachers, but I don't know. I really work very hard to get the good grades I make and I really worry and stew over my work. I can do it but it seems to take me longer than some of my classmates. I'm going to be a cheerleader next year and I'm just worried that I won't have time to do well in those subjects, but I know my parents would like for me to take them. But they don't like to see me get so uptight about things. Can I think about this a little longer and let you know in a few days? I know the school doesn't really allow this, but do you think I could possibly have two study hall periods next year so I could work on my homework?

Carl (a "C" type personality) — Mrs. L, I definitely want you to sign me up for the advanced classes. I've been working ahead in math and I'm going to be taking calculus at the [local] college first period, then I'll come to school for second period. Remember, we talked about this a few months ago and I'll be getting 12 hours of college credit with all my advanced placement classes. I've been working on a schedule for myself for next year. I'm going to be student body president and train for cross country after school, so I realize I've really got to plan my time and use it wisely. Can you give me Mrs. N, the physics teacher, for study hall? She has asked me to come into her classroom and work on physics projects for contests, so I thought if I had study hall in her room, I'd have time to do extra work for these competitions. Thanks.

Tornado Drill

One day there was a tornado warning at our school. My primary school children and I had to go into the hallway in case the storm came into our area. I remember many of the children being upset.

Yet my high "D" student, Edward, was very optimistic. He was telling all of the other children not to be such babies. In fact, he was very determined that no one would think he *might* be scared.

Warren, who is a high "I," was having a wonderful time! He was visiting with all of his friends from other classes. He could not have cared less if a funnel cloud had touched down and blown the whole school away.

Kristie, who is a typical "S," was so worried. Yet she still tried to calm her friends who were upset. As she gathered them up around her, she was very sweet and supportive of all of her friends.

Betsy, a high "C," was very concerned with the exact time the tornado had been spotted and how far away it was from the school. With Second Grade math, she was trying to calculate the exact time the bad weather would be in our area. Each time the radio came on, she was curious as to what the reporter was saying.

Although all of the children were fearful at times, these specific children could not help but let their high D-I-S-C personalities shine through. I hope I responded with comfort and support for each one.

The Science Final Finally!

Intro: The class of Fourth Graders is involved in a review session for their very first final exam. Because they have not had a "final" before, they are uncertain of what to expect. Just as anyone else, when we are presented with a new situation our primary personality traits are most evident.

A child we'll call "Big D" says, "Let's get on with the review. These finals are no big deal." He is unclear what all the fuss is about. "Big I" says, "Can't we hurry and finish this so we can go outside and play? I brought snacks for everyone — what are we reviewing *for* anyway?" "Big S" leans over and whispers to "Big I" that we are having a Science Final tomorrow. "Big I" says, "That's great! Everybody come over to my house tonight for a study party! You guys bring the drinks and I'll provide the snacks. I'll call you this afternoon...!" "Big S" sits in her desk with sweaty palms, combing the classroom with her eyes to make sure everyone has paper and pencil. She is making two copies of the review notes, just in case someone doesn't get them all down. "Big C" asks, "Do I have everything down correctly? Could you just check over my paper and make sure I've gotten everything?"

The recess bell has rung. Of course, "Big I" is the first one outside. "Big D" is second, commenting on the way out, "I can't believe the review session took that long. We've been over this stuff 20 times!" "Big S" is still at her desk, finishing up her notes. She knows she will miss part of recess, but that's okay! It's worth it for her friends. Besides, she'll have an extra copy of the notes should anyone *call* her tonight. "Big C" brings her page of notes out to the teacher on the playground. *What type of questions are going to be on the test? How many questions will there be?*

Returning to school the next day, the teacher allows them one more time to review just prior to the Science Final. "Big D" is asking for the Final, *now!* "Big S" and "Big C" are scanning their notes and making last-minute mental notes. "Big S" is also checking to see if the others have their notes. She sees that "Big I" does not have his review sheet on his desk and lays her extra copy on his desk — as she realizes she does not even see "Big I" *at* his desk at all! He is at his locker, getting a snack left over from last night's "study time," as he thinks, *At least I will have something to do until time for recess!*

A Real Trip

Mrs. S," Jessica inquired, "why does Carl feel the need to always push to the front of the line? It doesn't make sense. It's not like we're not all gonna be fed sooner or later."

I had taken the class to the agricultural museum, and we were waiting in line for a homemade biscuit filled with cane syrup. Carl looked back at us and barked, "Everybody get behind me!"

"Where's Sandy?", I asked. "She let everyone push in front of her, the dope," Carl said, his mouth full of biscuit.

"Diane, go back through the line and find Sandy — and don't stop to talk to everyone!"

A short time later, Diane returned with her arm around Sandy's waist. "Here she is, poor thing," Diane crooned. "Just stay by me, Sandy. I won't let everyone run over you."

After we finished eating, I thought it would be nice to see all the different buildings. "Carl, slow down! You're missing so many interesting things!" I told him. "I'm not interested in those stupid old buildings!" he yelled. "I'm gonna go see the animals." "Stay with the group," I warned.

"Mrs. S, why are they called 'build*ings*' when they've *already been built?* I mean 'building' indicates present activity, so the noun 'building' is really illogical." Did Jessica *really* expect me to answer that, or was she just being annoying?

"Ohhh, look at the little kitty on that window sill! He's sooooo cute!" Diane bubbled. She had found yet another friend. "Hey, Kitty, would you like to be held and cuddled?"

"Mrs. S, if cats hate water, why do they like fish?"

"I have no idea, Jessica."

Sandy crouched beside the kitten and started stroking its fur. "I wonder if he's lost..." she whispered. Sandy never talked above a whisper. It was a good thing since Carl was close by, and somehow I didn't think Carl was a cat's best friend.

"Let's hurry, girls. We need to catch up with the others," I said. We caught up with Carl just in time to see a llama spit on him. Sandy tried to stifle a giggle. "Shut up, Sandy!" Carl roared. "I'm sorry," Sandy said softly. "I really didn't mean to laugh."

I'm sure Diane would have laughed unmercifully, but we had lost her. She was probably helping a lost child find his mother. "Can I help?" Sandy offered. "Would you like me to check for her in the museum, Mrs. S?"

"Let's *all* look in the museum," I said. As we were walking to the museum, we noticed a large crowd gathering in the lobby. Carl pushed his way through the throng, and the girls and I followed.

To our surprise, there stood Diane. Her left index finger was pointing to a sign that read *Entrance.* Her head was cocked to the left... her eyes were as wide as saucers... her body was as stiff as a corpse... and on her face was a ridiculous grin not unlike the Joker's. She was posing as a "living mannequin," basking in the attentions of a rather large, captive audience.

Carl grunted, "Look at that stupid idiot." I just stood with the rest of the crowd, trying to figure out how to get her "unfrozen" and home without people realizing she was with me.

I Worry About A Few...

The scenario runs like this almost daily in my Third Grade classroom. I've never had a group like this in twenty-some years of teaching school. It certainly makes you entertain the thought of retiring. I'm one of those people who teach because

I love it — I do not consider it "working." I'm there early in the morning and I'm the last to leave in the afternoon. I've always written little notes to my students when I return their assignment papers. Former students have asked me to teach *their* children, so you know I've been at this awhile.

My "problem" runs through all aspects of teaching, from recess to math to language to history to science. *Whatever* I introduce, Michael is not interested in it and does his best to confuse the issue. He has been tutored four days a week just to help him stay afloat.

During any subject, he works on only two or three small tasks and then folds. In reading he causes some disturbance after just two or three words. Ellen (a sensitive "S" who *feels* for everyone) offers to help, but one by one, the other children have become disgusted with his misbehavior. *Why does Michael even come to school?*

Ellen wants to make sure everyone understands me and our subject. She always brings in extra information about whatever we are studying. She and her father make, draw, design — or find in the woods! — items she can brings to class with detailed thoughts about their workings.

Janet enjoys learning, too. She is a careful worker who reads a lot, and her "C" style does not have much patience with Michael and his disturbances.

I thought Michael was ADD and he may be — his mother is a teacher who blames it on an absent, divorced father. After reading *Positive Personality Profiles* last Spring, I see him at least as a high "I" out of control. In the classroom, he tries to be the life of the party by falling out of his desk, tipping it over, making facial contortions and grotesque sounds at every opportunity — while trying to enlist others in his "performance." Getting him to settle down and work requires my hand on his shoulder, helping him, talking about his responsibility. But this never lasts for long. Maybe I expect too much — he has been in two schools already and was retained in First Grade.

James is an excellent student who has made some wonderful progress this year after his parents and I established some boundaries for his "D" tendencies. He and Michael have been lumped together as "behavior problems" since First Grade. Being able to "group" James away from Michael has allowed James and other bright learners to move ahead. I hope to separate them next year. This may make it possible to get Michael with a group on his level — for James, I believe three years with an irritant in enough.

I worry most this year for Maggie, my highest "S," who hurts for everyone and consoles all the children I have to correct. She is so quiet… almost lost in the shuffle of the other children. She always wants to help and I know I can depend on her.

The other children in my class seem to blend in. But I am afraid these few students will be hurt if my "problem" continues any longer. Other teachers agree with me — we'll move Michael back to his level, and maybe he will be tested over the summer. I hope so. At least I see now how his behavioral style affects his ability to stay focused.

Wait 'Til Next Year

B arry showed all the traits of a high "D," and if I had understood this during his Senior year, I probably could have motivated him by letting him teach a section in my class. He was really smart but did not work up to his ability. In my Accounting and Computer Science courses, he never seemed to take the time to prepare himself — was he unmotivated by the "challenge" of my class, or just uncommitted? If I had given him more of an opportunity to be in control, I think he would have done so much better.

Matt had not been a good student until his Senior year, when he made the honor roll for the first time. The recognition seems to "turn a light on" inside his "I" compartment. He tried really hard in my Accounting class, right from the start. He often raised his hand and I called on him often to answer questions. Being a "central source" for information made him try harder. On Awards Day, I presented him with a special prize for being such an improved student. His parents and grandparents came to the ceremonies, and afterwards they stopped by to tell me how much he had enjoyed the class and how proud he was of his award. (This really happened!)

Beth was an excellent student in my 10th Grade Keyboarding class. If she finished her assigned class work early (and she usually did), she worked independently on increasing her speed. After our class had covered the fundamentals of the subject, I recruited her for help with the yearbook. Whether I understood it or not, I needed her "C" competence on the project! In her spare time, she would come to my classroom to do layout, to type copy, and to proof her work... which was always perfect.

Peter was a very quiet and shy 15 year old. He was in Keyboarding class with Beth. Early on, I realized he had a real knack for fixing minor glitches with our computers. It could have been "C" traits, but he seemed to take such pleasure in helping and being appreciated that I think his "S" traits caused him to help wherever he could.

I did not understand the "personalities" concept during the school year but looking back, this is how I see these students. I have really enjoyed learning about these styles and I am *almost* excited about school starting back so I can begin to implement some of these ideas on my new students!

Graduation Day

Waddlee-ah-cha, Waddlee-ah-cha, Doodle-ee-doo, Doodle-ee-doo

Those were the cheerful voices of the Kindergarten children as they practiced diligently for their graduation production. They had learned new songs, recited poetry and repeated the Pledge of Allegiance for many weeks in preparation for the big event.

We, the teachers, had discussed appropriate behavior, reviewing everything from how to shake the principal's hand to sitting nicely in "Sunday" clothes. With all our bases covered, we anxiously awaited the arrival of our six o'clock performance that night.

I should have known at 5:45 that it was going to be a most "interesting" evening when high "I" J.R. stuck out his tongue and began waving his fingers wildly behind his ears while fellow-"I" Daren turned upside-down in his chair with his shirt tail out and one shoe off.

I *very* patiently strolled over and unassumingly encouraged the boys to sit nice and tall. Using positive reinforcement, I praised *all* the children for their lovely behavior.

We made it through the welcome, Pledge and prayers. I was just beginning to breathe easily when I noticed Taylor swatting at something — *"Oh Lord, please don't let it be a bee...!"* Guess what? God answered my prayer and it was a soft, little feather. All right, *half* a prayer, because Taylor continued grabbing at it and the more he tried, the more fun it became to watch it float and dart away in the air.

Cathy, a "take charge D" personality, dealt with the problem by politely *pushing* Taylor down in his seat with a loud rebuke: *Shh-sh-sh!* Miss J said we have to mind our manners!"

In the meantime, Todd had picked up the feather and was blowing it up in the air, much to the shrieking delight of Adam and Josh, who were giggling uncontrollably. Even with all this, I had managed to stay cool and calm; certainly, the parents understood.

It was not until Amy began to cry that I truly began to feel helpless. You see, as everyone stood to recite the poem, Alecia noticed that Amy's sash was undone. Brimming with "S," Amy became deeply distressed because this was not part of the plan and she could not fix it or go to her mother for assistance.

Needing order and correctness, Alecia's "C" personality took over. Standing next to Amy on the front row, she bent low to tie, re-tie and re-re-tie the bow until she had it just right.

As the program was drawing to a close, I noticed that several of our children had folded their parchment diplomas into airplanes, while others had rolled them into telescopes. Thinking of course that nothing else could possibly go wrong, I graciously made my way to the podium to congratulate the children and conclude the program.

In my middle of my gracious remarks, one small boy — but don't ask me *who,* because by now I was on autopilot — began tugging at my dress. Unable to ignore him, I leaned down as he asked quite loudly "I have a present for you! You gonna open it *now?*" I assured him quickly that I would, turned back to the audience and invited everyone to celebrate with refreshments in the cafeteria.

Looking back, I have two observations:

1) It seems that this class had more than its share of *outgoing* personality styles, or maybe it was *just Kindergarten!*

2) We should have marched out to the song "(C'mon Baby) Let the Good Times Roll"!

The First Frog Story

I think back fondly to the day my First Grade class wrote a story for the first time at school. They had written sentences before but had not tried to make a paragraph. I explained that the title of their story would be "The Frog."

A mixture of emotions filled the room. Will, an "I," raised his hand as he bounced in his desk. I knew he couldn't hold back for long, so I called on him. He said, "I-ran-over-a-frog-one-time-then-my-sister-ran-over-it-too! It was gross!" The room filled with oooo-ooo-ooo! I said, "That's interesting, Will. I'm looking forward to reading your story..."

Cary, a "C," raised her hand. "Do I have to write about doing *anything* with a frog? I don't like frogs and I don't mess with them..."

Annie, my painfully shy "S," was looking really worried by now. I explained that they could write anything about a frog as long as it made sense. They could tell about a frog's color, size, age, name, what he does, how he feels, or something you did with him. "Write the title first, then three sentences," I said. "I know you can do more, but since this is the first time, we will write only three."

Annie looked calmer now, but Marc was noticeably uncomfortable. "Can I help you?" I asked the little "D-in-training." He groaned, "Can we get started *please?*"

I explained that if there were no more questions, everyone could begin. On my way back to my desk, I stopped by Annie. I put my hand on her shoulder and asked, "Do you have any questions?" She looked up gratefully and said, "No, I can do it." I smiled and said, "You sure can!"

They turned in some interesting stories that day.

Double "D's"

As a Fourth Grade teacher, I had never recognized the different personality patterns that make up a class. In a "normal" classroom situation, students will fall into each of the personality style groups.

My "D" example was double — *twins!* They were very strong-willed and very demanding. They ran over other children, did not want to take orders, and continually wanted to fight with others. Their behavior was much better if I kept them busy with activities that involved their hands or anything competitive. If only I had learned this information before I taught them, maybe I would have known how to deal with them more effectively.

I had a large group of "I's." They had great potential for being "straight A" students but were very talkative and wanted more to impress others than settle down and do their work. They were a fun, loving group always on the go, organizing what to do at recess... about the only "organization" I ever saw in them!

As any teacher deserves, I had a nice group of "S's" — very pleasant, dependable students who thrived on making good grades. I used these children to help other students. They were patient and it gave them a sense of being useful.

I also had a very classic "C" child, a very intelligent little girl who was very moody, unsociable and often irritated the other children. I was very concerned about her because she was so "cold" that she never seemed to enjoy anything.

Thanks to the information I have learned, I feel I will be a better teacher next year and will understand my students so much more!

Winning with Styles

In assembling any kind of team for any kind of project, it is a good idea to "know your players." Each of the personality styles can find a productive place on your team. Since coaching high school sports is of interest to me, these are the ideas I have about coaching football with D-I-S-C in mind.

Most coaches agree that successful teams win with defense. "Dominant" type people should make excellent defensive players. "D's" are good leaders, love a challenge and thrive on competition. They are energized by conflict and recharged by physical confrontation. Throughout the game, their emotions would be at a peak. "D" characteristics that would allow them to be most successful are: *dominant* (will to win, to dominate), *determined* (not easily defeated), *dynamic* (sometimes intimidating), *dogmatic* (they know what they think and will defend it), *dictatorial* (eager to lead), and *doers* (whatever it takes).

"Inspirational" type people will offer characteristics helpful to our offense. They are empowered by people and by being the center of attention. Offensive players are more likely to be in the limelight, thus recharging them should be an easy process. "I's" are good starters and if the defense does its job, a good start by the offense can give the team field position and even an early lead with momentum. *Leadership* is important and "I's" offer many excellent leadership qualities by inspiring their teammates.

"Supportive" type people make good linemen. They are motivated by helping others. They are good finishers, so combining them with the "I's" should keep a team competitive throughout the entire game. Their love is *teamwork,* which is paramount to football success.

"Cautious" type people can contribute a lot to our special teams. While the "D's" will not want to give up the football, the "C" players will be *competent, calculating,* and *consistent.* When we have to give it up, they will kick or punt using their perfectionist quality to be successful. "C's" dislike mistakes and good coaches know that mistakes in the kicking game can be devastating. This type will work and work to get it right.

A good balance of "D," "I," "S," and "C" styles will lead to success. We all expect skills and personality styles to be different, but good coaches can use this knowledge to their advantage.

Avoid conflict, strive for balance, and *just win, baby!*

Blood, Sweat and Tears

Situation: How my high school football team's personality styles were displayed in a game that could have qualified us for the playoffs for the first time since 1981!

Players' Personalities:
    D   Tad (star running back)
    I   Walt (running back/linebacker)
    S   Adrian (center)
    C   Joe (offensive/defensive tackle)

Before the Game: Tad ("D") was extremely focused; you could see it in his eyes. The rest of the team feeds off his intensity. Walt ("I") was *literally* bouncing off the wall with excitement. Adrian ("S") was near his locker, sitting down, really quiet, settling things within himself. Joe ("C") had his headphones on, using music to block out everything and to get himself focused.

Halftime: We were behind 7–0 in a closely contested game, but we were actually fortunate the score was not 14–0. Tad

("D") was really angry with himself. He had fumbled on our first offensive play after an 8-yard gain. The fumble eventually led to the only touchdown of the half. Walt ("I") had blown some assignments both offensively and defensively, which was not unusual. He was very withdrawn, actually *pouting*. Adrian ("S") asked me, as usual, how I thought the team — not *he* — did in the first half. His attitude was one of worry. Joe ("C") sat at his locker with no outward emotion and listened intently to our halftime coaching adjustments.

After the Game: Final score: We lost, 21–14. We botched up an onside kick attempt, with less than two minutes left, that would have given us a chance to tie or win. Tad ("D") was mad and disappointed at himself because he felt he had let himself and the team down. Walt ("I") was openly weeping because we had lost and he had made too many mistakes. Adrian ("S") also wept, but more discreetly, and again came into my office and wanted to know what I thought of the team's — not *his* — performance. Joe ("C") undoubtedly felt he had done his best, got dressed and left.

With these four young men, similar behavior was the norm for virtually all of our games. The importance of this one magnified their personality styles.

The Hallway Gallery

As a classroom teacher, I must keep in mind that each child is unique. We all carry around with us personality traits that can enhance us or hurt us.

The Second Grade child is at a very truthful age — or at least they have not learned subtlety, so they exhibit their "strong self" much more obviously in daily classroom situations.

One day I instructed my students to draw and color an imaginative, creative picture all their own. When completed, I told them I would pin their artwork on a clothesline in the hallway outside our classroom for everyone to see. Oh, what a motivating idea *I thought* this would be.

But to my amazement, Maria (a high "S" type) sat quietly in her desk and raised her hand. "I can't think of anything to draw," she said.

Bryan (an "I" type) was more than happy for the opportunity to draw his picture. He went on and on and on and on with his imaginative drawing, but his coloring left something to be desired.

Jared (a "D" type) completed his drawing and coloring in no time! It was as if he "conquered" it rather than created it.

Mindy (a "C" type) went to great lengths to be sure her drawing and coloring was perfect. It was not enough for her to *color* inside the lines; her *lines* were perfect, too!

These are just four examples of how this project developed — successfully and unsuccessfully. Oh well, just another day!

Junior English

After being out of the classroom for 11 years along with the changes in societal trends from the 80's to the 90's — and having no understanding of personality traits — I barely survived my first year of minute-to-minute classroom torture. I taught English to one section of Juniors. Three-fourths of the class played on the line of our championship-winning football team.

Danny, the highest "D" in the world (*now* I know!) challenged me every day from the moment his head appeared in the door until his feet took the final step out of the same door. Having a great deal of "D" myself, we butted heads most days. Danny would attack my teaching methods as well as the materials used. One day I was giving literature notes; repeatedly, I urged the students to take notes. Danny chose to take a nap. When I had an open-notebook test at the last part of the class period, Danny not only made a zero but informed me of the stupidity of the entire procedure. The year followed that same pattern. Toward the end of the semester, *his* "D" caused him to have several absences in my fifth hour class, and *my* "D" caused me to say inwardly *Praise the Lord!* for each absence. I would have handled Danny completely differently if I had understood our personalities. I could have given him some challenge and a little control without feeling threatened.

Greg, the high "I," kept the entire Junior Class entertained. I handled him a little better. Although I did not realize what I was doing, my teaching "auto-pilot" steered Greg away from being the class clown to providing the class with brief comic relief. I managed to guide him into some short-range goals. He would not take written notes, but he reached the point of mental notation. Just that little guidance and his own intelligence brought him from a *C*– to a *B*+.

Beth, a typical "S," never caused a ripple. She always wanted to sit away from the front, not be called upon or required to perform. Recitation in front of the class was a near traumatic experience. Since I was sensitive to her timidity, I fully explained to the class in advance my reasons for the assignment, and she made an *A* on that assignment.

Carley, a high "C," was also extremely quiet and agreeable to all. She was the class "patsy"; everyone ran off copies of her thorough, yet concise, notes before a test rather than take responsibility for note-taking on their own. She was very precise with her school work. The most evident example was when I announced that the nine weeks' test would be short answers rather than scantron. She scored 89, rather than her usual 98 or 99. Even though her *A* was not in danger because the nine weeks' test counted only one-fifth, she was furious because she feared her notes were not precise. On her exam she wrote the following: *I CANNOT BELIEVE YOU DID THIS!* But of course she demonstrated excellent penmanship....

A Day In The Life...

In this story, every individual's name begins with the letter that also identifies the personality style. I have taught for 14 years and have attended several recertification courses. As a Christian wife, mother and teacher, I feel blessed that I was able to take this course and wish that I had taken it a long time ago. With a little exaggeration, this is an example of a typical day with my family and an example of four students from my 5-year-old Kindergarten Class this year.

Carol begins her day very early. She already has everything laid out, lunches packed, and her list made of things to do that day. She wakes up her husband Ike for the second time as she is doing her hair. Her son, Donald Ike, is sleeping through his alarm *again!* Carol then wakes up Susan, who always greets her mother with, "Good morning...!"

Everyone is rushing to get ready except for Donald Ike, and Carol reminds him how important it is to be on time. She brushes Susan's hair. Susan cries, and then apologizes for crying.

Carol's husband Ike is discussing an upcoming fishing trip with son Donald Ike. Of course, Donald Ike has not eaten his breakfast or put on his shoes. **Carol** *again* reminds her son *and* her husband that they need to be on time.

It's time to leave, and **Donald Ike** has forgotten his lunch box on the table. **Susan** gives her Daddy one last kiss. **Ike** asks **Carol** what she would like to do during the upcoming weekend.

Carol and her children get to school early, and she begins to work on the following week's lesson plans. **Susan** colors quietly in the room, not wanting to disturb her Mom. **Carol** has **Donald Ike** help her by tearing out pages in her students' workbooks. He forgets to tear out half of the pages and then is frustrated that his mother asked him to do it. As **Carol's** children go to their classrooms, **Donald Ike** hits **Susan** on the head. She cries and then kisses Mom good-bye.

Carol's students begin to arrive. She greets them and reminds them where to put their things.

Matthew **I** comes in and begins talking to all of his friends. Lucas **D** comes in jumping up and down and "bopping" Matthew **I** on the head. As **Carol** greets Ashley **S**, the little girl just smiles. Carly **C** comes straight in and begins working, pausing only to ask for a second sheet of paper because she made a mistake.

During our opening devotional time, Matthew **I** has about ten prayer requests. Lucas **D** is poking Ashley **S** with his pencil as she holds back tears. Carly **C** asks questions about every paragraph of the Bible story.

At snack time, Matthew **I** doesn't finish, since he has talked so much. Lucas **D** knocks his drink all over Ashley **S**'s desk. She cleans it up. Carly **C** finishes her snack early so she can begin again on her work.

During recess, Matthew **I** "comes to visit" with all the teachers. Lucas **D** gets in a fight and **Carol** puts him into "time out." Ashley **S** falls down and tries not to cry. Carly **C** is playing school and has most of the girls in a single file line.

In the Reading Circle, Matthew **I** doesn't know where to read when it is his turn. Lucas **D** is on his head. Ashley **S** reads so quietly that **C**arol can hardly hear her. Carly **C** wants to know _why_ the characters are doing what they are doing in the story.

It is time to go home! **S**usan comes back to her mother's room and asks how her day was. As **D**onald **I**ke comes in, **S**usan also asks how his day was, and he just grunts, "Why?"

On the way home, **C**arol reminds her children of their afternoon responsibilities. **D**onald **I**ke left his Spelling book at school. **S**usan goes to her room and quietly does her homework. **C**arol is beginning supper as **I**ke comes home from work and plays with the children.

After an argument with **D**onald **I**ke about cleaning his room, **C**arol takes **S**usan to piano lessons and **D**onald **I**ke to his baseball game. He is upset after the game because his team doesn't win. **S**usan tells **D**onald **I**ke that it's okay he didn't win but asks if he had a good time.

Home again, **C**arol has a problem getting **D**onald **I**ke to get in the bed, while **S**usan wants to pray for everyone and kiss them all one more time. **I**ke wants to talk with **C**arol about weekend plans but **C**arol says she has papers to grade right now and needs some "quiet time."

Yet, she seems reasonably well-adjusted to her friends and family....

Class Of '92

I have decided to write about several Seniors in my American Government class several years ago. That class contained five students who were classic examples of the basic four personality types.

Chandler was my "D" type, but he was unusual in that he masqueraded as an "I." After some consideration, perhaps this is *not* so unusual. All good con artists must be "D's" disguised as "I's" since their intention is to impose their will on you while making you like them. In other words, I think they can make you *enjoy* being robbed! Chandler definitely fit into this mode, a rascal with manners. Very bright, he always wanted to rush through the chapters and criminal case studies. You could read in his eyes, *I understand all of this — let's move on to something new!* He always wanted his facts brief and straightforward with no elaborate details. Any objections were always sugarcoated with apologies and praise. He is now enrolled in a four-year college. I have envisioned him as the ultimate politician.

Roy, in-the-flesh, causes whatever image you have held of the "ultimate 'I'" to pale and wither in comparison. Have you ever heard the old Southern expression, "He would talk just to hear his head rattle"? As long as he attended our school we had no need of our P.A. system. In fact, "Telephone, Telegraph, Tell A Roy" was a witticism commonly heard around campus. Once teachers in the faculty lounge were disturbed by his voice reverberating down the hall. At this point, one of the coaches remarked that Roy would have blurted out something at the Crucifixion — I had an instant mental image of Roy, at this most solemn moment in world history, turning to the others with "How 'bout them 'Dogs?!?" *(Editor's Note to Yankee Readers: This is a familiar greeting among alumni and fans of the University of Georgia "Bulldogs" football team.)* American Government class was torture for Roy. Imagine sitting in class for 55 minutes without talking to the rest of the class! He was distracted by anything and everything done by the rest of the class. I helped him with this problem by seating him directly in front of my desk so he would have to concentrate on what *I* was doing. Projects like "Current Events in American Government" gave him an opportunity to *talk* and *learn* at the same time. He almost drove me crazy during the year, but on the morning following my mom's death, he was the first to call to offer his sympathy and to volunteer to take care of the livestock on our farm. Today, Roy works in his father's construction firm. All of us who had him as a student are convinced that wherever he goes and whatever he does, life will not be dull.

Francie was my "S" type personality. Steady, secure, sweet, submissive, sentimental — all of the "S" adjectives described her. A honey-blonde with big, beautiful blue eyes, and possessing one of the most radiant smiles I have ever seen on a child. That smile could brighten the darkest of teaching days. Pleasing others seems to have been her purpose in life. An overachiever, Francie maintained an *A* average by sheer determination. Her homework was always perfect. I am sure she spent far more time on it than the other *A* students. Mistakes made on an exam devastated her. Now I understand that it was not the lack of knowledge that upset her, but the fact that she felt she had failed *me*. Francie is now enrolled in a senior college and comes by our school occasionally to visit. I'll be sitting in my classroom and will hear a soft, Southern voice say, "Mr. W...?" Looking up, I will once again be treated to the glow of that unique smile.

Peter and Jerry are my examples of the "C" type personality style. Peter could best be described as a "C" with a strong dose of "I." Jerry fit the classic "C" mold. Both were brilliant students and served as co-Valedictorians in a class filled with excellent students. In class, they wanted a critical analysis of each chapter. Criminal case studies had to contain every minute detail. By the way, they drove Chandler, my "D," to the point of madness. They almost stopped me from including *True/ False* type questions on exams. They would dissect each question to the point that they would convince themselves that *True* questions were possibly *False* and that *False* questions could possibly be *True*. It took me a whole year to get these students to answer these questions as they were stated and not try to outsmart themselves. True to form, both were sensitive persons. I shall never forget the look on their faces as my mom's funeral. I felt that *I* should be consoling *them*. Peter and Jerry are both currently successful pre-med students at major universities.

With a teaching career spanning 25 years, there are many students I could have chosen to illustrate the personality types. I chose these five because they were members of a class that comes only so often in a teacher's life. Graduation night sometimes produces dry-eyed parents and a tearful faculty. The Seniors of 1992 were such a class.

The "People Equation"

The most difficult Physical Science lesson was now at hand: *balancing equations*. Although I didn't realize it before, this is just the sort of situation that drives personality styles to the surface.

When Kathy, a high "D," was unable to grasp the concept on the second example, she blurted out, "This is *stupid!* We will *never* use this in real life!"

When I tried to explain the significance, she interrupted to ask how many problems would be on the test. I thought I should console her and told her that we would have one or two at the most. Satisfied that this skill could not hurt her grade, she instantly quit trying and began working on homework in another subject!

Janie, a high "C," began asking every question imaginable: "How do you know where to begin? What are the steps? How do you know when you're finished?"

Angie, a high "I" said, "Mrs. M, I *love* doing this — it's so much fun!"

When the bell rang Sarah, a high "S," walked quietly out of the room. She didn't understand a thing that had happened, but she didn't want to ask in front of everyone.

This is a true story, but it would have been much different with my new "personality insights." I realize now that I should have challenged Kathy in some way, such as allowing homework incentives to everyone who completed the class work with a degree of correctness. I answered Janie's questions patiently, and I would not change that. I should have rewarded Angie by allowing her to demonstrate solving a problem on the board. Sarah presents a more difficult challenge. While I know that I can't personally check the work of every "S" every day, I hope I will do a better job of checking and offering encouragement, especially on the difficult assignments.

= Take Me Out Of The Ballgame =

At County Christian School, it was 1:30 p.m. and time for recess. As each row was dismissed, excited expressions and impatient gestures were made regarding who would be on the kickball teams of Joey and Aaron — both "D's." After teams were established, the game got underway. I noticed that Steven, an "S," and Donnie, an "I," had been chosen as pitchers. Since fielders usually see more action than pitchers, I could easily see that Steven had been coaxed into this position. He didn't seem to mind since Joey was one of his best friends. And Donnie... well he simply liked being in the center of the infield — right in the middle of the action!

While this was going on, Sam had been "squaring off" the playground, making sure the distances were exact and that everyone knew exactly where the bases were. Each base marker was put in place and Sam checked to see that the lineups were turned in. He was the official scorekeeper for both teams. Randy, also a "D" but not as dominant as Joey and Aaron, was the umpire. He loved to call strikes and outs with violent gestures and a loud voice, as baseball umpires did on TV.

The problem came when high "I" Rob got on first base. He began stealing before the pitcher released the ball — he *loves* the squealing cheers of onlookers as he manages to get into a "tie-up" between second and third. As he slid into third, umpire Randy called him safe. The riot began. No rules had been defined as to whether "leading off" and "stealing" were allowed. Since Rob was on Aaron's team, Joey stormed over to Aaron saying it wasn't fair. All the "S's" quietly murmured to themselves, "Let's quit all this fussing and play ball..."

Meanwhile official scorekeeper Sam had gone off to get the official rule book. Rob was still taking bows from third base for his performance. Joey and Aaron were about to start punching when the teacher called them both to her. She told them that they were captains and needed to take control of their arguing teams so the official ruling could be read.

The game proceeded at a relatively peaceful pace until a member of Joey's team missed an easy infield fly ball. Umpire Randy called him out, and Aaron came storming out to inform Randy that the infield fly rule does not apply in kickball. This sent Sam scurrying to the sidelines for the official rule book, so he would be able to quote "page 37, in the third paragraph..."

Recess ended before the game was completed.

Some of the hassles could have been avoided by going over the rule book with the captains and umpire *before* the game began. Also, by telling the captains that they were in charge of their teams and it was their responsibility to see that everyone got to play, they might have felt more of a sense of power and responsibility. By knowing the rules, they could have realized that the umpire was the final authority. This would have taught a necessary lesson about learning to be *under* authority in order to one day be *in* authority.

The Passing Of Old Bessie

This is an actual event in my Typing Class in the early 1970's. Of course, we had only manual typewriters. At the time this happened, I was a new teacher in my early twenties. I have kept this story in a folder with things students have done over the years:

The bell was ringing for the last period of the day to begin. Jack was seldom on time. He had too many other things to attend to — mainly locating his books and visiting with friends. Just before the bell stopped, he bounded into the room, made it past two desks, and then we all heard the noise — the third desk tipped over and the typewriter was literally in pieces all over the floor.

Startled, he dropped to his knees and began telling me how sorry he was and how he did not do it on purpose. Futilely, he pawed at putting shattered pieces in place.

My first thought was *How in the world am I going to explain to the principal an unrepairable typewriter?* He was not very receptive to foolishness or disruption in the classroom. *It was my responsibility to keep the students in place, but how do you keep a student like Jack in place?* It had never occurred to him that he was out of place, or that by nature he was a disruptive force!

I asked him how he thought I should handle this — take him to the office? have him pay for the typewriter? (It really wasn't worth anything.)

Jack's immediate response was, "Before you do anything to me, let's have a funeral for the piece of junk! After all, it has experienced a very tragic death and we will call it Old Bessie."

The class got in on this great idea. I am sure they were thinking if they played along they would not have time to do any class work.

I realized quickly that I was about to have absolute chaos on my hands. So I told them if they wanted a funeral for a typewriter, it would have to be planned and organized and we would have the funeral the next day. I explained that you don't immediately have a funeral after a death and that they could spend the night mourning Bessie's passing.

Bob (Senior Class President, Mr. Masters Degree, Beta Club member, football team captain, and incidentally, our PTO president as a grown-up dad) offered to organize it and assign roles:

Phil (now a pharmacist) was a quiet and rather solemn person who tried to do good work. It was decided that he would be the preacher. Since I was the teacher and the typewriters were my responsibility, I would represent the family. Pallbearers were to be two football players because you have to be strong to carry a casket. Since Jack had caused the mess, he would serve as undertaker and dress Old Bessie for her departure from the classroom. Nellie was in the chorus, so she would sing a short song. Mourners were to be two girls who were both very quiet and shy. This way they would not have to say anything. Tammi and Trish would prepare the script because of their wit.

After the parts were assigned, the preparation became their homework. Bob set up an orderly schedule for all to follow the next day. Each class member was to get a costume together.

The next day, our funeral service began with Preacher Phil saying:

> Dearly Beloved, we are gathered here today in the presence of all you nitwits to get rid of Old Bessie. I think she must be 100 years old and she has definitely lived a full and productive life. She really was tired of hearing the same old boring thing every day — *eyes on copy... ready... type* — and having people pound out *a, s, d, f, j, k, l, semicolon* in some fashion.
>
> However, I feel sure she was pleased when Matt sat in front of her. Matt has always thought it was stupid to type the same dumb drills and have to do them over and over again. He let her spit out other things when the teacher wasn't looking. In memory of her, I have asked Matt to say his last little piece of work.

Choked with "emotion," Matt rose to read the last words of Old Bessie:

> Little Bo Peep caught her a sheep
>> And made him a pudding pie
> While Jack and Jill went up the hill
>> To sit in a tree and wonder why
>> They weren't k-i-s-s-i-n-g.
> Little Jack Horner sat in a corner
>> Thinking Old Bessie sure is a goner!

We saw the different personality types in full display that day. Bob was a "D" with some organizational "C." Jack was definitely an "I." The quiet mourners were "S's." The teacher was more of an "S" than now, since she has learned how not to be so easily manipulated — now she can display some "C," too. I think Matt, the eulogy writer, was a "C" with a wry sense of humor and some "S" that was willing to be a part of the group. Phil was a "C," and the principal (who, thankfully, was absent) was a "D." He may not even have allowed Old Bessie's funeral.

Cleaning Up

As I walked through the cafeteria on my way to class, I noticed the mess — cups, boxes and papers covered the floors and tables, left from the previous lunch period.

Since this was my class's lunch period, I decided they would clean it and learn the importance of cleanliness. Of course, since my class was not the only group to eat lunch during this time, telling them my idea brought interesting responses...

Jon (our high "D") almost jumped through the ceiling. He made it known, quickly and loudly, that *he* was not going to clean it up. It was not fair for *him* to clean up the mess when *he* didn't make it!

Cheryl (our "I") was excited because we were going to do something — *anything!* — different from our normal routine. She had only two questions: *who* was going to help, and *who* was going to know we were the ones who cleaned it up?

Brianne (high "S") said yes, it did need to be cleaned up and if our class was going to do it, she would help. But she wanted to make sure no one would be upset by our cleaning the cafeteria.

Kevin (a classic "C") said if we were going to clean properly, we would need supplies: garbage bags, brooms, and towels for the tables. We would also need to decide who would be responsible for each area.

The class's final plan was to get all the "guilty" classes involved by rotating through a cleaning schedule. This would spread the responsibility for cleaning to everyone involved in creating the mess.

Jon was designated to go to the office for approval of the idea. Cheryl made the announcement and explained to the other classes what we were trying to do. Brianne made sure the materials were distributed to each class as they were needed. Kevin drew up a schedule for the classes to follow, with a list of cleaning supplies.

Did they all learn their lesson and keep in mind that "cleanliness is next to *godliness*"? Get real! Cleanliness is next to *impossible!*

I Went To College For This?

My first year of teaching was with Fourth Graders in a self-contained environment. I was hired about five weeks into the year, replacing a wonderful teacher who had left for another position. I was very apprehensive anyway... but *this* incident did not reassure me at all!

I developed a policy of keeping all old tests after the parents had reviewed them so my students would have them to use in studying for exams. Prior to exam week, I planned to pass out the old tests.

One student brought a note from his mother (a high "D") asking that I send home any future papers for her review — and asking that I return them again to her for safekeeping. From that day forward, I sent all of her son's tests home to her, as requested. However, I did not remember the tests I already had in my possession. I simply forgot they were in my files and did not send them home.

About three weeks later, I arrived at my classroom and the mother was waiting for me. I greeted her cordially; she was not cordial in return. She followed me into my classroom to "chat." Behind us was a fellow teacher, Mrs. Grimley (a "C" type) and her twin grandchildren both of whom were in my class that year.

Once inside, the mother screamed loudly at me, telling me how *stupid* I was for not sending home the rest of the papers. She also told me the other parents were angry because of my teaching methods. She continued on for what seemed like days. After she huffed out, I cried and could hardly even respond. I am an "I" type and she had hurt — no, *crushed!*— my feelings. She and the other parents didn't like me!

As Mrs. Grimley saw what was happening, she told her "C" type twin grandchildren to take their school stuff and go outside. Of course, they were very methodical in placing their belongings in the exact places they belonged — they even prepared their desks for class before they left the room! It seemed to take forever!

The little "S" student whose mother was so upset really just tried to sit in his desk unnoticed during the entire incident! In contrast to "mom," he was smiling and being nice to both of us.

In the end, the mother was still not satisfied and went to our principal before I could meet with him. Two hours later, I sat with him to tell my side of the story — how I had been pounced on like a wounded animal. Rather than being my defender, he (a definite "S") wanted to see what every other teacher did with their tests before exams and wanted us all to communicate better with each other, etc.

I learned a lot from this incident. Mostly, I learned to better defend myself in situations where I feel threatened, verbally or physically. I think it was interesting to see how the children reacted in this situation. And I can see now how their personality styles influenced their responses.

Free Reading Day

At the close of my third period on Thursday, I announced to my Sixth Grade Reading Class that tomorrow's class time would be spent in "free reading." During class on Friday, each student would continue to read his or her chosen library book in order to write a book report the following week. At the beginning of Reading Class on Friday, my observations revealed the following:

Reddy Dunnit had completed the reading of his library book on Thursday afternoon during seventh period study hall. Not only had he finished reading his book, but Thursday night he wrote his book report in final form. His final draft was complete — even though I had not yet distributed nor discussed the book report format. He proudly presented his final copy to me before the tardy bell rang!

Pogo Strider bounced into the room unburdened. Since we were reading library books in class today, he had come to class without anything. You see, at the close of class on Thursday, Pogo had given *me* his library book to keep safe until class time on Friday because he was afraid he might lose it or forget it in the meantime! It was very evident that he was excited about the assignment. In fact, he had brought Blow-Pop® candies for all his friends to eat while they were reading. What a guy! He even suggested that we play the radio for a little "mood music" while we read! I negated his request, and he attempted a second time: "How about headphones?" Pogo's enthusiasm manifested itself periodically during class. Each time he ran across a vocabulary word in his library book that we had studied during the year, he "po-goed" to my desk with his discovery. He showed the word in print to any interested students as he processed and recessed from my desk. He even suggested that if *everybody* would keep a record of vocabulary words in *their* library books, the student with the *most* words at the end of class would be the winner!

Serena Waters entered the classroom smiling and came to the back side of my desk, waiting patiently for me to look up. She handed me a stack of bookmarks with no comment whatsoever. I asked her if she would like to pass them out and she squinted her nose with a deliberate and definite *No.* I then got up to pass out the bookmarks for her, and she tapped me on my shoulder to get my attention. She uttered soft-spoken words of thanks for allowing her and her fellow students class time to spend in "free reading." Seeing Reddy Dunnit plop his finished book report on my desk, Serena immediately offered a sincere apology because she had not finished reading her library book nor had she completed her report.

Quest Chunn rubbed his chin as he flipped through his library book to see the number of pages remaining to be read. He glanced at the clock and mentally calculated that if he read one page every two minutes, he would lack only 27 pages when class was dismissed. As his eyes inventoried the progress of his fellow readers, Quest began asking the following questions even before his hand was fully elevated and he was recognized: "Exactly why are we doing this? Are we going to have a test at the end of class? Is silent reading a daily grade? Will we have to finish our library book over the weekend if we don't finish in class? How can you know if we are really reading?" By the way, Quest Chunn's chosen library book *just happened* to be one that had a correlating set of *Cliff Notes*® and had been made into a video… just in case!

My Quilt

They come in all shapes and sizes; variety is the spice of life. This thought popped into my idle brain as I entered my world of Eighth Grade kids, classrooms, and chaos.

There is Michael, arrogant in demeanor. He intimidated me a bit at first. Rumors had been circulating about his problems with Ms. Lincoln. Sparks flew every day. Even the Dean of Discipline had been called in twice. Both of these high "D's" wanted command of the same ship. I knew that Michael's parents were divorced and he was living with his "just a little spacy" mom... probably an "I." Being the sweet, supportive "S" that I am, I devised ways that Michael could command my ship without sinking it. Guess who became my responsible errand runner, my scantron grader, my right hand man? You see, Michael had become head of his household, the little decision-maker. How could he come to school and take a back seat in his environment? Did I have a problem with Michael? No, not one.

Adaptation can be acquired by others quite easily on the other hand. Christine was constantly ridiculed by "friends" for being the teacher's pet. But, as the song goes, "What's not to love?" about Christine. Caring, sweet and dependable — her natural traits. Career reports were putting us all to sleep, so Christine memorized her presentation, had a glitter-covered poster, displayed pamphlets, books, materials and tools, showed a short video — and wore SCUBA® gear, right down to the 20" flippers! "Above and beyond the call of duty;" was her motto, even at the risk of exposing herself to attention.

Oh, look — there is Spencer! You always know when he is coming. There is no doubt Spencer's running for student body president. His grades were so low, though, that he almost didn't qualify. *Everybody loves Spencer,* even the teachers who send him to the principal! He has such a way with people. He says he's going to be a preacher. He forgot to go to a church one Sunday where he was supposed to preach. He broke the speed limit to get there five minutes late. Oh well, that's Spencer.

Flashes of "kid color" I detect, but I don't really focus. There's poor Julia. She missed the first three weeks of Junior High with stomach problems. It's no wonder — she's a born worrier. "Meticulous in dress and academic performance" would describe Julia. She strives slowly but surely to create perfection on paper. A few weeks ago, she arrived at school with a pale, hopeless expression on her face. Someone told me she was sick in the restroom. Later on as I called roll, I put a big, red *A* for "absent" in her square. *Where had she gone? What had happened?* Upon entering that morning, she had seen all the kids studying for their science test. She had forgotten! Not Julia! She never forgot! If only I could have understood personality styles sooner!

My mind blinks back to reality and the vision of a quilt comes to my head for some reason. These kids are all different pieces to a sort of "memory quilt" my subconscious is creating within me. One thing, though, a quilt must have to exist is a foundation or a backing. Without that, the pieces can't unite; they can't be unified to build that final, completed whole.

Yes, teachers, we are that backing. What kind of quilt are we making? Hey, I've got to get to class. I'm late....

Our Magic Moment

Every teacher is blessed with magic, super moments, but this year took the cake for me. I thank God every day that a particular child is now a part of my life.

I'll call him "Lester." He has "Fragile X Syndrome." Research about his condition is in its earliest stages since it was labeled officially in 1991. "Fragile X" is a genetically linked, inherited syndrome which, with other characteristics, exhibits itself in varying degrees of mental retardation.

Our Kindergarten Class this past year included a myriad of personalities. Our range (as it see it *now)* was from an unbelievably high "D" to the sweetest "S" you will ever meet. With the high "I's" and more-than-competent "C's" mixed in, you could not ask for a more diverse group of little children.

In retrospect, the one event that occurred across the board for all of these children was that each of their strengths was manifested by their exposure to and interaction with "L." Each child accepted and feel in love with "L" in his own way.

The day "L" wrote his name for the first time was perhaps the most wonderful day I have experienced in my career.

I watched Megan (a high "C") relinquish her chair at the table to witness the event. Her loyalty to her new friend became evident, and her big tears emerging as he finished the last letter of his task made her sensitivity evident. Chad's easygoing manner and calmness established his steadfastness for his new friend as he supportively sat close by. This helped give "L" the encouragement he needed. Kyle's enthusiasm added the lighthearted fun atmosphere we all needed as the intense importance of the event became evident to each of us in the room. Dylan's confidence and determination became contagious to "L" as he realized that for the first time he would accomplish a goal he had set for himself — and that in his own way, he could *indeed* positively affect each child in the room.

Proof positive, I believe, that there are "angels among us." I am so very thankful for the little personality who helped me know that teaching children is where God can use me... and in doing that, *I* can grow.

P.S. The spontaneous standing ovation initiated by my high "S" Cal was more than I could handle!!! Too cool for school!

Speech(less) Class

It was the first day of school and time for Speech Class. This course is open to all at our high school and attracted 17 students who were glad to see their friends but sad to be back at school so early in August.

The "true colors" of our students shine through on their first day of Speech because each must stand in front of the class and make an impromptu speech introducing themselves, who they are and what they enjoy.

After welcoming the students and checking the roll, I made the assignment and gave my own introductory speech as an example for them. But their response reminded me of the old "Hee Haw" television show song, "Gloom, despair and agony on me…!" You should have seen the expression on their faces!

Only seconds passed before the first hand went up — you guessed it: a high "I." Allison asked, "Mrs. B., may I go first?" I nodded. She was seated on the back row but eagerly jumped up to come to the front. Of course, on her way she greeted everyone and told Angie where she had bought her new jeans. As she began her introduction, she interrupted herself: "Excuse me, I must remove my retainer so I can talk clearly. That reminds me of a story — you see, I was…" A "people person" from the word *Go!,* Allison talked nonstop for ten minutes! I thanked her for being so eager and ushered her back to her seat.

Immediately, Mitsy raised her hand and volunteered to go next. A definite leader, she was a cheerleader, class officer,

Honor Society member, star basketball player, etc. Mitsy strode confidently to the front and introduced herself to the class. Of course, she actually needed no introduction — she was a *presence* in our school. After detailing her two-minute family history, she explained her future plans, listing the 12 things she had jotted down quickly under the heading "Senior Goals." She was firm, direct and decisive — a high "D."

On her way back to her seat, she volunteered Cody, a gifted "C" type student. Being a loyal student, he approached the podium willingly but quietly. During the previous 15 minutes of speech-making, he had prepared a detailed set of 3"x5" cards and had them numbered and ready to go. His thoughts were logical and intense. He was very curious about the requirements for the course, questioned several of my earlier statements, closed out his speech and returned to his seat.

Next to Cody sat sweet, shy Mary. I called on her. She remained calm but seemed apprehensive about getting up in front of the class without time to think, prepare, and get her courage up. During her hesitation, two boys got up and interrupted. Although I stopped them, in typical "S" demeanor, Mary said, "Oh, Mrs. B, it's okay."

Actually, all the boys wanted was a "drop slip." They knew they would never get up in front of the class to speak — it was not their "style." *What would all the "studs" say?* So, I lost four students to fear on the first day. But I did find out a lot about the other 13 who were bold enough to stick it out.

Kindergarten Cop

As a Kindergarten teacher, I sometimes find it necessary to appoint a child as classroom monitor when I must leave for a few minutes. Throughout the year I call on different students to be my helpers and I have noticed different responses from each child, characterizing the "D," "I," "S," and "C" styles.

The first child I will discuss is Jill, with her "D" type personality. After telling everyone to be quiet while I was gone and giving Jill instructions to take names and leaving the class, I returned to find her in a heated argument with another child. She also had a long list of names and minor incidents to report on: one child had dropped his pencil and another had coughed. Only one had actually talked, whispering to her neighbor. I told Jill how thoroughly she had performed her job but that simply writing the names of children who talked would have been enough. I told her again how very much I appreciated her good job of helping.

Another day, I called on Jimmie to be the monitor. Jimmie loves to have fun and enjoys being in front of the class — a typical "I" personality. Of course, when I returned this time, the class was in an uproar. Jimmie and two other boys were playing tag around the room, and several other children were throwing wadded-paper balls across the room. After restoring order, I told Jimmie how very special he was and how God made him with a happy spirit to make people laugh. However, as I corrected him, I reminded him that when the teacher leaves the room it is not play time. I also thanked him for wanting to make our classroom a happy place.

Jeannie is an "S" personality, a very quiet, sweet and trusting child. When I returned to her "watch," the class was behaving fairly well, but she was in tears. One of the boys explained that Jill had gotten up from her desk and had been talking. She threatened to hurt Jeannie if she said anything to me about it. I immediately told Jeannie how much I appreciated her help as monitor and that she had done a fine job. I also told her not to let any child bother her and just do as I had asked her to do. I reassured her again that she had done a good job.

My last child is Jacob, a "C" type child who is very cautious and a perfectionist in everything he does. On his day as monitor, he informed me that *three* children had wiggled in their seats, *two* were not sitting up straight, and *one* child did not have his hands on his lap. I told Jacob that he had observed the class carefully and how much I appreciated his help. I told him not to worry about those children — he had watched them very well and I was proud of him.

Each child has a unique personality. God created each of us with special gifts and talents to work together in a positive way. We are different but wonderfully made. As stated in Psalm 139:14: "I will praise thee, for I am fearfully and wonderfully made."

Junior Achievement

To appreciate fully the differences of all the participants in this story, one must understand the overall curriculum in Junior Achievement Economics. This is a one semester course where students complete a fast-paced academic instructional program, compete in a computer-simulated sales and production program, and most importantly, organize a *Student Company* in which they must offer a product for sale and finish the semester with a profit. Bankruptcy is not an option. Students must compete for and/or be selected for the following company positions: president, vice president for finance, vice president for marketing, vice president for production, and vice president for personnel.

The initial phase is to have the class elect a company president. This is when the teacher begins praying for wisdom on behalf of the 11th Grade students who (we hope!) will select one of their own with a "D" type, leadership personality.

As luck would have it, Craig (a "D") was nominated and elected by the stockholder students. (The teacher, also a high "D," wanted to slip out of character momentarily and danced around the room like a high "I," shouting hurrahs all over the place!) The election of Craig is attributed to Divine intervention, since his position required someone with ability to lead and make decisions confidently. Craig is a star basketball player who displays these characteristics and more.

The president selects those who fill the vice-presidential slots. With very little direction from the teach, he grasped the requirements easily and matched students to those positions based on his perceptions of their abilities. The *Student Company* was formed early in the semester and progress began immediately.

Without benefit of any DISC training, this Junior Class student matched each position with a personality style that was able to get the job done.

For VP–Marketing, he chose Laurel, a friendly, personable, talkative girl who is everybody's friend and the life of the party. The *Student Company* cannot begin sales until Marketing gets its act together and conducts surveys to see what the customer wants. Laurel immediately jumped in front of the class and put together a survey questionnaire. Then she enlisted *Student Company* members to conduct surveys along with her in each homeroom. She could hardly wait for each morning, to stand in front of a class, explain the product offered for sale, and take orders from the customers.

Our VP–Personnel was quiet Melissa, who was dependable, efficient, practical, calm, and exhibited a keen sense of teamwork. She had to place the remaining students in positions as sales manager, timekeeper, etc. This required delicate negotiation skills so no one would feel offended and each person would feel comfortable in the position assigned to them.

Our VP–Production was Barbara Jo, who was extremely analytical, thorough, and an absolute perfectionist — she spent four to six hours at home each night, studying or completing homework. Barbara Jo was always disappointed if she scored less than 100% on any assignment or test. For the first time in our school's history, this Economics Class chose to make its own product. This meat the VP–Production had a tremendous responsibility in coordinating all activities to produce and distribute the product. No student could have done a better job. From the very beginning, Barbara Jo began estimating the cost of production materials and supplies, labor expenses, production site requirements and selection, and a completion timetable.

The *Student Company* ended the semester successfully with a nice profit, which they donated to the local Boys' Ranch. How did our VP's perform?

Laurel finished poorly in "individual sales," but she had a great time advertising the product and getting it in front of customers.

Barbara Jo saw all of her detailed plans come to a successful conclusion. The students had to work only two Saturdays for about six hours each day to generate products that grossed over $900.00. Sadly, Barbara Jo's quest for perfection left her mentally and emotionally exhausted, and she decided to attend another school that was less demanding academically for her Senior year.

Melissa led the class in individual sales of 13 items, totalling over $150.00. Who could resist buying from her with her sweet disposition? Based on her performance and productivity, she was awarded bonus points which gave her a grade of 100 for the second 9-week grading period and an *A* for the semester.

Angel Wings

It's a wonderful day in the neighborhood at "Presby Chris" — the nickname for our private church-sponsored school! Things are actually looking pretty good — kids' hopes and skills are high because Christmas is nigh!

Our Fifth Grade morning has started with a devotional talk on the appearances of angels in the Bible. Everything is going smoothly. As we come to a close, our heads are bowed reverently for prayer...

"HI, EVERYONE! WE'RE FINALLY HERE!" Annie has made her "grand entrance," not noticing our mood. "Did you know that we just saw an awful wreck in front of the school? An old, beat-up truck just bashed Miss Judi's new black Explorer — my mom almost freaked out!" Annie, to put it mildly, is an "I." Her entrance is the first of several happy comments that she will make today. By the time she has happily answered the questions that follow her announcement, her steady, stable teacher decides the students will have silent prayer. Her own prayer during this time is *Lord, make this day go as swiftly as angel wings flutter. Hold me close for I fear one of my wings will fly the wrong way...!*

Math class begins after Amber gets each and every one of her books and pencils in place. She is not an orderly "C"; she is an "S" making her comfortable "nest." As the stable, steady teacher reviews last night's homework answers with the students, the expression on Amber's face shows things are not going well with her paper. She makes no comments but her face is as red as her auburn hair. Before the teacher can reach Amber's desk to help, Blake — who sits directly behind Amber — blurts out, "She missed 10 of the 25 problems! She musta had her mind in the gutter while she did her homework! She got some *dumb* answers!"

The stable, steady, sweet teacher asks Blake to keep his comments to himself because he could hurt others. He is sorry, so he says, but the damage has already been done. Mandy, another sweet, steady, supportive girl, reaches out to comfort Amber and tells her that she will help with the missed problems.

The steady, supportive, sweet teacher presents the Saxon new concept for the day. She is patiently explaining the concept of "getting *unlike* denominators to *like*" when Tim, with his calculating "C" mind, announces that he has found a faster way. He triumphantly explains his method, but it unravels in demonstration. The class returns to its predetermined, charted course through the help of its steady, stable, supportive teacher.

American History is next — it is the teacher's love, so she introduces the Civil War in her usual enthusiastic fashion. She has plans for the class field trip to the final home of Jefferson Davis, the only President of the Confederate States of America, and explains his role in the Civil War.

Richard almost jumps out of his seat! "This was not a Civil War — it was the 'War Between the States,' or the 'War of Northern Aggression.' A 'civil' war is a war between opposing groups of citizens. The South was not opposing; it was only trying to withdraw from the Union. So," according to Richard, "please call it the 'War Between the States.'"

Ahhh, the sweet sound of the recess bell saves the steady, stable, sweet teacher. However, will not be surprised if high "D" Richard appears tomorrow with "an authentic Confederate Drum and Fife Corps" to prove his point!

An Innocent Assignment

Our librarian assigned our Third, Fourth and Fifth Graders to produce a newspaper, to teach them about headlines, bylines, etc. Different articles were assigned to groups in each grade, with each group's leader selected by the librarian. The project worked well for all the groups, except one. Several Fourth Grade girls changed their assignment when they decided the newspaper needed a "gossip column" — and with that, the trouble began!

The librarian selected Elaine (a high "C") to head this group. Samantha (a high "I"), Liz (a "D"), and Sherri and Terri (both "S's") were the other team members.

The first hint of trouble was late one afternoon when Elaine ("C") complained that Liz ("D") was bossing everyone and generally causing friction. Since Liz's style usually generated turmoil and since the assignment was to be done outside my classroom, I failed to heed the early warning signal.

The following morning, I received a call that Liz's mother (a high "S") needed to see me immediately. Fortunately, I had a free period and she came in at nine o'clock. She was most concerned that her daughter was going to be referred to as "a dog" in the forthcoming newspaper. Supposedly, Elaine had included it in the column and the others on the team had agreed.

I commented that this did not sound like Elaine, and Liz's mother handed me their notes as her proof. During recess, I kept the girls in my room, produced the note and asked for an explanation. These were their responses:

Elaine was horrified that Liz had gone through her purse. Elaine had not wanted to work in this group. She and Liz were on the outs anyway. Elaine was tired of being bossed around and bullied by Liz . "Everyone is tired of Liz," she said, "and we all agreed to call her 'a dog'!"

I looked at Liz and realized she was ready to charge all the girls. She glared, clenched her fists and smirked at the group.

Her expression and body language suggested *I am in control now! I have the note as proof!*

I glanced at our "Miss America," high "I" Samantha, with a questioning look. She twirled around and said she had been at the basketball game last night — she didn't have time to work on any gossip... "Yes, I knew Liz was called a dog..." Samantha seemed confused and unhappy by my puzzled expression and proceeded to pout.

Sherri and Terri (both "S" types) acknowledged they knew about the note and the planned article. "No, it wasn't nice," they agreed readily, but they too were tired of Liz. When I asked how they would like being called a dog, Sherri began to cry and Terri started biting her fingernails.

Needless to say, there was no gossip column in our first and final edition. I now understand why even the *National Enquirer* has an editor!

Jesse And His Cap

Our school was founded 25 years ago, and over the years our Board of Directors has modified our student code of conduct and handbook. Last year, in response to current fashion, a rule was added: *No caps are to be worn in the classroom.* I went over the handbook and carefully stressed this new rule to my students. Everyone in the room understood.

After our recess, all the students rushed back into the classroom and all the boys hung their caps up in the back of the room... everyone except Jesse. I reminded him of our new rule and he quickly removed his cap, quietly saying he was so sorry he forgot.

Glancing around the room, I saw that Brent was really enjoying the whole episode. He also made sure everyone else noticed Jesse's unexpected embarrassment and wanted to prolong his own fun at Jesse's expense.

Molly was sitting next to my desk and started questioning me about the hat rule. *Why was this silly rule made in the first place? Can our room change this new rule?*

Wendy said she could help the class remember all the new rules by writing them on a large poster so everyone could see them.

The class discussed which rules needed to be put on display. Molly and Jesse helped Wendy with the poster rules the class had selected. Brent excitedly volunteered to read the rules out loud before every morning recess.

Our "Personality Insights" course has helped me to understand that Jesse had an "S" type personality who wanted to please and fit in, Molly was a "D" who didn't like unnecessary control, Wendy was a "C" who was seeking compliance with the rules, and Brent was an "I" who saw humor in everything. Thanks to this course, I will be able to help many children in my classroom become their best.

A Secret Formula

The setting for this story is an elementary school science lab. The students are Fifth Graders. Excitement and anticipation are running high because it is the first day of Science Fair projects for three eager students. Plans for this initial "testing" have been in progress for several weeks. Research has been completed, experiment materials have been pre-approved and gathered, and 15 students are assembled with one teacher as the episode is about to unfold.

The students have been divided carefully into groups of four, with two students in each group prepared to begin experimenting today. As the teacher, I have made every effort to appear calm and collected in spite of feeling tense. I have carefully explained directions and procedures, knowing full well that most of my instructions went in one ear and out the other. My novice scientists are poised and ready to work with their "science buddy" at their side.

Sandy, Joey, Jeb and Cyndi are "Group A," and their project is the same as the other groups': "Can Homemade Toothpaste Clean Effectively?"

I signal for work to begin and I move casually from group to group, checking progress and answering questions — generally displaying my own "S" and "C" traits. Everything seems to be going well and I am feeling a bit smug that the work is proceeding exactly as planned. Mixing and measuring of ingredients had begin and "homemade toothpaste" is becoming a reality.

Sandy (an "S" type) apologizes that her mom forgot to buy peppermint as required by the formula, and explains that they are substituting oil of cinnamon in its place. My confidence level swells over the success of my "hands on" science project.

Science buddy Joey (a "D" type) pushes Sandy aside and insists on measuring out the oil of cinnamon. Things were moving much too slowly for Jeb (an "I" type), who feels he should measure and spur things on. He is anxious to draw the attention of the surrounding students, and in his excitement, he gets a bit carried away (as "I's" often do). He pours about *three times* more cinnamon oil than is called for. Feeling a bit overwhelmed, Sandy asks, "Are you sure about this?"

By this time, cautious Cyndi (a "C" type) has left her own experiment and is double-checking amounts and procedures, completely upset about the confusion. Joey is becoming quite perplexed and says, "Hurry up, Sandy — we want to get a taste before class is over!" They all converge on Sandy and convince her she should try is first since it is "her" experiment. Timidly, she agreed. She reluctantly sticks a finger in the mixture and places it in her mouth. "Wow!" she exclaims, "It's really hot!"

That did it! Every Fifth Grader in the room immediately ran to Group A's table, and more than half put "Advanced Formula Crud" into their eager mouths. Screams, hysteria and hives began emerging! Kids were running to water fountains and sinks, grabbing handfuls of water in an effort to stop the burning. Susie was hysterical. I was overwhelmed. Teachers ran to my door from other classes. *Pandemonium* — the nightmare of every teacher!

After 30 minutes of mouth rinsing and consoling efforts, all was well again in our little science lab, but the episode will never be forgotten by teacher or students.

Unobserved Observation

As Winter turned into Spring, it was a time for faculty observation and evaluation by our principal. This ordeal is something an "S" type teacher dreads from Christmas vacation until Memorial Day!

I felt I had prepared my class for his visit into our Kindergarten world. I explained that the principal would come into our room for a visit and sit at the back table to watch us play and work. They were told to continue whatever they were doing. I thought this was explanation enough at the time.

Writing detailed lesson plans, collecting support materials, and making an all out effort to give the Kindergarten room an unused, unabused appearance strained my limited "C" skills to their limits. I was prepared at eight o'clock for my principal to come and see me at my "Supportive/Cautious/Inspirational" best, and my preparations made me feel somewhat secure.

By nine o'clock, he still had not come to our room. The children had been working on their creative and wonderful tasks for an hour. Their schedule called for them to leave from nine o'clock to nine-thirty for Art Class. This is a class the children look forward to — and I planned to use this time to straighten the room, apply lipstick and brush my hair — just in case my appearance had a significant impact on my evaluation. But on this day, the Art teacher became ill just before our time. So, being flexible, I decided to shift my 10:30 to 11:00 plan to fill this half-hour.

Catherine, my high "D" six-year-old, wanted to go to the art room and teach the lesson herself. Justin suggested "indoor recess," a true "I's" reaction. Margaret, an "S," was stricken with concern about the welfare of their art teacher. And Kyle, my "C," was upset most because he already had all his supplies ready. By 9:30, still no principal — and my "I" had raised to the desperate point that snacks and recess looked mighty good!

As we were about to sit down, the principal walked in and seated himself at the back table.

Justin ran to hug him and announced, "The president is here!" If I had dug deep to find some glimmer of "D," I would have continue with our snack. But instead, I was concerned that he needed to see me actually *teaching* something — *anything!* So, instead, I decided to read aloud a favorite book of mine.

Catherine ("D") reminded the class that the librarian had

read that book to them on Monday, and that she hadn't liked it the first time. Margaret hugged her and reassured her that I had plenty of other books. Kyle commented that it was not circle time anyway and wanted to know why we were not eating the snacks he had brought.

I announced that I was flexible and picked up a book of fairy tales. I chose the shortest one and was horrified to find there were no pictures. My "S" took over and I suddenly felt threatened by the children, the principal and The Ugly Duckling!

Fighting panic, I said, "Class, this is a fairy tale... Now how do they usually begin? That's correct — 'Once upon a time...' And how do they end? Yes, Kyle (as he *profoundly* stated)... with a *period!*'"

Somehow I got through the story, fed them their snack and took them to recess. So much for the best laid plans of an "S – C – I" (no "D") with many unobserved talents!

Say The Secret Word

In my First Grade Class, we play a "Password" game right before lunch. I select one word from the new "Words List" on the chalk board. I print it on an index card and show it to the class. If a child whispers the correct word in my ear, they go to the cafeteria. If they miss, they get a second chance a little later.

This particular day, I ask Danny D if he would be in charge of picking the password for today. In his normal take-charge voice he says, "Yes, ma'am. I can pick a great one!"

Barely before he finishes the sentence, Iris I is jumping up and down by her desk, squealing "I *love* to play Password and I know what the word is!"

Carl C calmly raises his hand and asks, "Missus B, why is it necessary to say a password before we can eat our lunch?"

I tell him that it is a game that helps me find out how my teaching was that morning. If you say the word, I know you were paying attention. If you miss it, I'll know that I didn't so a good enough job getting you to pay attention and I'll try to do better tomorrow." (I move on quickly before another "D" suggests that if *they* don't know the word because *I* haven't done *my* job, maybe *I* should be the one to be late for lunch!)

Susie S is giving me her usual, adoring smile and has her hand raised. I call on her and she says, "Miss B, you are so nice. Thank you for letting us play games."

How The Teacher Got Thru The Day

After 13 years as a Kindergarten teacher, I became our school's librarian, responsible for all K–6 students instead of a small group of five-year-olds. 1 wasn't always sure what I was supposed to be doing, but I was determined to do more than check books in and out and shelve them according to "Dewey."

After several weeks, I decided a class of 3rd Graders was ready for an interesting assignment. So, after checking in their returned books I divided them into smaller groups by tables, and told each group to write and present a short story telling "How the Camel Got Its Hump," or "How the Leopard Got Its Spots," or "How the Tiger Got Its Stripes," or "How the Elephant Got Its Trunk."

I encouraged each group to be *very creative* in thinking through the idea. Everyone was going to participate in the thinking process, and then one person would write down their ideas and one person would present their story to the rest of the class.

My group divisions were part of the problem — one with leadership skills. Jamie, Stephanie, Frankie and Savannah were not going to write *or* speak. The "not me" virus spread to all the other tables, except one. But they couldn't create, write or even pretend to present anything with all the other commotion. This table seemed like a bunch of clowns escaped from a circus — their griping, grumbling and complaining over who got to speak and who was left out was almost slapstick.

As the period ended, my wonderful lesson plan lay cold and dead at my feet, and my feelings were hurt that no one had even been excited about my terrific lesson plan.

I could not give up! This was a bright and fun group of students. I *knew* they could really enjoy this type of assignment. What went wrong with my plan?

The following week, books were checked and the students were told to divide themselves into groups of five. Most formed around a strong leader who was not shy and would be willing to lead and speak.

To give them more control this time, I let them draw their own topics from a list of suggestions. They were also given a choice of writing and presenting their story, writing and acting it out on our library's play stage, or pantomiming the story and letting us guess what it was all about.

This time the lesson was a great success. We changed many variables during the semester and the idea caught on. Classes of all levels asked if they could write and act every week. We even wrote a play as a book report.

Until taking this course, I did not understand that my success the second time around was because my revised lesson plan gave all of the personality styles a motivational reason to participate and to find something enjoyable in the assignment. I ended up having as much fun as my students did!

Recess Melee

For most elementary school children, recess is the highlight of the day. I try to explain to my students that it is also a learning time just like a regular classroom session. During these times of play they are learning to get along with children of different personalities and are developing their social skills.

One day while on playground duty I was watching "my children" at play. Their game was a version of dodge ball. As they ran out onto the playground, Trent had possession of the ball and immediately began dividing the group into teams. Trent naturally assumed he would start the game since he had the ball. Chip, best described as a lively cricket, reminded Trent that he was first during their last recess. Trent happened to be the largest boy in the class. He informed Chip that he was going to be first and Chip was not going to tell him what to do! Chip might have weighed 60 pounds fully dressed and soaking wet, but suddenly he snatched Trent's ball and began running in all directions with the rest of his classmates giving chase.

Amid their squeals and running was a sense of play until Trent lost control. When he finally caught Chip, he threw him to the ground and the fight was on! Aleshia, who tends to "mother" everyone, stepped in to stop the fight and was hit by a flying fist.

By this time, I had arrived on the scene. After some discussion, Lori stepped forward and informed me that Trent was first during the last recess and it was actually Brian's turn because he scored the most points in the previous game. Lori explained that none of this would have happened if everyone had followed the rules of the game. She also brought to everyone's attention that if they didn't get started soon, recess would be over and no one would get to play!

As the game got under way, Aleshia apologized to me for everyone's behavior and explained that she was only trying to help. She assured Trent and Chip that she was not hurt or angry because she had been hit — in fact, she apologized for being in the way!

It is amazing how I now can understand these children and their personalities. Did you identify them as you read? Trent is a "D," Chip is an "I," Aleshia is an "S," and Lori is a "C."

A Square Root In A Round Hole

My fifth period Geometry Class walked into my room in late August and little did I know that my wife was changing. There were only twelve enrolled, but by the end of the first week I felt there had to be fifty! In all my years of teaching, I had never worked with a group like this — each person was so different.

By the end of the second week, I was sure someone had played a trick on me. There was no way these twelve students could have been registered in the same class without some serious rearranging of schedules.

On any typical day with this class, Kirk and Evan would start by asking why I could not move faster with the assignments. And why did I have to *explain* the lesson since anyone could read the book and get all the explanation they needed? They wanted me to give only one problem of each type because, they reasoned, if they could solve one, they could solve all of them.

Before I could explain the reason and need for a thorough explanation of every theorem, Marcie and Caroline would be planning an after-school trip — perhaps to the mall to look for prom dresses — and had probably invited half the class.

Adding to the circus, Carmen and Brandon often doubted the theorem proofs in the textbook, and would weigh in with suggestions that I rework two or three proofs, just to be sure.

These strain of these daily developments must have shown frighteningly on my face, because by this time Doreen would be assuring me that even though there were many interruptions, everything was going to be fine.

In the Spring, I attended a teachers' association convention and learned about different personality styles. Even while Dr. Rohm spoke, I was taking notes and thinking about this particular class.

With advanced math book assignments for Kirk and Evan, peer help for Marcie and Caroline to keep them focused, and a lot of "reworked" proofs, I survived the rest of the year.

I am prepared for *this* year!

Wild Waves

During a Literature Class, I had ordered *Robinson Crusoe* from the required reading list for all my students. I knew that some would love this book, some would like it once they got into it, and others would hate it altogether. One purpose in reading was to teach that we need to read — or do — things that we may not want to do.

We read by chapter assignments. They would read a certain number of chapters, and then we would discuss the material. We were well into the book. Crusoe and Friday had found each other. They also found that natives (cannibals) had come to Crusoe's island. Sharon, a "C" type personality, asked, "Why did the natives come over to this island to perform their ritual? Why didn't they stay on their own island?"

Several hands went up immediately. Looking around the class I saw Keith who was not raising one hand but waving both wildly. I thought to myself *Keith, I am bright enough to know that if you know the answer, holding up one hand will be sufficient.* He was looking around the room to see if anyone was being more demonstrative than he. I called on him. He hesitated, looking around the room, grinning. Finally he said, "…What natives are we talking about?"

"The ones in the story," I replied.

"I didn't read about any natives!" he exclaimed. (My questions apparently do not invite him to *answer,* only to *talk!*)

Wyatt, a high "D" type who had been sitting quietly while reading ahead, never looked up but commented, "It was because they wanted to eat out."

Nicole, who was sitting with her head down but her eyes up, caught my eye. She was a good student, wanting to please, so I called on her for a much-desired response. "I'm not sure but I think maybe they didn't perform this particular ritual on their home island. I didn't like that part, but I knew you wanted us to read all of the book, so I did…"

Wyatt interrupted with, "What was wrong this that part, Nicole?"

"If you liked it, that's fine…" she said in her non-confrontational "S" style.

Kevin was still grinning and looking around. "What's for

lunch today, Mrs. F?" Which probably caused Sharon to wonder, *Why did I ever ask this question during class discussion?*

Guess who my high "I" student was — wave both hands wildly over your head if you think you know.

Im-probable Games

My objective was to teach First Graders about "probability." I wanted to accomplish this in a concrete, hands-on way and let them have a little fun, too. So I decided to have them play a game and in the process learn a little about probability and tell about their results. This is how we went at it:

I planned to assign the children to cut five blue squares and two red squares from construction paper. Next, they would be told to put the squares in a paper bag and shake them up. Then, they would draw one square from the bag without looking — and repeat this action ten times, each time coloring in the color of the square on a little bar graph. Eventually, I planned that we would do the entire procedure three different times, changing the mix of blue and red squares each time. I was hopeful a pattern would emerge and with a little discussion we would discover what it meant.

As math time rolled around, I placed two sets of materials on each table in the classroom: a sheet of red construction paper, a sheet of blue construction paper, a small paper bag, and a graph sheet labeled *RED* and *BLUE* and numbered 1 to 10. As I was doing this, the children's questions started to fly: "What are we going to do?" "What are these for?" "Why are you doing that?" I just smiled.

When the materials were distributed I said, "We are going to play a game. First, find a partner." (This was my first mistake!) We had picked partners before, but this was the first time the partners would actually have to *work* together and produce *results*.

After the madness died down, we began discussing the rest of the plan. We went through the game step by step and practiced coloring in the squares on a big graph I drew on the board. Before long everyone assured me they understood and we started. But walking around the room, I soon identified three problem areas.

The first is Austin and Taylor who fell into a *huge* argument. Austin was already frustrated: "Mrs. S, Taylor is cutting the squares all wrong — they don't look like squares. Some don't *even* have four corners!"

Taylor threw his hands in the air and said, "Look, everyone else is halfway finished and Austin won't even let me put the squares in the bag!"

Behind me was the commotion of my second problem area. Marcie and Adam had cut out their squares, put them in the bag and started to shake the bag. At some point, the shaking evolved into Adam jumping around the table with the bag over his head, then handing the bag to Marcie, who pulled out a square. I asked them, "How many times have you pulled out a square?" They said in unison, "All ten times!" "Great!", I replied, "show me your graph!" Hands flew over their mouths — oops! They had forgotten all about the graph!

On the other side of the room, the third problem was waiting for me. Garner and Erica had the most pained and confused expressions so I asked what was wrong. Cautiously they replied, "We're not exactly sure we know what to do…" I asked, "Why didn't you tell me? Most partners are almost finished!" They were waiting for me to come around. Something was wrong — terribly *wrong* — with this picture!

If I had been aware of personality styles and that some work better together than others, I probably would have "encouraged" different combinations.

Austin and Taylor were a "D" working with a "C." Austin was a perfectionist and Taylor just wanted to get the job done. Marcie and Adam were both "I's." They started the project right away but soon got carried away with having a good time and forgot to do the last step. Garner and Erica were both "S" types, too sweet and shy to interrupt me. They had not even started.

Better combinations might have been:

Taylor ("D") with Garner ("S"). Taylor would have helped Garner get started, and Garner would have been a great finisher.

Austin ("C") would have been better paired with Adam ("I"). Austin would have helped Adam be more focused and complete the project, while Adam would have helped Austin loosen up and see it as a game.

Lastly, Marcie (also an "I") would have worked well with Erica (also an "S"). Marcie would have helped Erica get started while Erica would have helped Marcie to remember to finish the project.

These combinations might have made all the children feel more comfortable. Each of the children would have been more successful and their teacher might have had fewer headaches!

A Game For All

No matter what type of personality style you have, there is a football game for you. Let's check in on some games that go on during a typical football evening. Each game is headed by one personality style...

Duke charges $3.00 per person admission and game time is 7:30. His game would feature *two* teams but only *one* coach — himself. But he would also Quarterback both teams to make it fair. He would be easy to spot in the field since his jersey would be striped — he would also be the referee! His game would consist on two halves, each thirty minutes, with no timeouts and one five-minute break at halftime. This is all the time he would need to lead the band's halftime show, since he would also be the drum major. The game would end at 8:35.

Indy would have a free admission game, figuring more people would come. Game time would be 8:00 or so, following his thirty-minute interview with reporters and autograph session for fans. He would have four teams with five coaches each. Every team would be responsible for playing at least an hour. During the game, he would wander over to the concession stand, then up to "mingle" in the bleachers, then out to the field to talk with the players — and at the last minute taking up money to pay the referees. After the game, everyone would meet at his house for a victory party. But no one would know the final score because he had forgotten to turn on the scoreboard!

Sam would make sure his team was happy. If there were problems, everyone would meet at midfield and work it out until they were satisfied. No one would sit on the bench — tell Sam you want to play and he would say okay. After the game, people would be free to do whatever they wanted. Incidentally, *both* teams would be winners of the game.

Carl would charge an admission price of $7.29. Game time would be 7:31 to 9:03, using two teams and four quarters of play. One week before the game a committee, headed by Carl, would meet to draw out all the details. Everything would be determined at this meeting — plays would be drawn up in order and the play-by-play commentary would be typed up and ready for reading. The fans would be allowed to cheer only from their assigned seats and would receive refreshments periodically during the game since concessions would be included in the admission price. To know the final score, you would check the scoreboard as you entered the stadium.

Camelot And A Lot More

R ehearsals for the annual School Musical were under way — we were doing *Camelot*. With two weeks to go until the show opened, things were going pretty well, but not all of the cast had finished memorizing their lines. I sat them down before Thursday's rehearsal began and gave them a "pep talk" about it, pointing out that the performances would be here before we knew it. I told the cast I was a little disappointed that not all of them had taken the initiative in memorizing the script and set the follow Monday's rehearsal as the absolute deadline for memorization. I was winding up my speech with an admonition about personal responsibility — that we owe our best to ourselves and to our audience — when Judd interrupted me in mid-sentence:

"Can we get on with rehearsal here? You know we'll get the job done. We always do, don't we? I've got a big Chemistry test in the morning and I'll be up half the night studying as it is. My character's just onstage for Act I, so let's get started and I can get out of here. How about it?"

"Hey, you think you're the only one, jerk? I've got to read the first 80 pages of *Silas Marner* by second period tomorrow and do 20 problems in Pre-Calc, too!" This from Ben, who character was onstage practically the whole show, which meant he would be here until the bitter end of rehearsal.

"Judd," I replied, "I told you when I gave you this part that the show would require a big commitment, and besides, you've had a copy of the rehearsal schedule for five weeks. It's your responsibility to manage your time effectively. You could help me by calling the main characters together for some extra line practice on Saturday and making sure they've got everything memorized."

"Cool! Ben, Natalie, Don, Lou! My house, Saturday, two o'clock! I'll tell my mom she has to order pizza for us. You guys are going to get these lines down cold!"

"All right, folks, let's get started — Act I, Scene Three," I said, getting up from the floor where I had been sitting in front of them. "Judd, thanks for taking care of that."

I took my customary "rehearsal director seat" in the first row of the auditorium, called "places" for the actors, and rehearsal was under way, just five minutes late. As Lancelot and Arthur began their dialogue, Natalie approached me, timidly as usual — and waiting for me to speak first, she stood quietly in the semidarkness of the auditorium.

"What is it, Natalie?" I asked.

"Oh, Mr. L, I hope you aren't too mad at me. I know I ought to have my lines memorized by now, and I *have* been working on them, even at home every night. It's just that our English term paper is due next week, and I promised my aunt that I'd keep my two little cousins for her and Uncle Ken on Saturday night — it's their tenth anniversary and they're going out to dinner. But I promise I'll know my lines by Monday night! I don't want you to think that I'm not taking my part seriously. I love this show, and I don't want to let you down."

"I know you'll give it your best, Natalie. I wouldn't have chosen you for this part if I didn't have faith in you." I gave her a pat on the shoulder.

"Yessir. And... I know you're really busy... but, do you think you might have a few minutes to help me with my solo in Act II? I have the words memorized, but I'm having trouble with the high notes at the end."

"Sure I will. Let's work on that during activity period on Monday or Tuesday. How's that for you — okay?"

"That's great. Thanks, Mr. L, I really appreciate it."

"No problem, Natalie. We've got plenty of time to get everything together."

Forty-five minutes later, I called a ten-minute break before we went on to Act II. Most of the kids drifted out into the hall to the water fountain or to the bathroom. Sean walked over immediately.

"Mr. L, can I talk to you for a minute?"

"Sure, Sean." (Thirty-six on the A.C.T. and a scholarship to Harvard already.)

"Mr. L, I need to check with you about the rehearsal schedule. I noticed that the final dress rehearsal is on Saturday, the ninth of April. I'm also scheduled to go to Oxford with the debate team that day. We're going to compete in the State Finals at Ole Miss at 10:00 that morning, which means that we have to leave here at 5:00 a.m. The round should be over by noon, and if we leave Oxford right then, we can get back to Jackson by 3:00. Since our rehearsal is scheduled for 4:00, I could get here on time for makeup, warm-ups, and be in costume. I don't *have* to go with the debate team — they would be okay without me. And I *did* have the commitment to *Camelot* first. My question is, even though I can make both activities, do you think that if I went to Oxford on Saturday I'd be too tired for our rehearsal? I've calculated the driving time and I know we can make it back okay."

"Sean, I appreciate your willingness to support the debate

team and to honor your commitment to the show as well. It sounds like you've checked out the details. The debate team may do well without you, but we can't do this show without you. If you get up that early, drive to Oxford, compete, then drive three hours back, you could be so tired that you wouldn't be in any kind of shape for play rehearsal. I'll leave the decision up to you; use your practical good sense and do what you conclude would be most productive."

"Well, thanks, Mr. L. I'll think about it some more, but it sounds like you're right. Going up to Oxford doesn't look like the best thing to do."

With the break over, we spent the next hour on the first three scenes of Act II. rehearsal was scheduled to end at 9:00 p.m., but at 8:45 I called the cast together onstage, made a few observations about the night's work, and dismissed them. Most of the kids cleared out quickly, grabbing their backpacks on the way out. Ron hung back while I talked with Lou about a small section of his monologue. As Lou headed offstage, Ron "rolled" in my direction, doing his "air Michael Jordan" interpretation of the real star's gyrations to the basket.

"Hey, what's hap'nin,' Mr. L!"

"Well, Ron, it's the end of a long day, kid. Where do you get all this energy?"

"Hey, Mr. L, let's talk, okay?"

"Hit it, pal, I'm listening."

"Okay, look. I've been bustin' my buns on my lines and on that solo in Act I, right? How do you think I'm doing, huh?"

"You're doing fine, Ron. You've made steady improvement this week."

"Really? I *thought* I was getting better, but you haven't been talking to me as much as usual, so I thought you were mad at me or something. I thought you were ignoring me. Did I do something wrong? Usually you talk to me more and I thought maybe you didn't like the way I was doing my solo. Is it okay?"

"Yes, Ron, it's going fine. You seem to have the right idea about how to sing it, so I left you alone with it. You know, there are so many details I have to take care of to get this show ready, and your part is going along fine, so I haven't needed to give you any corrections on your solo."

"Yeah, but you've been giving Lou extra time with his monologue. And Natalie says you're going to give her extra time on her solo next week. I was just wondering, you know, why you weren't giving me some pointers or things to work on with my solo? Hey, did you see how the cast reacted when I did that scene with King Arthur tonight? It really blew them away, didn't it? Wow! I love that part when I come tearing out on stage with the sword! Really cool, huh?"

"It is, Ron, it really is. You give terrific energy to that part of the show, and I like the way you do it. I've been impressed with your hard work. Have fun with the fight scene! The audience is going to love it!"

"Look, Mr. L, let me sing me solo for you just one time before we leave. You don't mind, do you? I know you're tired and all, but can you listen to it just once more?

"Okay, Ben, one more time."

Ready, Set, Go

The morning my Second Grade class went to the Mississippi State Veterinary School proved to be very interesting.

Jimmy, a typical "I" personality, came into the classroom

talking as usual. He had forgotten his lunch and did not remember we were going on a field trip.

Brian, a very high "C" type, entered reluctantly. He was not sure if he had packed the right food. He also wanted to know the time when we would be leaving and returning.

Dick arrived next. The high "D" personality ran to his desk and began to jump up and down, yelling "Field trip — go, go, go!"

The classroom was almost full as Burton, an "S" type, arrived. He put down his belongings, then came to me and said he was sorry it was loud in the room. He also hugged me and told me I looked nice.

I began to get ready for the field trip. I asked Dick to stand in front of the class and call out rows for the restroom. We completed going to the restroom and the class was settled. The quieted classroom made Burton feel more secure. Jimmy was sent to call his mother to bring his lunch. Hang in there, Mom!"

All Shook Up

It was time for the Third Grade play dress rehearsal. Parts had been chosen and practiced for several weeks in the classroom. Finally the big day had arrived for the children to use the stage and perform for the First Graders as a trial run. The real show would be the following day.

As the practice began the teacher called for the announcer to introduce the play. The "D" child pushed his way through the others, grabbed the microphone, and spoke in a loud voice. However, the First Graders continued to talk among themselves. At this point, he shouted "Shut up!" to the younger group and continued with his script that he had rewritten. As he came down the steps, the teacher took him aside and questioned his behavior. His reply was that it was their fault he yelled because they weren't listening. He went on to say that he thought his rewritten script was much better than the original one. The teacher corrected him for speaking rudely but complimented him on his introduction.

The play began and a quiet little girl, who was an "S," nervously walked onto the stage. She spoke her lines carefully and quickly with a shaky voice. As she stepped down, she looked up at her teacher as if to ask *Did I do it okay?* The teacher smiled and winked with a nod.

The play practice was progressing nicely when the teacher felt a gentle tug. It was her "C" child who was bothered about how to pretend to play "four square" during his part. He asked several questions: "Who will take the ball up on the stage? Do we really need to bounce it? How many times should we bounce it? Who should hold it when we finish? What should we do if it bounces off the stage?" The teacher thought about it for a minute and decided it would be better to *pretend* to play the game — after all, this child was the only "C" in the group, and the "D's" and "I's" might try to really play the game just to see what would happen.

In the final scene, an "I" child appeared on the stage, dressed as Elvis. He was smiling and ready to entertain this room of cheering fans. He began his performance and stole the show as he sang and gyrated to the rhythm of the music. He turned to leave the stage, then paused, curled his lip and said in his best "Elvis voice," "Thank ya… thank ya very much!" The audience squealed with delight and clapped loudly as he stepped off the stage with a grin bigger than his pompadour. This was a day he would never forget.

The play ended and the teacher smiled as she looked over

her precious cast of children with such different personalities, each displayed in such a special way. This was a memory she would treasure always.

A Two-Week Project

I teach Fifth Grade Social Studies. I divided the class into groups to work on a project. Each group was assigned a European country. They had to research the country and present their findings to the class in the form of a play, a quiz show, commercials, etc. At the end of their presentation, they had to serve food and drink refreshments from that country. One group was composed of Patrick, Philip, Brenda and Jennifer.

"Patrick, Brenda, Jennifer! Y'all come over here!" yelled Philip as he waved his hands in the air. "This is great! We're going to have so much fun doing this!"

"I'll do whatever I can," Brenda said, "as long as you give me plenty of time. You know I have something every day after school, and I may not be able to go to the library anytime soon."

Jennifer thought, *"I wonder why Mrs. J put me in this group?"*

Patrick said, "If I had been teaching this class, our assignment would have been to find a way to gain control of this country's natural resources!"

"Oh, we couldn't do that!" Brenda responded, incredulous at the concept of "world domination" by the Fifth Grade Class.

Where there's a will, there's a way, thought Patrick. "Philip, you gather information on how the people spend their leisure time…"

"P-A-R-T-Y!" Philip said, attempting to dance some imitation of a Latin hussle. Patrick ignored Philip's enthusiasm and kept giving orders — he was immune to these contagious outbursts that frequently "infected" others in the class.

"Brenda, you be in charge of the refreshments and all that stuff," Patrick continued.

"All right," she said, "I'll try to find something everybody will like."

"Jennifer — you draw a map and put all the physical features and important cities on it."

"I just got a new atlas with all the information I'll need. And we could present it like *Jeopardy!* with questions and answers. I can write them so we know they'll be right!" Jennifer said, shaking her head in the direction of the still P-A-R-T-Y-ing Philip.

"Yes!" he exclaimed, "I'll be the announcer and come out first and introduce everybody. I'll even do a few commercials!"

"I'll be Alex Trebec," Patrick decreed. "I'll ask the questions. Jennifer can be the judge and Brenda can help our contestants."

"I would love to," Brenda said.

"And why do you want me to be a judge instead of the host?" Jennifer inquired.

Patrick just ignored the distraction. He has always been good at that.

Living Bible Lessons

It was a rainy Monday morning, a number of years ago. I really wanted to stay at home. How could it ever enter into a Bible Class teacher's mind to not want to rush to Bible Class every day? Well, it happened!

You see, I knew that I would have to face Daniel — *this* namesake of the Bible story Daniel would have had all the *lions* in the lion's den begging for protection! He was a wonderfully intelligent student, but he could certainly irritate me. He was *diligent* — there's a "D" word! — and very glad to remind me exactly where we left off and eager to correct me if I did not start where he thought we should start. It seemed to me his arm would get tired, but he had his hand raised most of the time, *determined* to ask questions that could not be answered. He seemed motivated to reveal my lack of ability to answer his questions, rather than having a thirst for knowledge. Ours was a clash of wills — he was so *confident* that at times I secretly hoped he would make a mistake. He could be extremely *arrogant*.

Thank goodness there were other types of students in the class, too. I thought of Ingrid as I stopped for a red light. She was just plain fun to be around. She was *talkative,* however. She seldom bothered to raise her hand — she was good at blurting out whatever she was thinking about. She was very *enthusiastic about* our lessons. She loved our Bible lessons and could get very *excited* about making them come alive. She loved it when I called on her to help with reading a story. However, she was also good at *daydreaming.* Sometimes I would have to remind her where we were in the Bible. Her *optimism* was *inspiring* to me — I knew she would lift my spirits when I walked into class, even on this dreary Monday.

I was going to be late! The rain was really coming down. I was getting more and more nervous driving on the slick streets. Then I thought of Shelly.

She was such a *sweet* girl. She could always *calm* me down by making me feel good as her teacher. She really wanted to *please* me and I knew I could always *depend* on Shelly when I gave extra work — she might work a little *slow,* but I knew she would always get it done, adding her special, personal touches along the way.

As I turned into the parking lot, I thought of Charles. He was a very gifted *student,* but boy!, could he be *critical!* He was very *thorough* in completing his work but also very *rigid* in conforming to the way he felt things should be done (namely, *exactly* right!). He was always full of *How do we know?* and *What if...?* kinds of questions. And he would stay at his questions until I gave him *quality answers!*

Recently, I was walking down the street of a large city near the small town where I teach. I passed by a very imposing building — over the entrance was a carved marble title: *Daniel* S. Johnson, Attorney.

I came to the city another time because I was planning to redecorate my home and didn't really know where to begin. An ad in the *Yellow Pages* had practically jumped off the pages at me: *Ingrid* Anderson, Interior Designs. What a beautiful job she did to brighten my home as she once brightened my classroom!

I needed surgery a few years ago. Waking up in post-op was the sweetest nurse: "Welcome back to the world!" Could it be Shelly? It surely was! As in our school days long ago, she could not have been more calming and helpful during my hospital stay. I often think of the lives she touches and blesses.

I know this last "coincidence" is going to sound wild — but it really happened! I won "big bucks" on *Jeopardy!* and knew I needed to invest my money. Yes, I turned to *Charles* Buckley, Stockbroker. I should have known years ago that he was headed in this direction.

My mind goes back to all the children I have taught and served, and how amazed I am to see that, over the years, they have taught and served me in return. They have found places of service that fit the pattern God designed in them. I think of Ephesians, chapter 2, verse 10: "We are God's work of art, created in Christ for the good deeds He has designed for us."

And that makes me glad that I didn't stay home on that Monday morning so long ago!

The Awakening

I began my teaching career thinking that my classroom of children could be divided into two basic groups. As I had watched my teachers group students, I planned to do as they had done, simply dividing the "sheep" from the "goats" and going on from there. My plan seemed to be working well... until my "Day of Awakening."

It came the day I asked my students to recite their favorite Bible verse. My "D" students were ready to recite right away — the only problem was that they all chose the same verse: "Jesus wept."

My "S" students asked if they could wait a little while, maybe even until the next day, to make sure they knew their verses well enough to recite them in public. Oh, and they also wanted to know if they could just recite them to me at my desk, rather than saying them in from of the whole class!

My "C" students were very agitated that I had not included this assignment in the "nine-week overview" handout at the beginning of the term. However, they were agreeable to giving it their best shot, and they did.

My "I" student made this assignment a production of "biblical proportions" — in this class there was only one true "I" type child, but he had enough energy to be his own group! He was the kind of boy who could eat raw onions on the playground and deny it right to your face... *literally!* Anyway, he thought and thought — for almost five seconds straight — and then began hesitantly: "Well, I don't really know the number of it... but it goes something like this... 'Don't squish — no...!,'" his hands clenched in terror, his eyes darted to the ceiling in search of divine aid. "Don't scrunch... uhhh, don't sk-k-k..." Then his eyes lit up, he stood up confidently, and he beamed with self-evident pride. "Don't squash the Spirit!"

When I deal with high "I's" these days, I remember this mangled verse — blocking it out isn't possible — and I make a special effort not to "squash their spirit," either!

Comrades, Arise!

Being a mathematics teacher is a challenge, in that math tends to be boring and does not lead to many exciting lesson plans. Therefore, if you were to ask my 14- to 16-year-old students about their favorite subject, most would probably not want to discuss Algebra I. Of course, some like math and see it as a challenge, while others frustrate themselves trying to understand it. Still others try to ride the coattails of others by cheating their way through. My story is based on a confrontation with a high "D" type student who cheated continually, and the responses of the other personality types in the classroom.

First, my students understand that accountability is important to me — if I give homework, I expect it to be done. I never expect it to be done perfectly, but a teacher can tell when true effort is put forth and when someone simply copies another student's work.

I operate on the theory that everyone forgets homework now and then and deserves one break or an excused assignment. So my point penalty list is as follows:

0–1 missed homework checkmarks   grade of 100%

2 missed homework checkmarks   grade of 85%

3 missed homework checkmarks   grade of 70%

4 missed homework checkmarks   grade of 60%

5 missed homework checkmarks   grade of 0%

This is an account of what happened one day when I not only *checked* homework but *collected* it for a grade.

It was the morning following a basketball game, and Ike (my high "I") was begging me not to check homework because he *forgot* his at home in the excitement of the game the night before. He conveniently forgot that I had given the class extra time in class the day before, with the option of turning it in then so they would not forget it.

For once, demanding Dominic (my high "D") was not complaining or remonstrating over the *checking* of homework — he had copied the work of Sally, his sweet, supportive girlfriend. (Can you guess her personality style?)

What Dominic did not plan was my having calculating Connie (my high "C") *collect* the papers. Of course, Connie didn't know I was going to do that either and such a "sudden" surprise caused her to start hyperventilating! Of course, she had completed her work and triple-checked it, but she still wondered if it was correct and now *needed* to check it once more, quickly, as the other papers were being collected. Of course, being the collector made that impossible.

Meanwhile, Sally was having her own tense moments — she had done something contrary to her honest "S" nature. Dominic had made her feel unsupportive and guilty, and she had shared her work with him. Her face betrayed that now she felt *truly* guilty. She just knew I would recognize that their answers were identical as I graded their work. But I already knew — Dominic was being *too* cooperative!

When he realized what was going on — that I would be grading their work and not just checking it off in my book — he responded predictably: he got mad! "Mrs. S, I will not turn in my paper to you — this is Communism!" He had a zeal of a revolutionary as he tried to marshal his "army" of fellow students: "You would think we were in Russia!"

I calmly laid down my book and walked to the door. "Dominic," I said in my controlled, "don't mess with me today" voice, "for you, you *will* feel like you're in Russia today!" The outside temperature was 36°F (just above freezing), and I gave him the choice of "exile" in the Siberia out-of-doors until (1) I was ready for him to return, or (2) until he could promise to control himself and remember his manners.

The revolution collapsed quickly — Russia did not feel too good that day!

Beside The Golden Door

Our class was reading a story about the Statue of Liberty. I thought it might be fun to create a bulletin board about the "Lady in the Harbor," filled with interesting facts. How the children's varying personality styles viewed the task was interesting to observe.

As we began drawing a large picture identical to the one in our book, our Third Grade "S" types (Beth, Jake, Brooks and Nancy) wanted to know if they could help to color the picture.

Since the illustration in the book was colored in shades of green, I decided duplicating this with green markers would be easier than having the students try to make it look like copper. High "C" Eilleen asked, "Mrs. D, why are they making the Statue green when it's made of copper — copper is not different shades of green?" Nat (a "D-and-a-half"!) jumped in with, "I don't understand why we're wasting time drawing the picture again anyhow. If somebody wants to know what the Statue looks like, just go look in the book again!" Bronson, Aaron and Bryce could not stay in their seats. They talked busily to the other kids about how much fun it would be to go to New York City and see the Statue and the big ships.

"Give me your tired, your poor, your huddled masses yearning to breathe free... I lift my lamp beside the golden door." I wondered, *Could this be a description of the teachers' lounge in the middle of a day like this?*

We finally got the bulletin board completed — but it felt as if recreating "Liberty Island" in our classroom had been at least as involved as Bartholdi's original efforts in creating "Liberty Enlightening the World" in Upper New York Bay!

Making The Grade

This is an anecdote from my Seventh Grade Art Class, made up of 19 daytime and boarding students. From what I gathered in the two "Personality Insights" seminars I have attended this year, I believe most of my students are high "D's" and "I's." But this story is about only five of them: Megan is a "D"; Laurie is an "I"; Ellen is an "S"; Christine and Kate are "C's."

First, I should explain that I took over this class in the last 12 weeks of school when their teacher left for health reasons.

I had taught most of these students in Typing Class and had known these five for several years. But I am primarily an English teacher. I inherited Art Class along with English classes — I know *nothing* about art, but I had to give them a grade for the final quarter. I am a high "D" myself, and I admit that my feelings color what I do in my class to a certain degree. To be fair to the students and to myself, I selected two grades to give to the students: a 95% or a zero (sort of like "pass or fail"). Arbitrarily, I decided to give them all 95's, assuming I would have no problems with this.

The morning I decided to award these grades, Laurie asked me what her grade would be. When I said she was getting a 95, she was thrilled. "Is that an *A?* Who made an *A — me?"*

Megan had a different response to her grade of 95: "What? Is that all?" I told her that her choices were a zero or a 95. She made the wise choice and went on.

Later that afternoon in class, I told the rest of the students their grades. Most were happy and satisfied, but three girls had questions. Now Ellen is my own daughter and that brings in more opportunities for conflict. She asked me if I was giving her that grade because she was my daughter or because she had earned it. Even when I told her that *everyone else* in class had a 95, she sill was not convinced.

Christine is fairly stable but leans toward the "C" characteristics. Her only question was why I picked 95, instead of some other number. I told her that I gave everyone else the same grade, but if that made her unhappy, she could have the alternative. Again, *why?* I tried to explain to her that my art background was not strong. She was not happy, but she took the grade anyway.

Kate is an extremely high "C." Previously in typing, I had given her a grade of 99. She wanted to know why she did not have an *average* of 100%. I had explained that I never gave perfect grades since the school did not like to use them. I also said that she had made *some* mistakes in *some* of her assignments. I got the crying then — so I was prepared for the fight in Art. When she asked me why she had only a 95, I explained that I used the same grading system our teachers use in Physical Education classes. Good behavior and effort put forth earns a 95. Her response was tears again. This went on for three days. Finally, she wore me out, and my "D" got the best of me. I told her she could choose her own grade from the two choices: 95 or zero. Again, *But why...?* Fortunately, her buddies saw that I was about to explode and explained to her that if she did not shut up, I would reward her with the failing grade.

If you decide to use this story, please change the names as I have absolutely no imagination and had to use their real names! *(Editor's Note: We did!)*

Team Effort

The day we did Creative Writing in groups was the day I recognized how different my Fourth Grade students really were. I divided my class into five different groups of four children. I tried my best to put a "leader," a couple of "middle" students, and a "lower functioning" student in each group. I hoped the extreme high would help the low and all would work together.

I went to each group to help them decide on a topic they could all agree on. However, the task was much more difficult this day than I had thought. I did not know that in one group I had placed four children who didn't like each other anyway.

Andrea, the "D" in this group, wanted to choose the topic, write the notes, listen to suggestions nervously and restlessly, and then write down what *she* wanted. She was very bossy. She kept repeating softly, to keep me from hearing her, "C'mon, let's do this. She's going to read the best one. Be quiet so I can think!" All the time she was writing down her own ideas, wanting everyone to be excluded but not exactly on purpose.

I approached the table in an attempt to involve the other children while trying to tone her down. I said, "Andrea, let someone else talk for a while. You have talked the entire circle time so far." She slumped in her seat and laid aside her pencil and paper. Resigned now to absolute failure, she said, "Okay, fine."

The other children breathed a sigh of relief — they felt I had "cooked her goose." Jeremy, my "I" child, sat across from Andrea with a smirk on his face that seemed to shout *Ha-ha! The teacher sure told you! If you had let me do it, the teacher would have liked it better!*

Amy is an "S," and her response was more like self-blame. Her expression was apprehensive — *Was this going to become unpleasant?* — and guilty — *Oh my! I should have helped. She got in trouble because of me. It's my fault.*

Betty, my "C" child, was disgusted by the time I intervened. Her expression said *I wish Andrea would be quiet and think before she speaks. If she had just started with an outline and had us jot down our thoughts, she could have had all our ideas!*

Everyone in the group was upset and frustrated. Andrea wanted to switch to another group because she had no help and wanted everyone else to do as she said. Jeremy wanted to go get a drink of water so her could "think better." Amy looked up timidly as if to say *I wish they wouldn't fight. It makes me nervous.* Betty raised her hand, modeling compliance with the rules, and explained that Andrea should have asked permission to lead, write and suggest her ideas. She should have made a list (like her own!) and been more organized.

I looked at the group and knew it would be a long year if they were unable to work together on projects. I explained myself: "What I really meant, children, was let's work together. I'm glad you took control of your group, Andrea. You are a very smart student, but let's use a different tone. If you're going to be a *leader,* let your group members help or there will be no group to lead."

Jeremy stood up and grinned with all his teeth as he said, "I had a *great* idea and I knew what to write. I forgot my idea, though. It was great!"

Amy volunteered, "I'll be glad to do what you want me to, Andrea. I might not do it perfectly, but I'll try. What can I do to help?"

Organized Betty said, "Let's start at the beginning. Let's get our thoughts together. Mrs. G, is this how we would begin? How long does it need to be? Can you give us some more suggestions?"

I looked at them calmly and said, "Andrea is going to start again. Betty, since you are so organized, why don't you make the list of everyone's ideas and write the final, revised copy? Jeremy, you do such a good job speaking, why don't you read the paper out loud to the class? As they write, you listen so you can gather what they're thinking, and you can spice it up. Thank you for smiling. I really like your attitude.

"Amy, thanks so much for offering to do your part. Your sweet attitude really helps everyone remember to be kind to one another. You all are good students."

As I walked away, I heard Amy say, "Let's work as a team." Betty added, "Who's first?" Jeremy asked, "Is it time for me to practice reading?" And Andrea said, "Let's do it!"

Everybody Line Up...

Kindergarten children are interesting to watch the first time they are told to line up. Some of them have not had "group experience" of this type before and their response to something new is either challenging, exciting, predictable, or questioning.

The "D" child can be spotted as his dominant and demanding behavioral style propels him to the front of the classroom. He folds his arms and announces arrogantly: "I am going to be first! I'm the leader!" The teacher then explains that the leaders are picked in alphabetical order. Today would not be his day, but his turn would come soon. (Even a "D" has to submit to the alphabetical order, whatever that is!)

The "I" child probably does not even hear the instructions to line up. He is busy entertaining all the other children at his table. If he does hear, he really can't be expected to interrupt his performance. He intends to do it... in "just a minute!" The teacher pulls him aside as says, "I am going to enjoy having you in my class this year. We are going to have a lot of fun together — and one of the things you are going to learn is how to listen and follow instructions. That will be great!"

The "S" child listens carefully to the instructions. He does as he is told and does not cause conflict at all. He smiles up at the teacher warmly and steps into line. It feels good to do what's right. The teacher says, "I really appreciate you. I'm glad you are in my class this year."

The "C" child responds by asking questions. "*Why* are we lining up? *Where* are we going? *How* long are we going to be gone? *Who* will be there? *What* do I need to bring?" The teacher answers the questions quickly — and completely — knowing this will move the process along...

And maybe, it will even move the kids out the door!

Clean Up Time

When art time was over, the First Grade children were told to clean up their area. Their responses varied according to their personality style:

David (a "D") was not through with what he was doing; therefore, he ignored my command and continued with his project. He was confident that he had the best idea in the room and he was determined to finish it before snack time.

Mark (an "I") was so busy hanging over the table and chatting with a friend that he never heard what I have said. When he tried to find the pieces of his project, they were scattered all over and under the table.

Andy (an "S") immediately started cleaning up everything around him. Since he never wants to break a rule, he made sure he had permission to get out of his chair before going to the trash can.

Jermaine (a "C") had his project completed and had cleaned up everything as he worked. Of course, his project was perfect.

When the children realized that no one would eat their snacks until the room had been cleaned up, they responded in different ways:

David was of the opinion that someone else should do it!

Mark was still talking and unaware of what was going on.

Andy was by then down on the floor, cleaning up after everyone.

Jermaine was busy analyzing the colors and shapes of the paper scraps to determine whose trash needs to be cleaned up by whom.

When the task was finally completed, they went out to the door in D – I – S – C order!

Playin' Hooky

This past year I taught an English Class of approximately 25 graduating Seniors. We were completing a unit on William Shakespeare's *Macbeth*. As we finished our test review, the intercom came on in my classroom. The principal interrupted my class to tell me that I had a long-distance telephone call in the office. (My classroom was about ten doors down from the office at the end of the building.)

I immediately instructed my Seniors to sit quietly while I slipped down the hall. I've taught long enough to know (17 years!) that they weren't going to be perfectly quiet — I just hoped they would not tear the room apart! It is never a good idea to leave a class unattended. Since the room was at the end of the building, I felt they couldn't cause much of a disturbance. None of them was what I considered a "trouble maker." And in the next classroom, the girls' junior/senior high basketball coach was available if things got out of hand. Of course, he more than likely could not hear my class because of the noise level in his own room! I threatened my students with their lives — and whatever else I could think of — and left the room.

The telephone call lasted about two minutes. As I finished and stepped out of the office and into the hall, I almost lost my breath. All I could see were the backs of some of my students as they sneaked into the gym. I realized what had happened immediately and rushed back to my classroom, to find only a few students talking quietly at their desks.

I looked at Valerie, a high "D," and asked, "Where is the rest of the class?" She replied, "I can't tell you!" I told her I would just have to give them a failing grade for the day. She stated, "You can't do that!"

Since I was unable to get any information from the few

students left in class, I headed straight for the cafeteria. *How dare they leave my classroom!*

Abruptly, I stopped the first escapee I saw and asked who gave him permission to leave my room. His response was short: "I dunno… It looked like fun!" *Obviously a high "I"!*, I thought.

I pushed on over to another girl with the same questions. Boy, was I in for a blow! *She* started asking *me* questions: "When exactly did they leave? Did you see them leave? How do you know they left early (now that the bell had rung)?" *I don't need questions from a "C" — I need quality answers!*

Eventually, I made my way to a girl who oozed "S." In order to protect her classmates, she took the blame and said it was her idea. She let her classmates manipulate her.

By the end of the year, the incident had become the class joke. Many times the Seniors reminded me of the time they "innocently left" near the end of class and how "bent out of shape" I got that day. When they told the story from their perspective, I began to see how illogical I had become in their view. I had become fearful that day. *I was losing control!* Ultimately, I learned laughed along with them about the incident.

I'm an "I" myself, and I wanted to be liked by all of them! The rest of the year was without a similar incident and we had no serious disobedience or classroom conflicts. Learning to laugh with them brought me something else a high "I" wants as much as to be liked: they learned to respect me on a new level as they learned that teachers are people, too.

Just A Glimpse...

Their favorite time of the day has arrived — *recess!* The children put away their materials and head hastily toward the door to enjoy some outdoor fun. Quickly, some find their favorite activity while others enjoy just talking with a special friend. As they busy themselves, I relax... and carefully watch their every action.

I notice as Jason, a "D" who is strong-willed, moves quickly from group to group, demanding to be in control of each activity. He is very persistent and very impatient. Over the year, as he realizes how this behavior is costing him friends to lead, he will slowly learn to change and adapt.

Freddie is an "I" who is having the time of his life. He is everybody's buddy, very outgoing and so enthusiastic about everything. He is glad to be out of class — so carefree! He plays hard but is quick to show compassion to those who fall or get hurt. Friends are indispensable in his recipe for fun!

Shana is on the swings. She is an "S" who is so dependable and efficient in what she does. She is also timid and shy, easily manipulated — this frustrates her. She keeps on swinging, because this has become "her place," and it is where she finds security.

And of course, there is Cary, a "C" who is a perfectionist about everything. He is even cautious in choosing his activity this morning. Whatever his final choice, he will be very careful and does not want any sudden or unnecessary interruptions to his routine. He observes his classmates from a distance as he "takes the temperature" of the situation. He is very curious about why they are doing what they are doing. Many questions bombard his mind.

Recess ends and the students (unique even in this) line up and return to the classroom. Once again I smile and am thankful to have this opportunity to recognize individual needs, and can give all my love and support to each little

What?   Who?   How?   Why?

For you see, I know it is not a matter of "good" or "bad" or "right" or "wrong." It's a matter of differences... *delightful differences!*

Up, Up And Away

For the past few years, my Eighth Grade students have looked forward to their study of the atmosphere. Learning about the different layers of Earth's atmosphere, and how warm air rises and cool air sinks — to cause weather patterns around the globe — would certainly create interest in the serious Earth Science student. This, of course, is not what the typical Eighth Grader waits for all year! They eagerly anticipate the opportunity to make and launch their *own* hot air balloons.

The week before the assembling begins, I always prepare students with necessary information. They choose one or two other students with whom they will work as a team. They receive written instructions and meet in their groups to decide who will buy the tissue paper. Buying it and bringing it to school is the only big, outside-of-class responsibility they have. The color of paper they choose is strictly their decision, but it has certain size specifications that sometimes require careful and extensive shopping. All of these requisites are discussed thoroughly, and the importance of bringing the materials to class before the project starts is highly stressed.

You would think that since this is a major *fun* project, *everyone* would be *prepared* to begin assembling *on time*. Not so! Year after year, I have observed my students and have come to expect the same results with each class. But until I took this course on personality differences, I didn't understand *why* my students were handling this project in different ways.

Monday morning arrives: My "C" type students convene with perfectly matched paper, the correct size, and have read — almost *memorized!* — their instructions days in advance. They are ready to work. "D" students are ready to tell "S" students how to construct the balloons. "I" students show up without their materials, but they are not concerned. They begin "networking" almost immediately. *Who has extra paper? Improvise!* It may take them a little longer to begin because they have to talk each group out of their paper, but in the end they always seem to put together a balloon that is ready to fly.

Watching each of these types work is also interesting. "C's" work *carefully, cautiously,* and *competently* on the project. "D's" are usually the first ones to finish as they have *directed, dominated,* and *diligently* progressed. "I's" are usually the last to finish. They do not follow written directions well and usually enlist me to tell them exactly how to put the balloon together. They are *impulsive, imaginative,* and *illogical.* They thoroughly enjoy talking and laughing their way to the finish line. Of course, the "S's" are *supportive, sweet* and *stable.* They are willing to help the other students as needed. They are the very ones who will help the "I's" who have forgotten their papers and step in to salvage the "D's" who get bored or frustrated.

Reading and following directions, measuring in both centimeters and inches, cooperation, responsibility for materials, cleaning the work area, and understanding the principles of why balloons rise and then begin to fall are just a few of the objectives. Successfully building and then launching these balloons allows each personality style an opportunity to work together in a way that helps each student to grow emotionally, as well as academically. What a neat way to learn Science!

The Fair Way

Field trips had gotten to the point where they were almost no fun anymore. Between the planning and fighting over where to go, I almost decided not to take any more.

We once had decided to go to a movie as a reward for being good, but the fight that broke out over our choices quickly stopped our trip. Denise, who liked to choose, wanted to go see an action film. Her choice was *The Watcher In The Woods,* which would have been an excellent choice except that the others in her planning group didn't want to see it. Chris, after some prodding, said that he really would rather see a mystery movie like *The Case of the Missing Dinosaurs.* This too would have been a good choice, but once again the others said no. Ida said she thought a better choice would be *The Party Patrol* because she heard that everyone really liked it and she thought a crowded theatre would be more fun. Simon didn't make a choice because of the arguing. He said, "Whatever you decide is fine with me." The final choice was "we can't decide," so the teacher — me — decided not to take in a movie.

This time, I decided I would help them with their choices. "What about the fair?", I suggested. Everyone agreed that *maybe* this would work. When putting the students into groups, the four original planning group members (who had dismantled our previous outing) ended up in one group. I didn't think this was a great idea, but it really was out of my hands. The parents had already arrived and loading the cars had begun.

The four children decided to try and work together so they all could have a good time. Each wanted to do something different, but they all wanted to have a good time. Naturally, Denise wanted to plot out the trip so they let her. The curious thing was that once she knew she was in charge, she became easier to deal with. Paul started to give more facts than needed when Denise interrupted, "Hey Paul, how about the short version?"

Paul looked a little disturbed, but he did tell them about the early crowds on the east end because of traffic from the streets. "It would be better if we entered from the south end, through the cattle barn, and miss the traffic. Also, the bigger rides tend to be less crowded during lunch so we might want to ride the best rides then. If we spent the early morning at the exhibit hall, we could miss much of the crowd and still get to see most of the fair."

Paul started to smart off but Simon headed him off with a quick, "Great idea, Paul. You sure seem to be helping Denise get this off to a great start." Simon liked peace best of all and he rarely got into a fight unless it was the only way to stop one. They all liked Simon.

No sooner had they walked through the gate than they noticed someone was missing. Ida was nowhere to be found. Denise and Ida were usually good friends but this was upsetting the plan and Denise was not happy. In fact, because of the anger in the air, neither Simon or Paul were happy either. Paul nervously stated that he might just like to go on back to the school. Seeing that her plans were falling apart, Denise came up with another one. She didn't like changing from the original, but she realized that she had to, and she was determined to have a good time.

"Hey, Paul, if you were looking for an exciting place where on the fairgrounds do you think would be the flashiest?"

"Well, personally, I don't like it but I think the tank where they dunk the clown would probably have a lot of people around. He always draws a big crowd by making fun of the people and they laugh and throw balls at him,

"You know," Simon said, "I think I did hear her say she wanted to 'clown around,' which might be her way of saying where she was going. She's pretty funny. I like clowns, so maybe that's where she went."

You like everything, Simon," Denise said, "but you're probably right. Let's go!"

They found Ida when they got there, but she wasn't watching the clown — she was *in* the tank, cracking jokes almost as good as the clown's! They could hear her laughter before they arrived.

Denise was still angry, but seeing Ida wet and laughing started her laughing, too. Soon they all were laughing. It's hard to stay mad at Ida. She wasn't always ready and rarely did she know where they were in her textbooks, but she was funny. Besides, it's hard to stay mad at a wet, giggling girl.

Denise started talking to the owner of the booth. "You know, we really had planned to enjoy the fair today. I think Ida is helping you make money, so how about sharing some of the loot?" Paul and Simon couldn't believe their ears. They knew Denise would say anything, but asking a grown-up for money was a bit much! To their surprise, he agreed — he didn't actually give them money, but since Ida was helping him by entertaining, he would buy them all lunch and give them tickets to return later and enjoy the fair.

"Gee, thanks, Mister," Simon said, "we don't want to put you out, but we sure do appreciate all you're doing."

On the way back to school, the conversation went like this:

"Ida, next time I wish you'd tell us what you're doing. This turned out great but I like plans to go like they should."

"Well, yeah, I guess so. I was thinkin' about the clowns and all the laughing and I just *had* to go then. I shoulda told you but I didn't even think about it. You know, I really like those clowns. I might even be a clown one day and famous. I'm good at things like that. It sure beats trying to stay quiet during math. You know, the other day when we were adding and it turned out to be four, I got to thinking how *be-fore* long we would be out of there and then I remembered that I was getting to go to my grandmother's house after school and all my cousins would be there and we would have a really good time..."

"'Scuse me, Mighty Mouth, but like I was saying, just tell us next time!" frowned Denise.

"I think it turned out great!" said Simon. "I always like the fair and we got to go together and no one got really angry."

"I was thinking about this," said Paul.

"I bet you were," said Denise.

"I'd say all in all, we had a pretty *fair* time," he smiled.

They all laughed.

A Morning Circus

The circus begins at 5:30 a.m. when the roar of the alarm clock goes off. Mother Chimpanzee (that's me!) arises to prepare everyone's breakfasts, lunches, clothes, books, etc.

When all of these trivial chores are done, I quietly go to awaken the Lion (my husband!) who swears he has been awake for at least 30 minutes. I'll admit he makes some weird noises when awake but not like what he has been making the last few minutes! He has to be awakened and out of his cage before the others. This is done for safety reasons. We now have no scaldings from too hot water — he's used to it — no wars over spilled milk or uneaten cereal, and most of all no explosion over the toothpaste cap not being replaced. I have taken care of each of these tragedies by the time he returns from his watering hole.

In the next ring comes the Parrot (my daughter!) with the telephone already attached — to be honest, I believe it is permanently attached. She spends the next hour preening for work as a dental assistant. You know, she must look great for all those people she will be jabbing in the mouth. I believe she totally enjoys her work because she sees and *talks to* a large number of people all day. She loves having the chance to talk — have you ever tried to answer a question while someone's fingers are in your mouth?

By this time, the three smaller animals are up. Timothy has the personality of a Giraffe. If this happens to be a school day, he absolutely must study again for every test he has that day. It makes no difference that he knew every possible answer eight hours earlier. You hope and pray that he doesn't send you to the encyclopedia to double-check the information. Finally he is dressed and fully prepared, because anything below 95 is failure.

Summer and Casey are now doing their performance. Every circus needs a clown or two. Casey, the five-year-old, is definitely letting you know that she is *not* going to eat, wear, or cooperate with anything you suggest. She certainly has a mind of her own. By this time, four-year-old Summer has probably painted the kitchen table with fingernail polish, and when confronted will respond with, "Did *I* do that?"

By this time, my "S" is exhausted and my "D" has risen to its full potential so we will be where we must be... by 8 a.m.!

Family Matters

I have not been in a classroom on a regular basis in fifteen years. Therefore my memories and recollections of my students are rather vague. So, for the purpose of this paper, I will limit myself to my own children, since they have three different personality styles that their teachers deal with on a daily basis.

My husband is a "C with S" and I am a "C with D" blend, which I am sure is hard to deal with from our children's perspective.

We have a 15-year-old daughter who is just now learning to drive and is totally immersed in adolescence. The "Ohhh, Mom!" is really here — I saw fleeting glimpses of it over the past two years but now I know they were only forewarnings of the real thing. After going through several similar studies, I have finally decided that she is a "C." We have always gotten along well and she has been really easy to deal with. I can remember telling her when she was six to "lighten up and be a kid." I said she was born mature, not really doing the silly little girl things, so in adolescence she will probably make up for it. She adjusted well at age five to a twin brother and sister. Our friends were amazed at how well she handled herself. I have always said that if one day later in life she does something really wild and crazy, she will probably say it was because "my mom had *twins!*"

My twin daughter is a definite "S." She is so sweet and kind. She loves her friends and has difficulty standing up to those friends who are "D" and "C" types. Her best friend is another perfect little "S."

She is so honest. In school last year, if she forgot to read even one sentence of a homework assignment, she would immediately confess and risk getting the dreaded "homework check!" In this grade, she had to build an igloo out of sugar cubes. Of course, the "C" in me wanted to make it perfect and so I did help "just a little." The teacher stated that parents really weren't supposed to help, so of course she confessed. She tore the entire igloo apart and reglued every cube "herself" — all 200 of those little sticky things!

She still prays for this teacher each night. We say if you ever get on her prayer list for any reason, you'll never get off! At times, I feel that she could easily be overlooked except for one tiny characteristic" we call her "The Gnat!" She constantly hums, sings, talks or buzzes around us, and this feature has made her very hard to ignore.

Well, as they say, I've saved the best and most challenging for last. This is the other twin, middle child and only boy. He's an "I with D" trying to live with "C's" — what a group! He truly makes good use of all of our parenting skills. He can bring us the greatest pleasure as well as the greatest pain.

He loves to entertain and will be "center stage" whenever possible. In the Third Grade play, he volunteered to be Elvis and did a memorable rendition of "You Ain't Nothin' But A Hound Dog!" The women went wild and he loved it. He wanted to wear the outfit every day that week.

This year his class went to the symphony and they were told to wear nice "Sunday School clothes." He wanted to rent a tux! Each school day, I do a pocket check. He has been known to get to school with some interesting items, such as a stopwatch, rubber bands, jewelry, food for the class, and — my favorite — perfume. It smelled so strong the teacher had to raise the window and air the room out. This class has really helped me understand him so much better and has probably saved his life! I should either arrange a "scholarship" for his teacher to attend a seminar or at least buy her *Positive Personality Profiles!*

Poetry In (Slow) Motion

A "D" and an "I," cautious "C" and slow me
Grouped together in English during period three
Were given ten sentences to check and correct
We had twenty minutes before they'd collect
The assignments we'd worked on as well as could we:
The "D" and the "I," cautious "C," and slow me.

The "D" split up the problems (he thought that he should)
Then scribbled his answers as quick as he could.
When finished, he tried to help out cautious "C,"
Who seemed to work nearly as slowly as me.
The high "C" got angry and corrected "D's" work,
So the "D" whispered meanly that the "C" was a jerk.
Why couldn't we hurry as quickly as he,
The talkative "I," careful "C," and slow me?

The "I" read his problems, then read them again,
A puzzled expression replacing his grin.
He asked "D" to help him, but didn't much care
That "D" wrote the answers on his paper there.
"I" took it and showed it to a group of his friends
Who copies "D's" answers and thanked "I" instead.
"I" chuckled and winked in conspiratorial glee
At the dominant "D," cautious "C," and slow me.

The "C" checked punctuation, the spelling of "scribe,"
His verbs showed action and his nouns described,
Choices of adverbs and adjective placement,
And if subjects and verbs were all in agreement.
He wrote everything over and handed it in
Just before the class bell would be ringing again.
He went back to his seat just as pleased as could be
Since he'd done so much better than "I," "D," and me.

I ignored them and did what I could to work on
Until after the bell rang and others had gone.
I examined the assignment and plodded slowly
Through the work, hoping no one would soon call on me.
I turned in my paper with the other three
Of the dominant "D," sparkling "I," perfect "C."

The Field Trip Committee

Each year in Second Grade we go on a field trip. I like to give the children some opportunity for input on the planning of the trip. We let them make suggestions on where they would like to go. These were the reactions of four of my students.

"Dave the 'D'" was the first to blurt out his choice: "I want to go to the zoo because I know all the animals. If we don't go to the zoo, I don't want to go!"

"Ida the 'I'" said, "I want to go to the Discovery Zone® because there is so much going on there. Do you think I could invite my best friends — I would love for them to go with me. I can show everyone how to play all the games!"

"Sue the 'S'" said, "Well, I don't care where we go. Since Dave wants to go to the zoo and Ida wants to go to the Discovery Zone, can't we go both places? I think we would all have so much fun…"

"Cory the 'C'" asked, "Well, what time will we leave school and when will we come back? Do we need to bring our lunch or are we going to buy it there? Are we going to take a bus or are we going in cars? Can we take our camera along with us? I will help make a list of what we need to bring to school for the trip. I know we all will enjoy this trip.

Going on a field trip is always an exciting adventure. You know with a mixture of personalities that it will be very entertaining.

"Lettuce" Find That Hamster!

The Third Grade always has a study unit on vertebrates and invertebrates in Science. According to my syllabus, the first class of vertebrates our class was to study was mammals.

Tim, a high "D," *insisted* for three straight days that he wanted to bring his pet hamster to school as an *example* of a mammal *and* a spine. By the third day — and against my better judgment — I relented and gave him permission to bring the hamster the next day.

With his pet in its cage, Tim arrived unusually early the following morning. Our high "I" students were beside themselves with excitement — it was like having a new friend! Bobby convinced Tim to let him hold the hamster. Almost immediately, it was put down on the carpet, and instantly it was off and running all over the room. Bobby loved running along behind it and commenting on how it was and how fast it could run.

Elizabeth, a high "S" type, felt sorry for the hamster and began to cry when it disappeared behind the bookcase. She also felt sorry for Tim because his pet was lost. She was worried and unhappy the rest of the day.

Allie, one of my "C" type students, quickly tried to think of a solution for this problem. She reminded me that hamsters are nocturnal, and reasoned that it would be awake and running around the classroom all night.

She made a trap, using a long wooden block and an upright plastic trash can containing a piece of lettuce. She explained to the class that the hamster would try to get to the food that night.

Sure enough, the hamster did fall into the trash can and was unable to climb out because the plastic was too slippery. The following morning, one mammal with a spine and fur was returned to its cage.

I don't think I will ever be talked into having another hamster visit for Science unless I have a class of 25 "S" students.

----Teaching... And Reaching----

It had been a typical Sixth Grade year with our "sweet" Fifth Graders becoming "typical" Sixth Graders. In our Presbyterian-sponsored private school, almost every parent *conference* became a *confessional* that began with, "My child has never acted this way before!"

A wonderful privilege in my class is that my students may sit where they like, as long as I do not have a discipline problem. From the beginning of that year I had noticed a few of the girls interspersed themselves among the guys. Usually, they divided themselves as girls on one side and boys on the other.

Two of my guys and one of my girls were really good friends — not girlfriend/boyfriend — but true friends. Zach was such a high "I." So outgoing, friendly, compassionate, and just a "fun" sort of person who came to school primarily for his friends and sports, school being secondary.

Randi was a typical "S" type. So sweet, dependable, easygoing, and so supportive of all of her friends. And while many of my students wavered from clique to clique, not Randi. She was not unkind to anyone, but she was so supportive of Zach and Ted.

You now know the name of the last "Musketeer," Ted. Very conscientious, a wonderful student, yet so sensitive to the needs of those around him. A definite "C" type, with his perfectionist trait being exemplified in his appearance.

We ended the year with our traditional Field Day activities: over 700 children on the field of our area college, participating in class relays, eating hamburgers, and having such a fun day!

Interestingly enough, I remember that particular Field Day because I was encouraging (yelling!) my class to go faster and faster as Zach ran over my foot with the wagon he was pulling with a classmate on board. But finally our part of the festivities was over — and thankfully, a weekend to recover!

Around noon the next day, my phone rang and it was Randi's mom, sharing with me about a tragic accident in which Zach had been tragically burned and was being flown by helicopter to the regional trauma center. Our parents had planned a hay ride that Saturday night for my class, and Zach's parents urged us to continue with our plans.

That night, as I rode on the hay wagon with my students, all of their true personalities were exemplified — they so covered me with hay that I had to grab a jacket to put over my head in order to breathe. Then later that night, my kids encircled a huge bonfire in the middle of an open pasture, joined hands and cried together as they asked God to heal their friend, Zach.

That night, I felt that God had "burdened" my heart to drive to see Zach the next day. I argued that I couldn't go on Sunday, but I did. We arrived at the Burn Hospital about noon and Zach died about three o'clock. I was never permitted to see him, but no amount of money could replace my just being there.

After the funeral, about a week later, one of my students came to my door and asked, "Mrs. W, could I see you a minute?" As the door closed behind him, this tall, handsome young man said to me, "I think I know why *my* life was not taken — I wasn't ready to meet the Lord!" And from Zach's death, another student found new life.

The Sixth Grade year ended with graduation as usual, but in memory of Zach. Ted and Randi went on to different schools but kept in touch. Randi had been sick quite a lot that year and was soon diagnosed with lupus. Eventually, the severity of her illness caused her to become homeschooled.

Readers from my part of Mississippi will perhaps remember the mission trip to Honduras that was sponsored by the

Brotherhood Department of the Southern Baptist denomination last year. The young man who was killed when the flatbed trailer he was riding toppled down a mountain was the same Sixth Grader who opened my door that day and asked, "Mrs. W, could I see you a minute?" *Ted!*

Not knowing my own personality style at that time, I would not have placed myself as a "D." But through these experiences, I feel God has changed my life — to make me more caring and even more focused, knowing what is truly important in this world. I am glad that I can teach and reach young lives, knowing that I can reach some in a way that will last throughout eternity.

Working It Out!

In teaching Fifth Grade, a teacher gets a variety of good opportunities to utilize the personalities of her students. On one occasion, I was sitting in my classroom when a sweet child named Corrinne walked in. She appeared to be crying and I asked, "Corrinne, is there anything that I can help you with?"

She replied, "Oh, Mrs. T, they are really being mean to me!"

I sat her down and rounded up the other people so we could work it out. Tony, an energetic, happy child, walked in first. Next was Kaley, who is generally a well-planned student. Finally, Monty came in and asked, "How long are we going to be in here? We're playing a basketball game and I'm the leader."

I said to all of them, "Please have a seat." I positioned them around me so I could see all of them at once. They sat there quietly for a short time. Michael broke the silence. "I know what you have us in here for."

I looked at him, waiting for him to continue. "Well, I told Corrinne not to be such a baby because she couldn't hit the ball in the game. We can't have babies on my team," he said.

"Okay, Tony," I inquired, "what's your take on this situation?"

"Mrs. T, I really appreciate you asking me that question. I love to talk to you. You are just so easy to talk to. Oh, yeah... how did I get off on that? What was the question? Oh, yeah — how could I forget?" He paused, then continued, "Well, all I can say is that we were having a really great time!"

Kaley was getting in a huff as she explained, "Mrs. T, what actually happened was Corrinne got up to bat and was doing just fine. She had batted twice and got on base both times. Monty was standing behind the base and started telling her that she was standing wrong, holding the bat wrong, and looking in the wrong direction. This frustrated her so much that she completely missed the ball!"

I asked them, "Do you guys see what has happened?" They all just looked at Monty. I continued, "Monty, how could you make Corrinne know how to bat correctly without hurting her feelings?"

He instantly replied, "I could show her how I want it done in private." He was starting to catch on.

"Good idea," I finished. "All I want you guys to remember is that you are all very special people, and each one of you is different and should be treated as such."

Late-Breaking Story

The students had gathered in Room 14 and were charged and ready for the day's activity. The emphasis was on current events at the local, state, national and world levels. These Eighth Graders always looked forward to this Social Studies activity.

Our newspapers had been delivered, the students had divided into their four groups (local, state, national, and world), and the stage was being set for the big search for news on their topic.

As the teacher moved around from group to group, she observed the "national" group carefully. Ray had taken charge immediately, giving orders and assigning tasks. Millie was sitting quietly, waiting to be told what she could do to help. Dan, the class clown and talker, insisted on presenting their oral report to the rest of the class. Ginny was becoming very concerned because she knew their grade would depend on this presentation and the facts it included.

The group was having difficulty even deciding on a topic. About that time, Dan saw a story that caught his attention — one that he knew for certain would command immediate attention from all the other students: "The Trial of Lorena Bobbitt." He could hardly wait to "perform."

After she read the article, Ginny became even more concerned. She wrote down all the reasons why this topic was not appropriate content for Eighth Graders. She felt some class members might be offended — and Millie wasn't going to offer her objections!

Realizing that time was expiring for gathering reports, Ray took charge and got the group focused. Ginny had found a report on a religious cult in Texas that had become involved with the FBI. All agreed that this story had a dynamic impact on the nation. She quickly and thoroughly jotted down notes. Then Dan looked them over and made a dramatic presentation to the class.

After the presentation, the "national group" was pleased

with its choice. The students felt they had made a wise choice and presented something of national significance... even if it wasn't joked about as much on *David Letterman* as Dan's story was!

Red Marks

en years ago, I took my outgoing, vivacious, never-met-a-stranger, high "I" six-year-old son, Chuckie, to his first day in First Grade. Because of his exuberant personality, I knew he would never be the quiet, studious type like his sister, but I was not prepared for the year that lay ahead of us.

When high "I" Chuckie and First Grade teacher Mrs. High "C" got acquainted the first week of school, it was definitely not good. There were *many* instances I could recount, but I will concentrate on the assigned writing papers.

As Chuckie did not stay *inside* the lines on coloring pages, neither did he stay *on* the lines of the First Grade writing tablet. (We were to learn later that this was of *utmost* importance to Mrs. High C.) Whenever there was a writing paper returned, it was covered with red marks and red notes. Nothing was ever good enough.

As a First Grade teacher myself (a high "S"), who had never placed much emphasis on perfection of anything — especially writing, and especially for a six-year-old — I was getting pretty ticked off! And it didn't help my feeling very much that my six-year-old was praying each night that Mrs. C would please like him. One night he said to me, "Mama, Jesus knows I can't stay on the lines all the time... Why doesn't Mrs. C know?"

Well, it was time for war! My child had gone from a happy-go-lucky, bubbly little boy to a dejected, miserable, frustrated mess. He had to spend recess (his favorite time of the day) in the classroom copying over writing papers; and no matter how many times he copied them, they never seemed to make the grade.

When Sara's mother called me to say that Sara (an "S") was crying and really sad because she couldn't do well in writing, I started asking around. Sara never got into trouble, but she was getting lots of red marks on her papers. Since Sara was very shy, she felt she could not ask for help and was sure everyone in the class thought she was dumb. She cried every day because she didn't want to go to school and she was positive the teacher didn't like her.

I knew that Drew (a high "D") was a very dominant and domineering child. His mother was pulling out her hair, for along with red marks all over his writing papers, she was enduring daily phone calls from Mrs. C. The only difference was that Drew was so self-confident, strong-willed and self-assured that he wasn't really worried about what Mrs. C said anyway! He told his mother Mrs. C didn't know good writing when she saw it!

Celeste's mother told me that Celeste was having a wonderful time in Mrs. C's highly structured classroom. She liked the very controlled atmosphere and the clearly defined tasks and writing assignments that required exactness and precision. What a surprise to learn that Celeste is also a high "C"!

I wish I could say that Mrs. C has changed her teaching style and that she has realized her room is filled with different personalities, and that she is an experienced teacher gifted with the ability to teach them all. But I am afraid she still delights in slapping red marks on writing papers and lowering six-year-old's self-esteem. And turning *butterflies* into cocoons...

Billy Bob And She Wolf

Ten years have passed since I was taught basketry by three Choctaw Indian master weavers. The Mississippi Choctaw culture is quiet, pragmatic and unassuming. Women are taught to be submissive, unassuming and obedient around men in general, and Choctaw men in particular. Their distinctive personality styles seldom flair outside of all-female groups.

Since their basketry skills are fading away because of tribal factory jobs, tribal casinos and the like, I am now spending part of my summer teaching basketry to young Choctaw girls. There is a generational and educational gap between the old master weavers, who have the knowledge, and the young girls. As an outsider, I seem to have good success at teaching the craft.

A few summers ago, I had a group of four sisters: "She Wolf," "Flitting Bird with Busy Beak," "Little Doe," and "Yellow Beaver." We often worked in a setting where outsiders could watch the process. This was considered an educational project for the general public, as well as for the young Choctaw girls.

We usually progressed smoothly unless our visitors became overly zealous with questions or breached cultural boundaries. This, of course, made the girls uncomfortable, and it was then that their individual personalities became apparent.

One afternoon, a guy we'll call Billy Bob decided to "sit in" on our class. His abrasive manner made the four sisters uncomfortable, resulting in eight eyes lowered and forty fingers working so busily that Billy Bob felt ignored.

As he tried to get the girls to talk, "working" the table, touching, asking questions, he zeroed in on Little Doe. He asked her how long she had been weaving. Eyes down, she whispered to me to tell him she began weaving two years ago. I wondered if she would crawl under the table to dodge his questions!

Then he asked Flitting Bird with Busy Beak if she enjoyed making baskets. Flittling Bird looked up and began to tell him how much she enjoyed weaving, although her sister Yellow Beaver had first talked her into coming instead of going to a Stomp Dance. As she moved into telling Billy Bob about the Choctaw Stomp Dance, he turned to Yellow Beaver. Without missing a beat, Flitting Bird transitioned to me, asking if I could come to next week's Stomp Dance — there would be a lot of people there, good food...

By this time, Yellow Beaver was explaining step-by-step how she learned to weave. No detail was ignored in her description of the weaving process. Billy Bob's eyes began to roll back in his head.

Seeing an opportunity to escape, he sat down by She Wolf who, I could tell, was rather "put out" with Billy Bob. His tone of voice had been very patronizing and condescending — she was steaming. Her cultural training was winning her internal battle until Billy Bob turned to her to ask, "So... what kind of Indians are you, anyway?" She Wolf raised her head, a gleam in her eye, and with all the venom she could muster said, *"Apache!"*

Needless to say, Billy Bob turned white — well, *whiter!* — started to say something, thought better of it and literally turned tail and ran. The three other sisters looked at She Wolf and, if it had been culturally acceptable, I am sure there would have been "high fives" all around. Instead, they lowered their eyes and went back to their weaving — a battle won.

Note: She Wolf has a bumper sticker on her car which reads *FBI (Full Blood Indian)!*

A History Project

Background: The school year was more than three-fourths over; it was time for the last Social Studies project of the year. (Remember that Fifth Graders are taught the rudiments of writing research reports during Language Classes after Christmas.)

During the whole year, Fifth Graders study "The United States — Yesterday and Today." After going through the geography and history of our country, each region is explored: transportation, agriculture, economy, etc. Now it was time for a fun way of pulling it all together.

Project Assignment: Here is your topic. You are to approach it in any creative way you would like. You may research information in nonfiction books, encyclopedias, or in magazines, record a program on television for us to watch, draw pictures or cut them out from magazines... (I made sure to describe all boundaries, set time limits, etc. I made sure that all of my students understood the assignment — even going over with some of them at recess or in privacy, "spelling out" ways that this could be approached.) Groups of four were asked to find all the information they could about one of the following topics from the years 1880 to 1940. (No later time period than that was allowed because I did not want them to be confused about "modern times" in these areas.) The topics included transportation, immigration, agriculture, household inventions, and others.

Performance: Ahhh, personality styles clicked in! "D" type students wanted to get the project finished yesterday! "I" students had no inkling of any reason to worry about their projects. "S" students could not find a starting place. "C" students re-did theirs, using umpteen pieces of poster board and supplies!

(Be kind to me; remember that I had not yet taken this course and learned about personality styles. I simply selected the groups based on how I felt they might work together, and who could help the "poorer" students.)

Believe it or not, hardly any group "copied" my instructions. They did some unbelievable work on their assignments. As I look back, I now understand that most of the credit for the type of work, the amount of creativity and the decisions about content that went into each project belongs to a particular personality styles.

Dennis, a high "D," was in charge of his group's transportation project. They were the first to turn in their assignment. He *did* most of the work on it and *demanded* that his ideas be used. He *dreamed* about how he wanted it presented, *dictated* how the work was done, and *dynamically* turned the project in. (I remember how he flew to the font of the class and *decisively* deposited his group's work on the table.) They had gone from the first transportation (other than feet) that was devised in the late 1800's to every possible method of transportation through the mid-1900's. Any pictures they could not find, he drew! Super job! They wrote under each picture the name of the transportation and the date.

Next comes "I." (No, not chronologically! They got started only after they saw the interesting "stuff" being turned in by their peers.) *Impulsive* Ian (whom I now see as a high "I" type), just happened to head this group, *influenced* by his high "I" mother — who just happened to be a teacher and thought her *important* child would not get an *interesting* grade! *Impressed* by the other finished project, Ian became *inspired*. (However, I never was sure how much of this work was done by whom!) He "made" a huge bulletin board, *interesting* and *imaginative.* This group had pictured all agricultural equipment from "Before 1900" and "After 1900," with old photos of farm families using much of it. (Of course, it helped that Ian's father is a farm equipment dealer and his mom could help Ian get the appropriate pictures from the dealership!) Ian was just plain fun to watch as he explained their project and ate up the response he got to his enthusiastic presentation.

Thirdly came the "S" project. (How I ever gave a student from each style the head-of-the-group role is beyond me!) *Sweet, status-quo* Melinda headed this one. Wow! *Steady, supportive, submissive* Melinda, backed by high "D" Laurel, made sure that each of her group members got "a piece of the action." They went to the library and researched almanacs to gain information about percentages of immigrants who came from wherever in whatever years. They made efficient charts and graphs to explain all their data. (If not for Laurel, that project would have been finished on the last day of school!) *Sentimental* Melinda, thrilled by the appreciation that seemed to come from group because of their finished project, crated and carted it home when it was ready to leave the classroom!

Now for Lillian, our high "C"! Whew! Analytic, idealistic, thorough, (and gifted) cautious Lillian caused my blonde hair to be streaked with grey! A zillion questions later, many recesses spent in her teacher-mom's Kindergarten room with her group-mates and thirteen poster boards, flannel boards, illustrations galore, and the "real" thing — a "telephone" made by stringing two tin cans together — careful Lillian was conscientiously correcting her detailed display on the top of the table and on the wall above the table. Her group had come up with a creative and meticulous method of showing every household invention from the telephone to electricity to can openers to movies to cars!

What a joy to work with different personality styles — and what an education to the teacher!

Seeing Eye To Eye

Meet Bobby Clarke. Bobby is an "I" student who comes to school merely for social purposes (recess, P.E. class, and Pee Wee Football). He is a nine-year-old boy with blond hair and blue eyes who hasn't got a care in the world. You gotta love him!

Meet Mrs. F. She is the brand new Fourth Grade teacher. It is still the month of August, and she is under the mistaken impression that since the first week of school went so well, this teaching business will all be a piece of cake.

After the morning devotional, pledge and prayer, Bobby raised his hand and told me he had just lost his contact lens and his mother was "going to kill" him. Immediately, I asked the students to stand perfectly still. I crawled to him on my hands and knees to gently check his shirt and the area around his desk. While lying on my stomach on the floor, it suddenly occurred to me that *Bobby doesn't wear contacts!*

The very first question that came to my mind was *How can I get out of this without looking like the biggest idiot God ever put on the earth?* I asked the students to remain still and quiet for just a few minutes while I left the room. Bobby's older cousin was in a classroom across the hall. I got him out of class for just a moment to make absolutely sure Bobby did not wear contacts. His cousin informed me matter-of-factly that not only did Bobby not wear contacts, he didn't even wear glasses! I felt totally reassured in the actions I was about to take. I would have hated to be a fool twice. When I returned to the room, I was able to see what the different personality styles among my students were thinking:

D – *What was the point of this? I wish Bobby had checked with me before pulling this stunt. I would have said NO!*

I – *This was a great joke! I wish I had thought of it myself!*

S — *I guess this was funny, but only if Mrs. F and the rest of the class think so...*

C — *Will Mrs. F think this is funny? This is getting our day started off late, and we'll be off-schedule all day.*

My trap was set. I told Bobby that the lens was obviously, hopelessly lost and that I was on my way to the office to call his parents. They could come right to school, pick him up, and take him to have his contact replaced. As I walked out the door and headed down the hall, I heard Bobby calling behind me: "Stop! *Stop!* **Stop! STOP!**"

As he tried to explain to me how he thought up this "joke" on the bus, I felt all of my four personality styles coming into play:

D — *I'm in charge here and I've got you right where I want you, boy! You're busted!*

I — *I'm sure that as the years go by, I'll look back on this and I'll think it is pretty funny.*

S — *Am I going to look stupid when I go back into the room? Will it be okay? I'll be glad when this is over.*

C — *I can't believe I fell for this! I must have "Kick Me" written on my back. I won't make this mistake again.*

Bobby Clark is a Junior High student now. Every time I see him he says, "Mrs. F, I think I lost my contact!" His mother and father still apologize *every* time I see them. And the "I" in me was right. Now, it *is* funny!

The Science Poster

I assigned a Science poster project on mammals. I wrote on the board *five* things to include in their project, and the due date was in two weeks.

The "D's" were thinking *Two weeks! Give me a break! I can't believe you would need two whole weeks to do one poster project on a mammal! Only five things — get real!*

The "I's" were thinking: *Boy, two weeks! I still have thirteen days before I have to start! I know, I'll do the bobcat! I'll get to stand up and talk — everyone will be looking at me! This is great!*

The "S's" were thinking: *I wonder what mammal Mrs. E wants me to do? What is her favorite mammal? What is her favorite color I can use for my poster?*

The "C's" were thinking: *Okay, I have five things to do for this project. I will need first to choose my mammal and go to the library. I'll write short summaries on each topic. I need to ask a few questions about this before I start.* Then he raises his hand and asks a *million* questions!

On presentation day, the "D" student presents his poster like Sgt. Joe Friday on television's *Dragnet*: "Just the facts, ma'am." No details. Takes thirty seconds at most.

My "I" child not only brings his poster of his mammal (which by the way is not too neat and has one or two things missing from the "must have" list of five), but he also brings a stuffed bobcat to show us everything. Finally, I have to tell him we would like to go to lunch *today* in an effort to get him to wrap it up.

My "S" child gets up with an eye-catching poster and has everything I have asked the class to do. It is very neat. I know she has spent a lot of time on it. She makes a good impression.

My "C" child raises his hand and has a question about "S's" poster. He asks, very cautiously, "Is a *duck* a mammal? I don't think it has tracks and I know it lays eggs!" The "S" child is devastated! She breaks into tears and I think she may hyperventilate. I tell the "C" child, "No, it is not a mammal, but she gave an *excellent* presentation on what *she* thought was a mammal."

At the time this incident happened, I didn't know about the different personality types. As I look back on how they reacted to the incident, I can see clearly each student's personality type. And believe me... I'll know from now on!

On The Way To The Museum

I recently chaperoned my son's Kindergarten class on a field trip to a museum. Since this was my first opportunity to have a car *full* of five-year-olds for a two-hour trip, I knew I should be prepared.

My riders consisted of two "D" personalities (who insisted on sitting side by side), one "C" type, one "I," one "S," and the driver who is an "S."

The night before our trip I loaded our car with coloring books and toys. My first mistake was that no two books or toys were alike. The two "D" boys always wanted a book or toy someone else had (just until they got it). There was always conflict between these boys and someone over the crayons, books, etc., but the conflict always ended as soon as the "D" children won. The "S," "I," and "C" children never *really* minded giving up as long as they had one toy or book to replace the other.

The little "C" girl always wanted to know how much farther it was, how much longer it would be, and where we would eat. The entire trip, she tapped my shoulder and said, "Missus, Missus, may I ask you a question?" When we got to the museum she did the same with the tour guide.

The "S" child agreed with everyone in the car. If a "D" wanted his coloring book, he *automatically* gave it to him and got started in a new one. He definitely was not into battles or arguing! It amazed me to see a child like this.

The "I" child *literally* talked her way to the museum (two hours)! If her mother knew the things she told, she would go into hiding!

I am very glad to be able to understand and identify these types. I wish I had know this eleven years ago when I began teaching.

The Whistleblower

My youngest daughter has a "D with I" type personality. She has always wanted control and we have been battling for years. One day, Sherry complained that she was too ill to go to school. I, of course, made her go. School let out early for our basketball championships that afternoon, and I thought it would be a perfect time for me to take her to the doctor. She, of course, had gotten much better throughout the day because her "I" wanted to be with her friends at the ball game.

I instructed her where to meet me after school. She said she would not be there and she wasn't. My "D" was rising rapidly as I approached the gym. I found her among the students in the stands; they were packed in like sardines. I motioned *Come on!* and she motioned *No!* One more confrontation.

At this point, I made my way through the huge crowd, finally reaching her, and issued my ultimatum: "Sherry, let's go... or you will be sorry." Toe to toe... "D" to "D"!

Her response: "No."

Then I realized I was truly backed into a corner. I was her mother — and a teacher among students. I had to show some authority. I gave her one more chance. What a joke! She said, "I'm not going."

I realized I had my whistle on my key chain and thought *Blow the whistle! This will get her!* It did. She bolted up, screaming, "Mother!" At the same time I realized I had also stopped the championship basketball game — it was incredible! Players, coaches, referees, students, Sherry and I were in shock. The game continued and we went to the doctor.

I know now not to confront a "D," especially among hundreds of people. Given the chance, she would have gone to the doctor later that day, but I did not give her a choice or an option.

This year, an "I" student, Frankie, was one of my favorite kids. He was "I," and "A.D.D." and precious! He did bounce off the walls. One day another student in class said, "Teacher, you and Frankie really compete for attention." I realized that he and I were a two-man entertainment package, and he was as good as I with the "straight lines." Needless to say, that class was "wild." I really believe I could have recognized his humor and ability and perhaps have calmed down both of us by having a "private chat" — letting him know that because I had "the big desk," I had to be in control.

"S's" are my dreams, hopes and wishes — and a constant reminder that somehow "God" perhaps made things a "little" unfair for me. I have three "I with D" combinations at home and am a single, "I" parent. (Oh well, "Miss Scarlett" will think about that another day.) I always tell my "S" students that I wish my children were like them.

When I do this, Frankie the "I" says, "Supreme Wise One, do you even *like* your children?"

My response was always: "I *love* them dearly... but *like* them...? Mmmmmm..." (shrugging my shoulders) "...sometimes!"

"C's" are really great in my classroom because somebody has to stay on task. Like Edward: "Mrs. M, if you tell another story we won't be able to finish our notes!" I love them, too.

Me: "Okay, Edward," (200+ I.Q.) "you're right — thank you..."

The "S's" are relieved. The "I's" feel let down because it's time to work. The "D's" think *She can't get anything done — I'm outa here!*

Me: "Back to the Great Wall of China... Where are my notes?"

Edward: "I believe you left them on the projector before you went 'rabid' about Chang Kai-Shek..."

Me: "Edward, I love you..."

The Boys' Beauty Pageant

The Senior sponsor met with her class to discuss its fund raising project for their Senior Trip. When she mentioned to them what the project was, she had quite a variation in reactions. She announced: "We will have a Senior boys' beauty revue!"

Darrell thought: *This is ridiculous! How degrading! I won't do it. Just let every Senior "foot" his own bill!*

Ivan just loved the idea: *Boy, to get on stage in front of an audience!* (His sister) *Ida has a long dress she wore in a wedding. I can use it! Great Aunt Sadie has a wig if I can get it off her. I can get some shoes that fit on the dollar pile at the discount store... if I can find two that match!* He said aloud, "I bet I'll win!"

Sharon thought it was a good idea if that's what the class wanted: *Will everyone agree? Will everyone participate? Will this be hard to plan?* She told the sponsor, "Let me know how I can help."

Charlie started reasoning: *Will this make enough money? Will people come? How will they find out about it? What night and time would draw the best crowd?*

In realizing the work this project required, the sponsor decided to call on some of the students to help.

She told Darrell, "I know you probably feel this is very childish and immature, and you really don't want to participate. But I need your help. I don't want you to be a contestant. I want you to be in charge. You will choose committees for each area. Before I turn it over to you, I just ask that you let Sharon be the follow-up person on all committees and allow Charlie to do all the public relations work. The rest is in your hands. I'm confident that you can handle this — of course, you already know you can. Just remember to be patient with those who don't work as fast as you."

The sponsor caught Ivan later that morning. She knew how excited he was to get his outfit together. She asked him to really "talk up" this pageant, get people excited about it, and encourage boys to participate. "Also, if any of them have trouble finding clothing, maybe you could ask around and help them find what is needed. I know you can do this, Ivan, and do it well."

Later that day, she saw Sharon showing a new girl around school. She stopped to tell her she had heard some Senior girls talking about getting boys' suits and being escorts that night. "Would you be interested in doing that?" the sponsor inquired.

"Whatever the girls decide to do is fine with me..."

"I've put Darrell in charge. What I want you to do is follow up on all the committees. Make sure they are on schedule and know their deadlines. Encourage those that get 'bogged down' and offer to help them. Darrell knows you are to do this, so you don't have to worry about him telling you to 'butt out.' Will you do this for me, Sharon?"

"If that's what you need me to do, I will be glad to. Anything else I can help do?"

"Not at this time, but if I see any area that needs support, I will get in touch with you."

At the end of the day, as Charlie was at his locker, studying the contents, the sponsor asked him if he could be the public relations guy.

"Charlie, we really want this to be a success and a good money maker. Could you just make sure that the parents and students are notified about this event? Make sure the posters get up — those the art committee is doing. We're not sure when we need to have this pageant, but be sure it gets on the radio and television stations' 'community bulletin boards.'"

He replies, "I'll start on this right away. Notices will be sent home in all the students' backpacks and lunch boxes. I'll need to pick a night and time that doesn't conflict with any other functions. When placing posters, I'll decide which stores will give us better exposure by deciding where most people shop. I'll get some friends in Speech Class to write some advertisements to be aired, and I'll make sure the English teacher proofreads them before delivering them to the stations."

"Charlie, you might want to get someone to help you. This is a large job. But if you choose to work alone, I'll understand."

As the sponsor leaves for the day, she is confident that

all areas are being handled by the appropriate individuals. Remember, it's not "the right person for the job," but the *right job for the person!*

Ode To Rohm

The assignment is spoken, get out paper and pen,
Now, what to say? Where to begin?
How about teacher's first day of school
At Brookhaven Academy where none would dare fool
Around with taking charge and running the class
'Cept those determined or those with brass.
The "D's" are dominant, say, Jerry's the one
Always in front, the first begun.
On day one of school he's assigned all the seats,
"That's the way that it's done. Don't you know, Teach?"

Our inspirational "I's" will take
Front row, center, a stage and just for the sake
Of order, he's assigned Sara S. status-quo
"It's her place from First Grade."
Wouldn't you know!

Christy G, a very capable "C"
Is sitting up front, next to me.
She's competent, cautious, careful, correct
And now she is ready to select
Those problems all others will dodge
Or hit or miss or at least submit a hodge podge
Of papers and homework and such
Proving Rohm's theory of blends, combos and much
More. And that's the way of "D," "I," "S," and "C" —
Personality Insights of Rohm, Ph.D.

Staying In Your "Seat Work"

I give "seat work" to my class each day. Assignments are written on a board for all to see. "Seat work" can be done at different intervals during the day, not during class time but to be finished by recess at 1:45. It usually consists of what would otherwise have been homework, but since it is finished in class, the homework load is lighter. For example, the children come into the room at 7:45, and after putting up their books and belongings, they begin working on an assignment such as answering history questions at the end of the chapter.

Gary, a "D" personality, hurriedly puts up his books and gets to work with the goal of finishing quickly — full steam ahead. Seth, an "I" type, "tries" to communicate with others in the class as he leisurely puts away his books. He plunders around until the eight o'clock bell rings. Sandy, an "S," makes sure everyone in the classroom is okay. Then she check with me to make sure she understands what to do and begins her work. Cassie, a "C" style, puts everything in order and then with her cautious and conscientious mind, she starts to work.

By the first bathroom break, Gary has almost finished; Seth hasn't started; Sandy is so concerned with her neighbor that she points out the answer to the question he is wondering about; and Cassie is making sure she finds the best answer to the questions.

After lunch, Gary has finished and wants to have his work checked. A few answers are wrong and he disgustedly corrects them. Seth has started now, but if someone drops something, he's distratcted. Sandy has almost finished and as her answers are being checked, she says to me, "I'll find *another* answer if that's not right..." Cassie is still searching faithfully to make sure each answer is correct, and *will* be finished by recess.

Everyone does finish before recess, except for Seth. He wants to me check the ones he has answered so far, so he can get recognition for either being right or wrong. He would really rather discuss them, but now he realizes he *must* hurry to finish by recess.

Now I understand the personality styles of these children. Recognizing their differences will help me to be a much better teacher in the future.

The Art Contest

As our school's Art teacher, I enter the children's artwork in various contests. I try very hard not to emphasize winning — the "eye" for drawing is a God-given ability, and some students will never be able to win no matter how hard they try. I don't want them to think that is the purpose or goal of "art" or my class. A great feeling of failure can be produced if students receive no praise except for winning. But contest entry time does come around — and as the children finished their artwork and brought it to me, I was reminded of four pictures...

Sean's artwork was colorful, complete with a background and foreground. The moment he handed his picture to me, he asked, "When are you sending these off? When will I know if I won? Are the ribbons big or little? Can I show the class? I know I will win!" His comments and questions continued until I said firmly, "Sean, I will let you know the minute I hear the results." Every time he passed me in the hall, met me in the store, or saw me at the gas station, you know what he asked. Sean is the most competitive "D" type child I have ever met.

Ervin's picture was interesting — very bold shapes, funny

lines, and vivid colors. In typical "I" fashion, he had to be reminded *several* times to quit talking and get to work. He enjoyed showing his picture to others and looking at theirs. His drawing needed to be cleaned up a little and have a complete background. He commented, "I hope you like this! It's so pretty — look at these colors! When do we get to go outside? I'm ready to play!"

Tabitha's high "S" picture was clean, without a lot of detail. I have encouraged her to explore different media, but she is content with what she produces now. When she brought her picture to me, she remarked, "Here's my art. I love art, but it's okay if I don't win. Sean's and Ronald's pictures are the best. Can I put away the paint for you. You're a good teacher, Mrs. S. I love you."

Ronald's picture was equally as good as Sean's but neater and with more detail, befitting a high "C." He asked me quietly if I liked it and then returned to his seat. He's a quiet child, never interested in any sports. Torment, to him, would be having to compete against anyone. God has blessed him with tremendous eye/hand coordination, and he is very creative and precise.

When the artwork was returned, the first place winner was Ronald. He acknowledged it with a simple "Thanks" and returned to his desk. Sean won second place and said, "What? His picture was not as good as mine! That stinks!" Tabitha's picture placed third. "Ooooh, I got a ribbon!" she said. "But I know Sean is mad. I wish he wouldn't be upset. Thank you, Mrs. S. The honorable mention ribbon went to Ervin. On his way up to my desk, he "high-fived" his classmates and skipped the rest of the way. He waved the ribbon around the room. "Check this out — I won something! Art is fun, art is fun, art is fun!" Then he "high-fived" his way back to his seat and handed Sean a box of Kleenex — "Use these if you need to!"

Trick Or Trig

In teaching Trigonometry I have found it very difficult to lay the groundwork by having my students memorize the six trigonometric functions. But without the basis of these functions, students struggle throughout the course.

Last year, I began by asking my one highest "D" student to teach the introductory lesson to the class. He was thrilled to be in control and his lesson went well. He enjoyed teaching and the other students liked having a *student* teacher.

The following day I reviewed the lesson and used techniques to reach the remaining students who still didn't get it. I challenged them to come up with a trick for remembering the trig functions. They were enthusiastic and the "I's" benefited especially. Their best and most memorable trick was creating sentences using the first letter of each word in the functions. After this, my "I's" never forgot their trig functions!

Finally, I promised that several pop quizzes would be given the following week, assuring that my "S" and "C" students had sufficient reasons to memorize the information.

I have found that this method, having "D's" teach new information, then making a game of learning for "I's," followed by quizzes for "S's" and "C's" is very effective in teaching trig.

The Little Ghost

Miss T's was planning her Second Grade class's annual Spring play, "The Woody Woodpecker Revue." The children eagerly awaited her announcement of players for the different parts.

RayAnne always thought she should have the most important role, so she was very disappointed when Miss T assured her that Woody would be played by a boy! However, she was given the supporting role of The Squirrel, with many lines to speak. This pleased her because she knew she could memorize and deliver lines better than anyone.

Harvey was cast as Woody. He was a natural entertainer. All of the children liked him, and he liked being liked. Miss T said Harry would make a great Woody, and he basked in the attention and praise brought by this wonderful moment.

James was chosen to play The Raccoon. He was reading a book at his desk and did not even hear his name called the first time. He did not know why he had been chosen for this role, but he would study and try to give it all he could. He asked many questions about why The Raccoon would do this or that. Finally, Miss T told him not to worry so much. It would be fine.

She continued calling out the other parts, until she came to The Fairies, who would wear beautiful pink costumes and dance around Woody on the stage. All of the girls liked the idea. Mary was a surprised and a little embarrassed when her name was called, but she thought playing a pretty pink Fairy would be nice.

The children practiced their roles for weeks, and every day Mary got more and more nervous. Her mother was already making her costume — she didn't want to disappoint her and Miss. T. They had both worked so hard, but she had a secret wish. She wanted to be The Ghost. Brenda got that part, but she didn't want it. She told Mary she wished she could be a Fairy. *Why not?* thought Mary.

She just wasn't sure how to ask her mother. But that night she told her mother that she loved her and thought the costume was lovely, but she really wished she could trade parts with Brenda and be The Ghost. Her mother asked if she was sure that was what she wanted to do, then called Miss T. They decided that if both girls were agreeable, it would be fine.

The next day, Brenda's mother picked up the half-finished Fairy costume and left a sheet with two small holes for eyes. Mary thought it was lovely to be in there, hidden from view.

On the night of the play, the school auditorium was full. RayAnne was there, informing everyone that the tail of The Squirrel's costume was stiff, as it should be, because her mother had used *real wire*.

Harvey was in costume as Woody. He practiced taking long, low bows and waving to his friends in the audience from behind the curtain.

James was there as The Raccoon. He was asking Miss T a question about his lines when RayAnne told him his tail was sagging because it had no wire in it.

Brenda was beaming in her Fairy costume, and Mary was glad that Brenda was happy.

Mary was excited as she slipped the sheet over her head. Later, as she ran around the stage and shouted "Boo!" at Woody, the audience laughed and clapped. Afterwards, she thought, "This was great, and I wasn't embarrassed on stage because no one could see me under the sheet." This became a very happy memory for the little Ghost — I know because I was that little Ghost in 1953!

I think RayAnne was a "D," Harry was an "I," James was a "C," Mary was an "S" — and I'm not sure about Brenda. RayAnne grew up to become a high school principal. Harvey went to West Point and later to Viet Nam. James became and engineer. Brenda became a legal secretary. Mary became a Third Grade teacher.

Lab Frogs

Today in Biology we will be dissecting the frogs. The students are paired into groups and this is how some of our students' personality styles play out.

Ethan has a "D" personality and has been "fighting" the teacher all week in her efforts to build the class up for today's lab work. His first negative words of the morning are, "I don't even know why we are doing this. What we're going to see is in the book!" The other students in his group hear the comment and rolls their eyes. He does the dissection quickly, not pausing to review the organs and their functions. Overall, it is a good dissection — it had to be, *he* was in charge.

Ricky bursts into the room announcing, "Let me see, let me see! I want the biggest one you can find!" He is ready to cut before the frog is even on his pan. He did not read the lab material last night, and as a result his frog is being massacred. He jumps from one system to another with no organization. I spend half the period telling him to go back to his station because he is visiting with all the other groups. His response is, "I just wanted to see their frogs."

Shannon has been very apprehensive about today. Perhaps if she stays very quiet I will forget to give her group a frog. Even though her stomach is queasy, she did her works diligently through squinted eyes. She certainly depends on her partners.

Thinking about Bruce makes me smile. He is my "question child." He takes his time and reviews his lab manual over and over before continuing. Every incision is precision and he takes care not to puncture any internal organs, constantly calling me over to check his work although he knows it is correct.

Now if you were a surgery candidate and all four of these

students *somehow* made it through med school, which one would you want to operate on you?

Math Mayhem

inal Mathematics exams were given on Tuesday, May 23rd. That made Friday, May 19th very significant as the last day of regularly scheduled classes. Naturally, students assumed that disciplinary actions for the year were over — at least *some* of the more mischievous of our group did.

In reviewing the incident, I will attempt to relate our "players" to their personality traits. This connection is made in retrospect since my knowledge on the subject has been broadened only this week.

I have not bothered to change the names of our "characters" because it does not appear that enough of them are innocent to be concerned with protecting them. *(Editor's Note: We did anyway!)* Also, it seems that I will have to work through a bias I have formed over the past twenty years. At this time, it is obvious to me that I do not respond well to students who have high "D" or high "I" personalities. That conclusion is drawn after many years of attempting to deal with students different from me and totally misunderstood by me. Maybe now I can do better.

Basically, this is what happened that Friday in Mrs. C's Eighth Grade Pre-Algebra Class. A "small segment" of the class decided not to take advantage of their final opportunity to review for the exam. A "larger segment" of the class got caught up in the activity. The details are better left out in case this book falls into the hands of a student who uses it as an operations manual. It is sufficient to report that total chaos resulted!

Zoe, our "I" in this fiasco, started by *simply* wanting to *play hard* during the time set aside to *work hard*. No malice was intended. She understood the importance of the setting but had no intention of settling for a simple "going over" of the assigned review sheet during this, her final performance of the year. A spontaneous party was ignited by her in celebration of the pending end of school.

Manny, our "D," loved Zoe's plan but couldn't stand the thought of her being in charge of such a delightful event. He felt compelled to lend his leadership abilities to the mutiny. But as momentum built, his "shark-like smell for blood" led him out of control to the point of being exiled to the hallway.

Jake, our anointed "C" continued asking Mrs. C about the content of the exam. Even though he was "almost" innocent, his volume knob cranked in attempting to be heard above the din.

Frank was rewarded for holding his supportive "S" position. Either because he is by nature "reserved" or possibly because he is Mrs. C's next door neighbor, he was included among the "cleared" four. He seems to enjoy not being part of the fracas.

The end result was that Mrs. C: *1.)* Blew her cool; *2.)* Threatened her class with a harder exam; *3.)* Wrote down 21 of 25 class members as being participants in the uprising; *4.)* Administered a multiple choice exam to the remaining four and a related "short answer" exam to the "infamous 21."

How we dealt with parents and tried to "fix" Mrs. C's error in judgment is a story for another day. Our faculty has profited immensely from our new understanding of personality styles.

My Dilemma

Problem: I have read both of the books and completed the other parts of my assignment for Dr. Rohm's course in "Personalities: Teaching and Learning Styles for Better Educational Results." It is now 10:30 on Thursday night and I am exhausted. Should I write my "DISC Story" to get an *A* tomorrow, or should I go to sleep now?

D: My "D" stomps my foot and yells, "It's not fair! Too much homework!" I pout and whine to anyone who will listen. But I am impulsive and very competitive when it comes to grades. I remind myself of Greg, my high "D" student this past year — how many times he blurted out the answer very loudly because he was so excited and enthusiastic — how many times he ran from his seat to tell me he knew the answer — how he pouted and was such a sore loser when I wouldn't give him even partial credit — how he was so proud of himself when he caught a mistake of mine! All he needed was a challenge. I gave him one: he is in accelerated courses next year!

I: Back to my original problem: Should I do my "DISC" paper? (I'm sorry my "I" kicked in and I started rambling on and on.) Well, I had good intentions for doing the paper earlier in the week. I got sidetracked by talking on the phone and then I got an invitation to a birthday party earlier tonight. I get recharged talking to friends! Maybe I can act like my high "I" student Esther and Mack, who would go to the party and forget the homework. They were relaxed and happy, but really disorganized and irresponsible — what a disruption to the class. And waste time? Always tardy, always needing to sharpen a pencil and talking to everyone on the way over to the sharpener, never bringing supplies to class. Wild excuses for not having their homework, like *losing* it! *Imagine!*

S: Now here is my "S" saying I'd rather be like Terri and Joanie — steady and stable, always dependable. They always listened when no one else did at the end of the day. They never argued about right or wrong answers. If they found a mistake I had made, they acted embarrassed when they politely asked me to rework it, or sometimes they never even brought it to my attention. Terri and Joanie would write the "DISC" story! But I want to make my friends who are settling for a *B* happy. And I want to make my friends who are working for an *A* happy, too. How can I make everybody happy?

C: Wait, wait — now my "C" starts talking. I have always set high goals and standards. I would really disappoint myself if I fell down this time. I am so methodical it makes my friends crazy. I have so many lists it makes my husband scream. The perfectionist in me reminds me of Brady, a high, high, high "C." I swear, he will have a heart attack before graduation. I've tried all year to convince him it is all right to miss one or two problems! I have failed miserably. He has panic attacks if he makes a 96 or a 97 instead of his usual 100. If I call out, "The answer to number 28 is six..." Brady raises his hand to ask if he has to count his wrong — he wrote 6.0! I have started to understand how my husband feels. *I* want to scream!

Well, my "D," my "I," my "S," and my "C" have said their piece and I still don't know what to do! Should I write the paper or not?

He Must Have Been Asleep

Every year I require my class to read and report on different types of books. This time, the students were required to read a biography and give an oral report use using a visual aid.

Even though I had drilled the students all year on the essentials for a biographical report, I still went through my entire spiel.

I could tell that my "D" student, Dale, was thinking *I'm so tired of hearing this over and over again! I wish she would shut up!* At the same time I could see expressions of appreciation on the faces of my "S" students. They were so thankful that I was going over it one more time.

The day for the reports came, and Jeff, a "C" type, was the first to speak. His report on the life of Abraham Lincoln was thorough and carefully organized. His visual aid was a perfect miniature replica of a log cabin.

Howie, an "I" type, was eager to be next. After making sure that every eye was focused on him he said, "I read *Rip Van Winkle* for my report." Needless to say, he talked on and on and on. I had decided to take him aside later and break the news that his *fictional* subject was not exactly right for a *biographical* report. I was beaten to the punch by Dale who forcefully raised his hand and said, "Excuse me, but I don't think *Rip Van Winkle* is a biography. That's not fair. I had to read a biography — why didn't he?"

Libby, an "S" type, shyly raised her hand and asked, "Can't you just give him another chance? Maybe he didn't understand." In the middle of this, Jeff spoke up. "We are wasting time. Will we get through with this before recess, or will we have to finish tomorrow?" Most amazing was that Howie just sat there saying, "What's going on? What are they talking about?"

My class was in total chaos by this time. I was very upset with Dale. If I had known about the four personality styles, I could have brought the situation under control more easily. I would have understood their feelings better. I know this Fall will be a new adventure, and I can't wait to view my students from my new perspective!

─ ─ ─ ─ Bubba And The Squirrel ─ ─ ─

For the first few years I taught at our private school, we had no cafeteria so the students brought their lunches and ate at picnic tables on a patio near the principal's office.

The principal was a young man from a military background who had no experience in dealing with children. He was definitely a "D" type who was very arrogant, egotistical, and often intimidating. I was the new Sixth Grade teacher with a very diverse group of students from surrounding counties.

One of my students was a big "teddy bear" of a boy called Bubba, who was large for his age. He was very a gentle "S" type. His three favorite activities at school were lunch, snack time and recess. To him the class work was just an unpleasant necessity to be endured while he enjoyed the other three things.

One day, as the children were talking and visiting with friends and unpacking their lunches on the patio, the principal appeared in his doorway. In "Hitler" mode, he announced loudly that there was too much noise and called Bubba's name out of the 60 others students who were also talking and ordered him to throw away his lunch and return to class.

Now Bubba had just opened his Thermos and lunch box in great anticipation of his hardy meal of warm beans and fried squirrel, which he had been lucky enough to shoot the day before. He had told the class excitedly about his hunting trip and had the proof of his marksmanship in front of him.

Bubba looked at the principal in total disbelief and big tears came into his eyes at the very thought of throwing away food — *his* food!

All the children became very quiet and watched with shocked expressions as Bubba was marched back to the classroom without lunch.

When the others' lunchtime was over and they returned to class, a little girl named Cheryl tried to comfort Bubba over the loss of his lunch. In "C" type fashion, she also expressed concern for Bubba's mother who had gone to the trouble and expense of packing his lunch only to have it thrown away.

Richie, a very outgoing "I" type friend of Bubba's, tried hard to cheer him up by saying, "We'll all share our snacks with you at the afternoon break, and on Saturday, you and me will go huntin' and kill more squirrels than anybody can eat!" (Nowhere but in rural Jefferson Davis County, Mississippi could this actually happen!)

Fifteen years later, Bubba is grown and married with two daughters, and he has a successful career in the oil and gas business. The principal has had many unsuccessful jobs, an identity crisis, became delusional, and is now battling anorexia. From a Sixth Grade teacher's point of view, this may be the ultimate example of poetic justice! *(Editor's Note: See why we subtitled this book, "My Students Are My Best Teachers"?)*

Rhonda Rebounds

Being the "I with S" personality that I am, teaching First Graders was one of the most rewarding experiences of my life. After a couple of weeks into my second school year, it did not require much observation to realize what a diverse yet extremely bright group of children I had been blessed with.

My instincts about children inspired one of those speeches "from the heart" — something I *now* know I had not done enough of in the past. Well, I proceeded to tell them what a joy they were to have in my classroom, how incredibly sweet, smart, and fun they all were. "There is *no* doubt in my mind that someday one of you will be Valedictorian of your Senior Class — that's how much I believe in you," I said.

The response to this praise was amazing. Missy ("Miss–C" student) quipped, "What is a Valedictorian?" When I answered that question, of course, she followed with numerous others — "What exactly *is* a Senior?" "Will I know how to read good by then?" "Will we have lots of homework all the time?"

…Then there was Trask, my "D" type child, who interrupted her line of questioning with, "Well, *of course,* the answer is 'yes' to all of those questions! Don't you know anything, Missy? Get your goals in order — I have!"

Bert, one of my high "I" profiles chimed in to ask, "Wasn't that the recess bell, Mrs. S? I think I heard the recess bell. I'm *sure* it was the recess bell!" We ignored him. And Archie ignored us — a little boy later diagnosed as A.D.D., who just smiles and stared into the ozone throughout all of this "excitement."

And then there was Rhonda. I remember her sweet smile, her big brown eyes, her extreme attentiveness. She was that "perfect 'S'" who carefully dotted every "i" and crossed every "t" in a way that said she cared — perfect penmanship, always doing her best, as she *so* wanted to please me and everyone else in the class. Rhonda was absorbing my every word but never opened her mouth. She simply nodded and gleamed at me throughout my speech, as if to say *Okay, okay, now I see just where I am headed.* That she did!

Though I started a family of my own and took an eight year leave of absence from teaching, I tried to inquire about my former students through my teacher-friends. Interestingly enough, the personality patterns of these children had continued through the years, pretty much as one would expect. Sadly, I continued to hear from Fourth through Eleventh Grade that Rhonda had suffered much unnecessary grief and turmoil caused by several of her classmates whose extreme *jealousy* of her kindness and dutifulness had gotten out of control. How it broke my heart when her mother phoned me one night and cried on the other end of the line. She told me Rhonda had seldom gone to bed in weeks without crying because of the merciless, horrible pranks some of the girls at school kept doing to her. And they had somehow manipulated half the class into joining in the "persecution."

My own high "S" first responded with tears, but then I felt my strong "I" take over! I told her mother to please tell that sweet angel child before bedtime every night that I loved her and I would be thinking about and earnestly praying for her — but that whatever happened, I *knew* Rhonda would endure it. She must hold her chin up. I know it's not in her nature, but she must "toughen up" that "S" of hers. I also reminded Mom that this behavior was a part of others needing to "catch up" to Rhonda's maturity level. Though it was hard to see, she would overcome such hard times and her good qualities would be appreciated by others — *they* just had to *grow up!*

Well, guess what?! Guess who was Senior Homecoming maid, cheerleader, Miss Academy, Friendliest Girl, Miss Hospitality, winner of the Daughters of the American Revolution Good Citizenship Award, STAR student, Most Likely to Succeed... and yes, you guessed it — Rhonda was also Valedictorian of her Senior Class! As others grew to appreciate her strengths, she developed her other combination traits — learning to "raise" her "D," "I," and "C," while getting her "S" under control.

Later, her mother wrote me the kindest note, explaining to me how Rhonda had never forgotten that day in my First Grade class, when they were told how special they were and were encouraged to become Valedictorian. Rhonda shared with her that she had set her goals that very day to make that inspiration a reality. (Perhaps even Trask's rebuke became fuel for her fire.) "Thank you seems so inadequate," her mother said. Do I have to explain my exhilaration at that moment, especially as she continued, "Rhonda has always wanted to be *just like you.*" What an impact that has made on my teaching career for the future, such a strong reminder of what a *tremendous* part we play in our students' lives. What we determine is just how positive or negative a part we play.

How I Saved My Family

My Dear Grandson:

Here in writing at last is the story you requested about how, as a boy, I saved the entire Normal family from certain ruin.

In the old days (just before the dawning of the new Millennium, when I was just a lad in Umbro's), life was quite sad. Back then, only a few fortunate ones had learned of the "DISC" behavioral analysis system, and though the good word was spreading, that year of 1995 was filled with horrific strife borne of ignorance.

As I have already recounted to you many times, my family was of a type common in its day — ordinary, yet extraordinary. My dad, your Great-Grandpa "Abb," an optimistic but driven man, had a compelling nature that at times was domineering and even inconsiderate. He was what we now know as a "D." In spite of his arrogant and reckless youth, he had the excellent luck and prudence to marry my sweet, softhearted mother, Your Great-Grandma "Simmy." She, of course, was his opposite, an "S."

Your Great Uncle "Sub" was my classic older brother — a tyrant who was not only bright and idealistic, but also moody and unsociable; also a classic "C," he criticized me relentlessly.

As for me, well... I was a darned near-perfect teenager — lively, funny, a really spunky fellow who talked and talked. In our current enlightenment, we all know that being an "I" is a special blessing. But at the time, I simply knew that someone had to rescue my quarrelsome family, and *I* was just the one to do it, having acquired *The Key* — info about DISC!

Well, one halcyon evening after Great Grandpa "Abb" had returned from his CEO's meeting, we four headed out to the nearby park for his relaxing hour of speed-walking, as was our practice. Great Grandpa "Abb" always claimed he couldn't really rest until he had stretched his legs and had a good visit with his "three favorite people."

My brother, your Great Uncle "Sub," as usual annoyed my dad almost immediately by asking, "Why... just tell me *why...* do I have to come on this stupid walk every day when you know I have important studying to do for my locksmith's examination?!"

Before my irate dad could respond, my resplendently affectionate mother interrupted. "Boys, boys, we all know this walk is our tradition. 'Sub,' please try not to be negative, and lower your voice. You are making people stare at us."

Then dad bellowed at us, "'Simmy,' 'Sub' — and you, too, 'Sorta' — remember that I'm the head of this outfit, and our family walks, and walks *fast!* I don't want to hear another word from any of you!"

Poor Mom, that was too much for even her. She stopped and turned to face your Great Grandpa 'Abb' and calmly said, "This dissension is making my head hurt, and I'm sick and tired of all this yelling and whining. Right now I'm not sure if I want to stay in this foursome any longer. And, 'Sub,' if you step on my foot one more time..."

Here was my chance! This was a desperate group who needed someone to *give* to them, *explain* to them, *elaborate upon, act out* and *illustrate* for them some true insights on our relationship.

As it happened, that very day at school, I had been introduced to "DISC" by a wise teacher who expressed concern about my rabid vocalizing in her Calculus class. Smiling with enthusiasm, I urged them impulsively, "Take a seat on that bench so I can help each of you begin to understand your true selves, for only then can we all begin to understand one another. We are not all *wrong* as a family; we are simply *different!*"

Of course, I enjoyed my initial presentation of "DISC" to my family, which has resulted in a happy history of success and mutual appreciation.

> With love,
>
> Grandpa "Sorta" Normal

Carpe Lunchum (seize the lunch)

On an otherwise typical Spring day in Second Grade, getting ready for lunch took an unexpected turn in my classroom. I had wandered to the back of my room to mark milk tickets and do "lunchy" things when I noticed that one of my "D" girls had slipped behind my desk at the front of the room. She sat straight in "my" chair and announced, "Rows 1 and 2, you may wash your hands. Please do not play in the soap, and use only one paper towel." I continued to watch as she called the next two rows, told them to get their lunch boxes, take their seats and get ready for the blessing. It was as if I was watching myself.

As a teacher endowed with "S" traits, I didn't want to hurt

Donna's feelings, although I knew it would be hard to do that anyway — her self-esteem was so high it would take a lot even to dent its shell. Then she told the class clown, an "I" personality to sit down and be quiet. She blessed the meal, moved the class to the lunchroom and continued her — *my* — duties.

As the students continued to follow their usual routine, with a *different* leader, no one even seemed to be bothered, except for one small "C" who walked past dutifully and murmured, "Do you think Mrs. M gave her permission?"

Frankie And A Net

The setting is the gym. The cast is four high school age kids: Matt is a "D," Spike is an "I," Jess is an "S," and Frank is a "C."

After practice one day, I told these boys to stay and help me put new nets on the basketball goals. I said, "The quicker we get started, the quicker we will finish."

Immediately, Matt told Jess to go to the storage room, and then meet him at the south goal to put up the net. Jess ran to the storage room and got the ladder. Matt then said, "I'll hold the ladder while you climb up to the goal. I'll tell you if everything is going smoothly." (He might have done the job himself if he could also have held his own ladder!) Jess has almost finished when Matt pointed out that he had missed a loop. They finished their job quickly. But, Spike and Frank were a different story.

Frank was sitting on the floor, counting loop holes on the net. After that, he counted loops on the rim just to make sure they matched. While Frank counted, Spike fooled around on the side practice goals. I yelled, "Spike, what are you doing?" He replied, "Just having fun while he counts those stupid rings on the rim!" Matt yelled across the gym in disbelief, "Frank, if *my* net fit, don't you think *yours* will too?" Frank replied calmly, still focused on his work, "I've just got to be sure…" Jess kept whatever he thought about it to himself.

Both groups got the job done, using four different approaches and two very different techniques.

─ ─ ─ ─ ─ Birds Of A Feather ─ ─ ─ ─ ─

While studying a unit on birds with my Third Graders, I went into great detail about birds' nests. We discussed and even collected and brought in nesting materials birds used. One afternoon, I divided the children into groups and asked them to "make" a nest themselves. I gave each group a box of materials and some water (in case any group wanted to make mud), and outside we went!

As long as Lance could keep Drake from checking out the other groups, he was in control, telling them how it should be made. Andrew questioned me constantly as to how *I* wanted the nest made and whether his group had all the right materials. I assured him he had what he needed. Brent kept going over the instruction sheet to make sure they were doing it right.

I found the project fun and the students enjoyed themselves, but it was almost impossible to complete. Lance was acting like a *hawk,* while Drake was behaving more like a silly *goose.* Andrew seemed like a *parrot* incapable of an original thought, and Brian was more like an *owl,* so stuck in a mode of hesitation and uncertainty *(Hoooo-hooo?)* that he couldn't get started.

Only My Teacher Knows For Sure

By way of background information, I am a Sixth Grade teacher. This incident occurred just after we had returned from Spring Break when my students and I had been apart for almost two weeks.

Gert, my high "D," asked in her loud, critical tone: "Mrs. R, do you dye your hair?"

Bonnie, an "I with S" blend turned to Gert and remarked, "Her hair *always* looks darker when she wears that outfit!"

Grace, my aptly-named "S" students, came to my defense: "She did not. Her hair always looks curly and bouncy." Later she told me privately, "It does look a little darker, but I like it."

The high "C" in our class is me. My response was none — I ignored all comments and did not give them an answer. After all, they were being critical and "C's" don't like to be criticized! Besides, it was none of their business!

Ups And Downs

I am a Fourth Grade Math teacher. I assigned my students to cut out graphs from newspapers and magazines. I said they could also make their own graphs on a computer for extra credit. Students responded to this opportunity in different ways, according to their personality styles.

My high "D" child reacted by saying, "I don't need extra credit so I'm not going to do it. I've got an *A* already!"

My high "I" child was excited about the assignment and asked if there could be an extra (or "happy") recess for the person who brought in the most graphs. In other words, *how can we make a game out of this?*

My high "S" child sweetly asked if she could bring in a lot of magazines and newspapers for everyone to cut graphs from.

My "C" child questions what kind of graphs I wanted to see. "Do you want color pie and bar graphs from our computers or black and white line graphs? How much extra credit will we receive?"

I guess it's true that there are no lazy students, just unmotivated ones. My "D" wasn't really lazy, but he had already reached his goal and needed further motivation. My "I" could do it if he saw the fun in it. My "S" was happy if she could please me by helping others. And my "C" wanted a clear graph indicating the bottom line return on investment!

A Flying Start

It's our first day of school, and from the start I can see that each of my students is going to need some special attention.

Student "D" arrives with everything labeled and sharpened. He wants to know before we start what the homework will be tonight because he has plans for the evening.

Student "I" arrives with nothing. "Oh, did we need to bring stuff on the first day? I never dreamed we'd get right to work!"

Student "S" has not arrived. But a note arrives from the office. It says he had a "nervous stomach" on the way to school and his mom is in the parking lot building his confidence. When he finally comes through the door, he brings me an apple.

Student "C" has arrived early to copy the schedule. He has already determined the length of each session, play break and lunch. He points out quietly that our clock is one minute fast according to his watch, which he is sure is correct.

The Daily Journal

As a primary grade teacher, I believe our class "journaling" time is very valuable. The children work at their own speed and level, and this offers them opportunities to be creative. Therefore, we journal almost every day in class.

Most days, I give them a specific assignment or a choice between two or three topics. What they really love is when I announce a "Free Journal Day." The only thing I encourage them to do is use their time wisely and do something they feel is important.

Debbie, who is a high "D" child, can't wait. She is in her element. She loves to write and begins immediately, composing a detailed story about her weekend trip.

Jordan, who is a high "I," chooses to write a story featuring herself and a friend. She relates her adventure to the others at her table as she works. After writing just a few lines and finishing quickly, she begins illustrating her work. She draws a large happy picture of herself first, then starts on her rendition of her neighborhood friend. However, as the others at her table realize they are not going to be included in either her story or her picture, they voice their great disappointment. She hurriedly begins to pencil them in. "Is it time for recess yet?" she asks, hoping to be rescued from her situation.

Ellen sits at another table, a sweet "S" child. She looks around the room for a few minutes, weighing her options, and finally makes her decision. She dutifully begins writing out her "color words" (we have been practicing hard on them). I realize she has taken to heart the instructions and is laboring over writing them neatly. Because I know she really might have wanted to choose her favorite activity which is coloring, I praise her for her neat handwriting and suggest she might want to draw a picture with her crayons at the bottom of her page. Her face brightens and she gives me a hug.

Last, but *never* least, is Larry. As an extremely strong "C," he is usually last to begin and last to finish when an original or "experience" story is called for. He spends his time thinking everything through carefully before he begins. But today, since he is in charge and it is his idea, he chooses his passion — *numbers!* He begins writing with "0" and continues past 100, past 200, past 300. He also distinguishes the odd numbers from the even. As expected, the numerals are written perfectly and are organized into neat rows, making the most use of the paper. He is a happy camper! When recess arrives, Jordan is relieved, but Larry begs to stay inside and finish. When I ask how far he plans to write, he states, "To infinity!"

It didn't take Debbie long to write two detailed pages. Pleased, she asks our student teacher, Miss G, to come listen to her story. While at the table, another child asks Miss G how to spell a word. But before she can respond, Debbie interrupts and spells the word for her classmate. A third child asks if Debbie is correct and Miss G replies, "Almost, but you actually spell the word with a 'C.'"

"No, you *don't,*" says Debbie. With that, the second child proclaims, "Debbie, Miss G goes to college and you just go here. She's right and *you* are wrong!" Believe me, the thought that she could be wrong honestly had never occurred to Debbie. (Please note that she has *not* answered rudely. She was just stating a "fact.") Her mouth falls open.

Satisfied thoroughly with her paper, Debbie picks up on Larry's idea and immediately begins her own numbers list. However, she decides to write "even" numbers only. The race is on! Debbie announces, "I just love my journal!" With that, I smile and tell the students to line up for recess. Debbie sprints (not runs) and beats Jordan to the back door. Can you imagine trying to teach without understanding your students' personality styles?

Mississippi, State of Confusion

My Fourth Grade class's Social Studies assignment was to create a booklet about our State of Mississippi that would include data, drawings, maps, and reports. The students had three weeks to complete the assignment. I explained that their booklets would be graded on content as well as skill in research, organization, paraphrasing, grammar, editing and spelling. The students were given a detailed outline to follow and then an opportunity to ask questions. Their facial expressions said it all!

Danny "D" looked "put out" because it would be a waste of time since the whole class lives in Mississippi and everyone already knows all about it. But he listened anyway because he was determined to finish his booklet first. Danny was competitive both inside and outside of the classroom.

Irene "I" glowed with excitement because she knew this could be fun. She was already thinking about working in groups and even baking a Mississippi Mud Cake to serve the day the reports were due. Wow! What a neat way to celebrate! She whispered to Sarah "S" about her plans and told her about the last time she baked a Mississippi Mud Cake at her grandmother's house in Carthage. Oh! not Carthage, Mississippi, but Carthage, Texas, where she was born. She commented that Carthage, Texas, even had a great shopping mall!

Sarah "S" just smiled and tried to listen to both Irene and the teacher. She didn't want to be rude to either of us, and she even whispered her offer to help make the cake.

Cathy "C" had a very serious look on her face. She listened intently but was worried about whether she could do it correctly. After asking fifteen questions, she started budgeting her time to be sure she could complete her booklet during the three week period. She took out her calendar and scheduled a trip to the public library for additional resource books. Sarah told Cathy that she would be happy to share her books with her. Danny interrupted to shout that he needed them first!

Irene jumped up and said, "Let's *all* meet at the library and work together — we could even go out for pizza! By the way, what subject are we going to work on... English?"

I knew it was going to be an interesting three weeks!

Diorama Decisions

An assignment has been given to make a diorama showing how a group of Native American Indians lived. Each student may choose a particular scene he wants to show, and the completed project is due in five days.

This is right up Dynamic Don's alley because he likes challenge and having control of things. He determined as soon as the assignment was announced that he would present the adobe homes of the Southwest. He will rush home, fly through the house collecting all the materials he needs and start immediately on the first day. Before the sun has set, he admires his completed project and is ready to turn it in the following morning.

Impulsive Irene has a different impression of the project: "Oh, great! We can all get together at my house and work on our projects!" At recess, she will get plans rolling for the gang to come over, and after school they'll head to her house — but they are high "I's" like her and will forget why they are getting together. Nothing will be accomplished, and their second, third and fourth day efforts will show the same results. On the day before deadline, Irene will panic and quickly throw together a teepee for her project.

Sweet Susie decides to do her project on wigwams. She will collect all her things but won't quite know how to start. Should she make it big or little? She wants to be right, but she will be too shy to bother her teacher with clarifying questions and will struggle with it on her own. Ultimately, she will choose the most practical way and do it very efficiently.

Competent Clarice is going to begin her project by checking out every book she can find, making sure precisely how she should proceed. After several days of researching and deciding exactly how to do it, Clarice will carefully calculate and measure the miniature logs she needs to make her log house of the Northwest Indians. Each log will be cut to the correct size as she puts them in place. She will turn it in on the final day, and it will be absolutely perfect... almost ready to be inhabited!

= A Real Blast (Off!) =

The Fifth Grade at our school takes a special field trip each year. Approximately 100 students and 32 adults make an overnight trip to Huntsville, Alabama, to visit the "U.S. Space and Rocket Center." This is the culmination of our week-long study of the space program. It is also the first trip many of these students have made with all their friends but without their parents.

After returning to school, the children are always asked to give their impressions of the trip, to tell their favorite part of the trip, and offer any suggestions they might have for improving the trip for the following year's Fifth Graders.

Here are two "D" responses we received:

Student 1 – I loved the fact that our groups got to go wherever we wanted during free time. We got to choose the rides or museum simulators we liked best. We could try them as many times as we wanted!

Student 2 – The SCAT was so cool! We got to try out all the equipment they use in Space Camp and to train astronauts. I did a great job on all of it! The group leader took lots of pictures of me!

Two "I" type responses were:

Student 1 – I had a ball! The bus was so, so, so much fun! We didn't have assigned seats. I say by Mary, then Jane, then Sue, then Polly, then Tiffany, then Caroline, then Mary Beth. We could talk and talk and talk! It was so great!

Student 2 – The Habitat was unreal! It is shaped like a rounded Space Station. We got our pillows and slid down the walls. It was awesome!

Two "S" types offered this feedback:

Student 1 – It was a great trip! I liked everything we did — everyone else liked it too! The parents said we were so good they would chaperone us again.

Student 2 – The SCAT was so fun! The SCAT counselors told us just what to do on each simulator. They said we were the best group that weekend! Everybody liked the SCAT because they gave us all an equal turn.

Two "C" types analyzed it this way:

Student 1 – This was the greatest trip! We got to spend two hours at the SCAT, one hour at the Omnimax® movie, two hours at the Redstone Arsenal, and six hours in the museum or rocket park. I learned so much!

Student 2 – The bus trip to the Redstone Arsenal was the best part of the trip. The bus drivers know *everything* about the Space Center. Most of them are retired workers from the area. One of them even had known Werner VonBraun!

Getters, Starters, Readers, Recorders

In our "hands-on" Science Class, we work in groups of four or five. On the first day of class, I have all the students sit in alphabetical order. But this year, it was readily apparent that this would not work at tables two, four or five.

Table two had a high "D" and three "S" type students. The "D" child took over control of all experiments and the "S's" let him. Table four had two "C's" and two "I's." The "I" students played and joked with each other, and the "C's" were very frustrated that they could not makes these two cooperate.

By changing our seating and giving every student a job, things went much more smoothly. I tried to make sure that there were not two "D's" at any one table. This was easy to do since there were only two strong "D's" in the class. Next, I tried to split the "I's." This was harder because there were six of them. I put only one "I" at each table and tried to place them so they could not visit with their "I" buddies at other tables. My ten "S" students and eight "C" students were evenly distributed as "buffers" among the tables, and they suitably blocked the "I's" from direct contact with each other.

There were four jobs that, once learned, were rotated around the table. This gave each child a chance to be the *Getter* who gets all the materials for the experiment; the *Starter* who starts the experiment but also makes sure that everyone has an equal chance to participate; the *Reader* who reports the group's findings to the class; and the *Recorder* who writes down the group's findings. By doing each job, each child has been able to do not only what they are comfortable in doing but experience things that are unfamiliar, learning to work together and to depend on each other.

Reformation Celebration

Reformation projects are a *big deal* in Seventh Grade Bible Class of our church-sponsored school. After being introduced to the Protestant Reformation and some of its key figures and events in their Sixth Grade Bible Class, the Sixth Graders are then treated to the Seventh Graders' presentations of their projects. So, most students start their Seventh Grade year asking, "When do we get to do Reformation projects?"

After a more thorough historical introduction during the first two months of the year, project worksheets are distributed. Selections are varied and students may choose to work individually or in small groups. The worksheet not only provides students with choices but also with deadlines for making their selections, deciding on their format, conferring with their teacher about a plan, and more.

Andrea (an "I") has been ready to start since August, inviting people to work with her. The only problem is she has no idea what she is going to do! However, she eager to start and knows it will be fun!

Brad (a "C") has known since seeing a presentation in Sixth Grade exactly what he wants to do for his project. He has been assembling dates for a time line that will top those he saw last year in at least two areas: manner of presentation and content. He has noted the various deadlines in his plan book, plus a few additional dates of his own. He intends to work alone even though Brian has been talking about their working together.

Brian (an "S") is uncomfortable. He has seen Brad confer with the teacher several times in the two days since the project sheets were distributed. Brian's own project sheet is blank, and he is worried. At recess he approaches Brad and explains that he has brought poster board to school so they can start. Brian even shows Brad the dates he has organized from his class notes.

Brad assumes a posture and tone that hurts Brian's feelings, enumerating reasons why he needs to work alone, without Brian. Brad also points out that Brian's approach will result in a time line that is no better than those presented last year.

Marta (a "D") has an ambitious video project: "Lives of the Rich and Famous," including "on site" interviews with Mary Tudor, Anne Bolyn, William Tyndale, and John Wycliffe. She includes two commercials, one a satire on the sale of indulgences and the other a sales pitch for Reformation music.

When the plan sheets are distributed, Marta immediately corners Andrea to work up the indulgence commercial. Andrea is enthusiastic, but she makes it clear to the teacher that this involvement is just for fun — she wants to do her *own* project for the grade.

Marta also recruits other students for various roles. She has already arranged for video taping at the historic First Presbyterian Church and has also set the wheels in motion for after-hours access to an art museum for taping. The director of the museum has been putting her off, ignoring Marta greatly, so now she begins pressuring her father (who is a board member and large contributor) to secure the needed approval.

How does it all turn out? Brad's time line is ready early and is such an involved multimedia presentation that he is asked to show it to the Tenth Grade Western Civilization Classes. Andrea has had a blast creating her commercial and filming with the group. When it finally makes its debut, her part in Marta's video will rock the class and kids will try to buy indulgences from her the rest of the year! Meanwhile, Marta is fuming because she can tape inside the museum on only two evenings. She enlists Brian to help behind the scenes with props, costumes, lighting, and keeping parents informed about schedules. Andrea has the whole crew over to her house for a wrap-up session to hoot and holler at the unedited version of the video. Marta doesn't come because everyone is fed up with her bossiness.

Still, Andrea wants *her own* project, but time is running out and all the projects are done so well, though some are a bit stuffy and dull. At the last minute, she decides to finish out Project Week by throwing an early birthday party for Martin Luther (his birthday was in November). Since she invites the other Seventh Grade Bible Class, last year's Seventh Graders, and the rising Seventh Graders, the party is held that Friday night in the school gym. Even Marta comes.

A Touch of Class

I had a precious Fifth Grade class this past year. In retrospect I realize one reason it was so sweet was because it was filled with "I's" and "S's" and only a few "D's" and "C's." Of course, this also accounts for the slowness of the class as a whole, since my best students academically were all "C with S" combinations who had lots of questions and constantly wanted reasurrances.

New spelling words were given on Mondays, with a test on Thursdays. If we had a spelling bee, it was usually on Wednesday and served as our review. The children in our story are Zeke (an "I"), Helen (a "C"), Lori (an "S"), and Abbie (a "D").

Every Monday, Zeke would ask, "Mrs. M, can we have a spelling bee?" My reply was usually that we should wait until Wednesday so everyone would have time to write the words and study them. But this went on most of the year. Zeke usually scored 85–95% on written spelling tests and, on occasion, much lower. Guess what?! Zeke won the Fifth Grade spelling bee and placed very high in the District Spell-Off.

Of course, my own supportive "S" praised him, but my "I" and "C" teased him good-naturedly by saying, "Zeke, I won't accept anything less than 100, or you will have to write your words fifty times each before the next test." He would play the game with some verbal affirmation predicting his score. However, he usually fell short of the mark because he made careless mistakes on paper. But when he could shine in front of his classmates, his ability to spell came alive!

Helen, on the other hand, always made 100 or even 100+ (with extra credit) on written tests. In weekly spelling bees, she deliberated over every letter before saying it, and oral competition was not a game for her because she simply did not want to be less than perfect with her responses.

Lori was a meticulous student who turned everything in, beautifully neat, and she made excellent spelling grades. Lori practically *whispered* her answers in our oral bees — she almost stuttered her letters! She was second runner-up for our big class bee. This was a really big deal because Lori's grades were high only for subjects in which she could memorize exact answers.

Lori would smile sweetly, glancing at some of her friends whenever she won. Zeke, on the other hand, always won with a lot of emotion, as if he had just received the Academy Award. Helen, who was quite a loner, smiled almost to herself, although she was quite aware of her capabilities.

Unfortunately, Abbie was a poor student by choice. She blurted out answers, right or wrong, in a very loud voice any time she wanted. In spelling bees, she was very bold with her answers. She possessed an innate confidence that far surpassed the quality of her spelling.

(Although she also made poor grades in Social Studies because she rarely turned in written assignments and did not study for tests, she blew us away on our Fifth Grade trip to Washington and Jamestown. When our historical guide asked questions throughout her tour, Abbie was the only one who answered loudly, immediately, repeatedly, and *correctly*. Many of the questions had answers of which even I was not certain.)

Helen was such an excellent student, and she always worked alone and with her own precise (if time-consuming) agenda. I allowed this because she was our top student academically and was so deliberate and thorough. However, this hurt her on her I.Q. test. When everyone had finished and time was called, Helen still had an entire section to complete because she had thought through each question two or three ways before answering. *(Editor's Note: This should give teachers real insight into the way students take test and how to help them accordingly)*

Lori received our "Striving For Excellence" award. She not only did everything exactly as I asked, she also had the neatest work anyone could have, and she never did one thing that she was not supposed to do the *entire* year. Her friends said she was chatty at home. At school, she was always smiling and sweet and so quiet.

Zeke received the "Good Citizenship Award" in our room by a landslide vote by his classmates. He came in from recess on day, all upset. He said, "Mrs. M, I have to talk to you." Tears were welling in his eyes. We went out in the hall, and there he said in a most matter-of-fact tone underneath his tears, "I'm afraid none of the girls is going to play with me anymore. There has been a misunderstanding. I just can't stand the thought of losing any of my friends..."

His other classic, daily response was, "...but Mrs. M, I *know* that I had my homework this morning. It's not in my notebook — have I already given it to you?" He would always find it later, usually at home. On the other hand, Lori and Helen always had every paper precisely when I asked for it. Again, Abbie did her work selectively and turned it in on a few occasions, and her grades reflected her choice to neglect her schoolwork.

In all fairness, I have to say that although my class was slow, they loved each other and me. My two "D's" were not terribly disruptive. The large number of "I's" provided a very warm classroom spirit. The "S's" fit right in, and my two "C's" were not arrogant or antisocial... I suppose I'll probably get *all "D's"* next year!

Around the World

A favorite game played in my Second Grade classroom is "Around the World." Two students stand side by side and compete to see who can be the first to answer a flashcard correctly. The loser sits down and the winner moves to challenge the next person on the row. This continues around the room to see if anyone can go "around the world" by beating everyone in the room.

To my surprise, a typically quiet "S" came out the winner the first time we played! She is very bright and knows all her addition facts very well. Of course, her victory did not set well with our competitive "D's," nor did our "I's" like all the attention she was getting. The "C's" were always right there, wanting to know if she was following the rules and making sure I didn't make any mistakes. I told all the students to practice their facts and we would play again the next day. My story is about how each personality style "rose to the occasion."

The "D's" took the challenge and all had improved by the next round. They weren't going to let an "S" beat them! One "D" boy did come out the winner, and they seemed to take the game more seriously than the others. They turned something meant for fun into serious business.

The "I's" did seem rather competitive, but they also just enjoyed the whole experience. An "I" typically had something funny to say when he lost, and if he won his whole body glowed with excitement. Even the "I's" who didn't know their math facts very well always got in there and tried — unlike the "S's."

The "S" children didn't show the same enthusiasm as my other students. They did not shout out their answers like the others, but calmly stated them. The game seemed to challenge everyone except these children. They didn't care if they won or not. On several occasions, several opted not to participate at all.

The "C's" paid close attention to the game. They watched the cards closely even if it was not their turn. They always remembered where I stopped last time and they didn't like losing. Because I have learned that "C's" always like to be right, I know this next quote was a typical "C" statement. After several unsuccessful attempts, one of my "C's" approached me discreetly and asked, "Miss P, do you think you could tell everybody to let me give the right answer next time? That way I can win!"

Assigned Seats

In my First Grade classroom, the students sit at tables arranged in groups, rather than at individual desks arranged in rows.

I have 26 students divided into six groups. Therefore, there are two groups of five children and four groups of four children.

How interesting to look back now, after analyzing each student's personality, to see how they reacted within their group. They worked each week on getting my "Quiet Table Award." I declared a winning table every day and on Friday I announced the weekly winners, who were awarded with candy on their way home. We always had two tables that "ran neck and neck," and of course there were several tables that always struggled.

I understand now that I had arranged my room like this:

Table 1 had a girl "S" and a girl "C" on one side; a girl "S" and a boy "I" on the other side, with the fifth child, a boy "I" at the head of the table, as far from the other boy "I" as possible.

Table 2 was another five-child table, with a girl "C" and a girl "I" together on one side, a boy "C" at the head of the table, then a girl "S" sitting between him and a boy "S" on her other side.

Table 3 had a girl "S" and a girl "C" on one side and a boy "S" and a girl "S" on the other side.

Table 4 had a girl "I" sitting next to a boy "C" on one side and a boy "D" sitting with a girl "S" on the other side.

Table 5 had a girl "S" paired with a boy "I" on one side, with a boy "S" and an "I" girl sitting on the other side.

Table 6 was arranged with two girls, an "I" and an "S" on one side, and it had an "S" boy and an "I" girl sitting on the other side — the "I's" and "S's" were diagonally opposite each other.

There were 16 girls and 10 boys in the room, and I tried to arrange them in boy/girl order as well as in what I hoped would be "best work" teams.

Table 4 always was the best until I moved the "C" boy to their table from Table 2. The high "D" boy at their table urged everyone at Table 4 to win and they did. The "C" boy I placed at their table had been moved several times during the year because he had difficulty cooperating with any group. They always said they couldn't win with him at their table, and most of the time they were right. I put him at Table 4 figuring if anyone could shape him up and keep him in line, this balanced "D," "I," "S," "C" group could — and they did! After a few weeks, they began to win again. I also see why Tables 5 and 6 won very infrequently until they got their "double I's" under control.

With the information I have learned about personality styles, it will be less "hit or miss" in pairing my students next year. What a fun and helpful tool this is going to be! *(Editor's Note: Teachers, do you think personality combinations in your classroom make any difference?)*

When You Hear The Bell...

Outside play time is an important part of a Kindergartner's day. When it is time to go outside, we ring a bell and let the children know that it is time to line up at the playground gate and return to class. Watching the different personality styles getting their place in line can be quite interesting.

As soon as the bell rings, the "D's" immediately drop whatever they are doing and scramble to get to the front of the line to be the leader. Whatever it takes to be first, they are determined — even if it means running over everyone else!

The "C's" also come right on to line up because the bell has rung and it is the correct thing to do. They will jockey for position, but they are not "dead set" on being first. Their main concern is getting everyone else to line up in an orderly way. A "C" will usually be the first to tattle if someone is not doing it "right" or is trying to "butt" into the line (a word we would like to expunge from Kindergarten vocabulary!).

The "S's" are scattered throughout the line because they know when the bell rings it is time to go. However, there will be a few "D's" who are not quite fast enough to get a choice spot in the line, and they will prevail upon or bully "S" children to let them into their spots. "S's" are generally very agreeable and usually move back to give up their position.

As we start to walk back to the classroom, we can look out over the playground and notice that a few high "I" children have not come to line up. They have not heard the bell ring, nor do they *want* to hear the bell ring! They are busily playing and talking, oblivious to what is going on. They would prefer to spend the entire morning on the playground and just forego any work that might interfere.

A Peter Panoply

In the school auditorium, the parents, grandparents, brother and sisters of Mrs. B's Kindergarten Class await the presentation of the Annual Spring Program. Mother sit nervously and fathers beam from behind video cameras, as brothers and sisters fidget in their seats while pulling at stiff collars and ruffled sleeves.

Backstage, the children (who are festooned in absurd costumes devised and constructed by a gaggle of nervous mothers now seated in the audience) anxiously pass the fleeting moments before the curtain is raised. Damon, Iggy, Susie, and

Constance (the Personality Style Poster Children for the New World Order) are demonstrating some classic behavioral patterns.

Damon seems ready for the challenge, relentlessly pacing back and forth behind the drawn curtain as if he is angry that a mere layer of cloth could keep him from his appointed task. Susie lends support by following Damon as he paces, careful to stay one step behind. Iggy is peering through the split in the curtains and waving to his mother. Constance, being ever-practical, questions Mrs. B as to exactly why it is necessary for each and every child to be dressed as Peter Pan, when there was only one in the video.

As the curtain is raised and the program begins, the pretentious personalities carry on. Iggy shamelessly breaks character by waving his pointed, green felt cap and loudly hissing "Hi, Mom!" in what was apparently intended as a tactful whisper. Damon promptly commands him to "shut up and be still!" Constance covers her eyes in dread as Susie tries to calm the ensemble by directing their attention to Mrs. B, who is now kneeling in front of the stage.

During the climax of the program, a raucous rendition of the song "I Won't Grow Up," the exhibition of diverse personalities reaches its crescendo. Damon sings loudly and proudly, while Constance mouths the words feebly, wondering how it is possible for a person *not* to grow up. Susie dutifully sings on cue and in key, as Iggy gestures wildly with his arms and create new verses.

The song comes to a merciful end and the curtain closes, the proud parents applauding the brilliant performances of their gifted offspring. Free at last, brothers and sisters scurry for the exits and drinking fountains.

Backstage, bedlam ensues as budding personalities reach full blossom. Damon pronounces the show a tremendous success and suggests an ambitious encore to the beleaguered Mrs. B. An exuberant Iggy prances the stage bellowing an extended solo of "I Won't Grow Up," pausing periodically to embrace his classmates warmly. Susie timidly thanks Mrs. B for her masterful direction and praises her fellow performers for their excellence. Always the critic, the horribly embarrassed Constance points out the shows shortcomings and provides corrective advice for future programs. The personality parade abates as the parents storm the stage to congratulate and cajole their weary thespians.

We're On A Roll Now!

At 8:15 on Monday morning, I began taking First Period roll. Less than ten seconds later, my progress was halted by Bruce (a rather zealous "C"), who wanted to know the day's assignment so he could start right away. I assured him that I would give the assignment as soon as the roll was taken.

When I got to Stephan's name, I noticed he was leaning back in his chair, feet on top of his desk in arrogant "D" posture. And he was throwing something repeatedly at James, an "S" who just sat there smiling. In order to rescue James, I walked over and asked Stephan to take his feet off the desk, stop leaning back in his chair, and stop throwing things. As he complied with my request, he told me he had been thinking... and if I would grade the *right way,* he would have an *A* and not a *C–* in my class. He went on to say that he should be teaching the class and asked if he could help me teach. Just to appease him, I said he could run the slide projector. As I turned away, James told me he would be glad to take my absentee report to the office for me. How could I say no?

Again, I returned to taking the roll. And once again, I was interrupted by Bruce. This time he told me he really needed an *A* in this class and wanted to know the day's assignment so he could get started in order to make sure he had enough time to finish. I assured him that he would have plenty of time to finish the assignment. Just to accommodate him, I said I would give him an extra credit assignment that he could work on outside of class.

Wearily I returned to taking the roll. Just as I was filling out the last name on my absentee slip, in walked high "I" Mindy, late as usual. She stopped, smiled and said, "Just put me in detention, Mr. B. I don't have a note." Then she tried to find her chair. I say *tried* because Mindy seems to have a problem knowing the difference between a friend's lap and an empty seat.

It was at this point that I decided it was time to start Mindy on a step-by-step walk through the class assignment. After all, we do want to make sure Bruce has enough time to finish.

Ship Ahoy!

In the Fall of 1993, during a series of lessons about Columbus, explorers, and treasure ships, I decided to do something "fun" with a Fifth Grade class. The lesson would involve research and some hands-on experience.

The following week, I announced the project. First, the class would research how a ship is designed to float. Then, they would be asked to design a ship with a foot-square piece of foil that would float in a tub containing two gallons of water. This ship had to be designed in such a way that it would hold as many pennies as possible before it sank.

Karen (our high "D") stood up immediately to take over. "I will bring the foil, the plastic tub and the pennies — how will I know how many pennies to bring?" I explained that this would be the "fun" part — we would have to estimate.

Nat (our high "I") promptly asked, "We are going to have *real water* in the library?" Then Judy (our high "C") reminded me that I had said not to get water near the books, and she inquired why we were doing this project anyway.

After explaining that we *would* have real water and that the books *would* be safe, I thought it would be good to give Nat the assignment of designing a foil ship that would hold the most pennies since he seemed so interested. He accepted excitedly: "Yeah!" The class was given one week, until their next library day, to get ready and to estimate the number of pennies needed.

In the week that followed, Karen assured us all that she had the necessary items for our experiment lined up and ready to bring to school. Nat said "Yeah!" each and every time he was asked about designing a ship, and Judy kept coming to the library to read about ships.

Library day arrived and sure enough, Karen came in very proudly, carrying everything she had proclaimed she would bring. We had the foil, all cut and ready to go, the plastic tub for two gallons of water, and plenty of pennies. The items were placed on a library table in front of the class. All the Fifth Graders gathered around very excitedly as I poured the water into the tub. Then Nat was asked to step forward and demonstrate his design for the ship.

"Ship? What ship?" was his incredulous reply. He had completely forgotten that he was the one to design our vessel. The whole project seemed to be lost until Judy stepped forward

and announced that she had been reading and thought she had figured out the best way to fold the foil.

She flattened out the 12" by 12" piece and carefully turned up a 1" lip all around the edges. Then she placed the ship in the water. The whole class was amazed that it floated.

Chantell (our high "S") volunteered to help pass out the pennies. One by one, each student took a turn placing a penny on the ship. They all took several turns as pennies were placed side by side to cover the bottom of the ship, following Judy's instructions. Then she told them to place pennies on top of each other, starting first at the four corners.

Chantell placed the *seventy-eighth* penny on the ship and it finally collapsed and sank. She was crushed that *she* had ruined the project. Judy wanted to do it again because she didn't see how the last penny went on. Nat was applauding the whole project because he had so much fun — "Water in the library! Oh man!" To conclude the experiment, Karen began giving orders on how the library should be cleaned up.

It is going to be interesting to watch these students grow up and fulfill their unique niche in life.

What A Day!

A poem based on one truly gullible day I had with my imaginative four-year-old class in pre-Kindergarten:

The last month of school — time drawing near
To children and teachers it seems so dear!
A story unfolded, personalities so clear
Listen very carefully and you shall hear

D-I had tubes in his ears put in
But not down very long when
Determined to be back in one day
He awoke from his surgery, ready to play

Lo and behold *HiDee* had a wreck that same day —
Her will so strong she was at school right away.
We were so glad when she came back
Though on her head was quite a whack!

"Now, children," the teacher said,
"Let's draw picture for *HiDee* and *D-I*.
We'll make them feel better
So they'll laugh and not cry."

"Oh, boy!" the children all said,
"We can color them so pretty —
They will take our pictures
And we won't even get them dirty!"

Later, as our Phonics we read
And our teacher sat quite proud,
Ifun suddenly burst forth with tears
Like rain falling down from a cloud.

Our teacher didn't know
What was bothering her so.
"My dog!" said *Ifun,*
"He's gone. We don't know where he'd go!"

But our teacher said,
"Why, *Ifun,* someone will feed him, I know!"
So her tears went away
And *Ifun* didn't look so low.

Then *S-will* calmly said, "My mother
Did to the hospital go —
When she'll be home
I don't know!"

"The stitches are this long —
All the way down here —
Could we draw her some pictures?
I'll take them to Mother, dear."

"But, *S-will,* that's not true!"
Said *C-S,* really quite clear,
"My Mother talked to your Mother.
You need have no fear."

"So while more pictures we draw
The teacher softly asked,
"S-will," whose taking care of you?"
"My daddy — he said
He'll wash my head
And put me to bed."
"But," said *C-S,* "I know that's not true!
And I've already told you!"

Carpool came and *Ifun* said,
"My mother burned her arm —
Can we make her pictures?
It really did her harm!"

Teacher called parents just to check
Parents called teach, what the heck!
"No!" said *C-S*
"Yes!" said *S-will*
"What? Why?" said *S-will's* Mother,
"All those pictures my car did fill."

Meanwhile my teacher on *Ifun's* dog did check.
They found him — on someone else's deck.
"But how is *S-will's* Mother?" asked Mother of *Ifun.*
"Just fine!" said my teacher, who was coming undone!

S-will's Father called and felt right bad
About *S-will's* story that was so sad.
"Don't worry!" my teacher said, "It is so... funny
I'm the one who feels like a dumb bunny!"

Next his Mother did call.
"Did they draw pictures for the Mothers, one and all?
I'm so embarrassed," the Mother said.
"We're putting *S-will* right to bed!"

"Whoa," said the teacher, "He meant really well.
Just meant you were special, though a story he had to tell."
"Well," said his Mother,
"He'll say he's sorry, of this I'm quite sure!"
But another story came out, so innocent and pure.

The story went on and on through the night
Giving many lots of laughter and delight!
"S" in my teacher — she's one of those kind
Though "sucker" is the word that comes to mind!

On The Line

About twelve years ago, I was teaching high school girls' basketball in Louisville, Mississippi. I was in my second or third year at the school, so by this time my girls knew me pretty well.

One day before the season started, we were trying to get ready for the opening game of the season. Practice was not going very well. I kept trying to get the girls to work harder and do what I wanted them to. I finally reached my boiling point. I had seen enough. I then uttered those four dreaded words they always hated to hear: "Get on the line." They knew me well enough to know that I was mad and that they were going to run line drills. Although I didn't know about the styles then, I understand now that it influenced the way each of the girls ran their line drills.

Kelly was my "D" type. She ran hard but was mad because she had to run — mad at the team because they had not been doing what they were supposed to be doing and mad at me because I was the one making her do something she really didn't think she ought to have to do.

Alisha was my "I" type, running with a *smile* on her face! She liked to run and was the fastest player on the team. I remember he passing me once and waving, all the while turning in a circle and running at the same time. Carrying on, she still beat everyone to the finish line!

Pam was my "S" type, a player who always did what she was supposed to do. She ran her line drills and did her best while at the same time encouraging the other girls and clapping for them.

Lydia was my "C" type. She was also running as hard as she could, but with tears running down her face. She felt the punishment was her fault because the team was not doing what I wanted them to and that she was the main one to blame. She also was the first one to apologize to me after practice.

By the way, this team worked great together and was State Tournament runner-up that year.

Teamwork Works

It is recess for Miss Sensitive's Third Graders. Various thoughts enter her students' minds as they prepare for play time.

Dynamic Don has been thinking about kickball all morning. In his mind, he sees himself as team captain, picking the best players and winning the game by a large margin.

Likeable Larry has been daydreaming in class. It has been hard to concentrate on the lengthy assignment. He's ready for recess so he can be with his friends and have a good time. He needs to release some energy.

Supportive Sam thinks, *It's recess. I know we boys will play kickball. I hope everyone plays fair today and doesn't argue like yesterday.*

Calculating Cal has figured out the reason his team lost the last kickball game. He can't wait to organize a new game and put his ideas to work.

The bell rings and the students head for the playground. As the boys line up to pick teams, the new student, Cathy, comes up and asks, "May I play?"

Now the students know Miss Sensitive's rule about kickball: Any student who wants to may play the game. If any student is not allowed into the game, then no one may play that day.

Dynamic Don stomps his foot on the ground and says, "I don't want Cathy on my team. She'll probably make us lose! Girls don't belong in boys' games!"

Likeable Larry has been talking to Cathy and finding out about her last school. He says, "Let her play. We'll still have a good time." Likeable Larry is also thinking *This could turn out to be more fun that I thought — girls run in such silly ways!*

Supportive Sam says, "Let's not yell and argue." He turns to Cathy and taps her on the shoulder as he says, "I'll help you. I'll explain the rules of the game to you."

Calculating Cal says, "Look, if Cathy plays, then the teams will have the same number of players. If we don't let her play, Miss Sensitive will make us stop the game. Do we want to stop playing kickball because of one girl? Why not give Cathy a chance? In fact, I have seen her run and she's really fast!"

Miss Sensitive has been observing what is taking place on the kickball field. She comes over and says, "Today, I will help you with the selection of the teams. Line up." She gives each student the name of a color, alternating red and blue. All the reds are on one team and all the blues are on the other.

The game begins and the students are playing well together. Miss Sensitive is pleased to see everyone so happy and having such a good time.

And, as fate would have it, Cathy and Dynamic Don ended up on the same team!

Kings Of The Wild Frontier

Before Mrs. T's Second Grade Class begins its reading lesson, a short biographical sketch of Daniel Boone, she attempts to motivate them. While their books remain closed, she reviews their previous lesson on the thirteen colonies. She asks if anyone can find the colonies on the classroom map. "Me, me, me!" shouts "David D," waving his hand frantically. After he points them out, she begins to guide their discussion toward reasons why the settlers might or might not have wished to leave the comfort of the cities and move to the western wilderness. "Irving I" says it would be a fun adventure to go to a new place with your friends and ride in the wagon train. "David D" says, "Yeah! They might get to fight some Indians!" The teacher notices that "Sally S" winces at David's last statement and "Carol C" rolls her eyes a bit.

Mrs. T then asks how they might have gotten to their destination if there were no maps and none of them had gone before. Irving guesses, "Maybe they could ask the Indians along the way?" David laughs loudly and says, "Duhhhh!" as he points to Irving. The teacher calls on Carol, who says they would need to find someone who had gone before to lead the way — someone like Daniel Boone or Kit Carson. David now has his book in his lap and is already reading the story. Irving is beginning to chat with his seatmate about fighting Indians, so the discussion is ended and books are opened.

Mrs. T explains that she particularly enjoys reading about Daniel Boone because her ancestor, Rebecca Boone, was married to him. Irving raises his hand and announced, "I'm kin to Dwight Eisenhower..." After guiding Irving back to the topic, the class then reads and discussed the story.

The following morning, "Sally S" brings a book about Daniel Boone to the teacher. Irving comes in wearing a coonskin cap and carrying a toy flintlock rifle. He asks if he may play his Davy Crockett tape and teach the class the song. Mrs. T suggests that he ask David to help him act out the verse and then they could lead everyone in the chorus. Can you guess who was the bear and who played Davy?) You should have seen the bear's great dying scene!

A week later, Carol's parents laugh and explain to Mrs. T that her statement about Rebecca Boone caused them to give Carol and abbreviated sex talk earlier than they had planned. Carol wanted to know if Mrs. T was related to *Daniel* Boone if her ancestor was *Rebecca* Boone. When told the relationship was only by marriage, she wanted that explained as well... et cetera, et cetera, et cetera!

Deck The Halls

One day several weeks before the Christmas holidays, I announced to my Eighth Grade homeroom the rules for our decorating contest. The class became very excited especially when I read the prizes for first, second and third place.

Before I could finish asking for suggestions, Janelle was taking the chalk from my hand and drawing her design on the board. Over her shoulder she was assigning duties to others in the class: "Jerry, since you and R.J. draw so well, you'll be in charge of drawing the village. Hillary, you're in charge of gathering the paper and other supplies for the door..."

Suddenly, Louis was out of his seat and marching to the front of the room. "Why is Janelle always in charge? I'm the class president — I should be leading the discussion!" The next thing I knew, Louis was planning a decoration party during History Class the next day. He was bringing the Christmas music and Shellie was bringing the candy. We could get in the Christmas spirit while decorating!

Not sure of what colors Janelle had in mind, Hillary returned from the storeroom with samples of all available paper colors. Janelle's reaction was, "Make a choice; we don't have all day!" When others began expressing their opinions, Hillary decided that the class should vote on the colors.

R.J., who had been sitting quietly, observing, decided he needed some answers before he could draw a village. Was this village Bethlehem? Is there to be a star? Will there be a close-up view of the manger scene in the stable?

Mercifully, the bell rang to end homeroom and the students jumped up and dashed out the door to first period — taking their chaos with them down the hall.

Acting "Annual" Retentive

I am our high school annual (or yearbook) sponsor. Because our yearbook is designed completely on the computer, we schedule student work on the project as an actual class for credit. The nature of this class is very free with only *necessary* structure (to induce creativity, of course). However, this is one of the factors in sponsoring this activity that creates a lot of stress in my life. I am the "C" in this story! My profile is actually a "C with S," but at yearbook time, I am neither *serene* nor *sweet,* so for the sake of this discussion, I'll be *just* a "C."

Of course, this also means I am a deadline person. We will meet our deadline even if it kills you *and* me! We were working fast and furious on this particular day as deadline was approaching fast. I have only three computers for this project, so I have established a schedule in order to complete our work. Of course, there are often corrections, adjustments, and design changes to be made before we can do our final "paste up." Before too very long, the students are really ready to finish their layouts.

On this particular day, "Debra D" and "Susan S" were finishing their designs. "Isabelle I" needed to finish but was socializing because she was just happy to be there.

Debra had finally finished. I checked and made one little adjustment (because the pictures *have* to line up!). She sent her pages to the laser printer. About the same time, Susan finished her pages, completed her work, and sent her information to the printer, too. Of course, it takes the printer a minute or two to process the data.

Debra was anxious to see her layout because she knew it was perfect and she was not making *any* changes. I was ready for her to be finished also, because some else needed to use the computer and meet their deadline. We were standing there watching indicator lights blinking, waiting for everything to print. Susan was just sitting there, not wanting to get in the way.

Isabelle came over, still feeling "sociable." As she walked by the printer, she suddenly said, "What's this button for?" and pushed *The Button!* The printer top popped up and disconnected the power. And the information that was going to print? Gone! It all happened so fast!

Debra shrieked, "I was printing! Now I'll have to do it again!" (It really wasn't that big a deal, but it was to her!) Susan continued to sit there. I was in shock, thinking that after months in my class she had picked this opportunity to pop the top!

Isabelle's reaction was, "I didn't do anything!" Debra lost it! "You shut the printer down!" she bellowed.

I was still catatonic. Susan was still just sitting there. Isabelle thought for a second (you could hear the gerbils whirring around in her skull!) and then explained, "I know — I've got to go *tee-tee* and I'm nervous. Yeah, that's what made me do that!"

Recovering my presence of mind, I said, "Isabelle, that doesn't make sense!" But she just smiled at me nervously and shifted restlessly (she has to *tee-tee!*). I decided she would never understand and said, "Just go!" She smiled her own "disconnected" smile all the way out of the room.

We restarted the printer. Debra said to Sue, "I'm sending my pages first and I'm not doing anything over!" Sue responded passively, "That's fine. I'm in no hurry." We printed and pasted with no further problems, but I still wonder what would have possessed Isabelle to do what she did, because *I* would *never* touch *anything* on a computer that I didn't know about.

By the way, we finished our yearbook and sent if off to the publisher one week before final deadline! Debra is going to be our yearbook's senior editor next year. I made this decision before I took this course. Now that I know she is a very high "D," I know she will respond well to the challenge... if she doesn't run off or murder everyone else of the staff! But that's next year....

== Bored Of Education! ==

I have been teaching for 22 years and have two children on my own, a 21-year-old "high D" and a 17-year-old who is probably the most delightful child I've ever known. All of this has helped me tremendously to see the vast variety of personality styles that exist. After hearing Dr. Rohm speak to our education convention and taking this course, I feel enlightened and relieved to know that there are many ways to deal with these personalities… but first I must deal with *myself*.

I love teaching! To me, it is getting a salary for being "mother" to 20–24 children for nine months — wow! Can you imagine a more rewarding and fun job, not to mention the extra three benefits: June, July, and August.

Nothing will ever replace a warm, loving teacher in the classroom, with the influence she can have on her "babies." The responsibility that goes with this job is, as my son would say, "awesome," because I know what the Bible teaches about rewards and accountability for those we lead.

I could tell several stories from my teaching experience, but this year was particularly challenging. I do a lot of hands-on in my class, besides the traditional teaching. Examples would include our ant farm, planting avocado seeds, "raising" cocoons into butterflies, and lots of reading to my class. I especially like *The Value Series* books on famous people (Beethoven on the value of giving, Lincoln on the value of respect, etc.), and we use maps of the United States and the world to pinpoint where they lived and travelled to tie our reading into geography. I feel I do a good job with bringing in these additional resources, and at the end of the year (and periodically) I evaluate myself to see if I need to make adjustments in my teaching, personal relationships with my students, etc. I know we all can improve.

I had a high "I" in my class, "Jim," who tested me beyond my limits. He was never sitting in his desk longer than thirty seconds, and he made noises and facial expressions constantly. (I ruled out *Tourette's Syndrome.*) I had a conference with Jim's parents early in the year and they seemed to be going to do some of the things I suggested. But they didn't do anything to help him exhibit self-control.

Not only did I have problems in my class, but I absorbed problems he created elsewhere, as he was sent back to my room frequently from art, band, music, library or other classes when he was disruptive. He failed to do classwork assignments or turn them in daily.

When I met with the parents again, the mother had her list (She was a "C") and the father was with her (a "D"). I felt something must be amiss at home, but I was not sure. I went the "full nine innings" and more to help this child, but his parents were so defensive. They went so far as to say that it might be I who had a "personality clash" with this child. *No way*. I just wanted them to see that he had a responsibility to complete a certain amount of work and to behave properly. Mother's list did not include personal responsibility, but it included that he wasn't being challenged — he was bored. The rest of us had no time to be bored. We felt like firefighters at a four-alarm blaze!

My bottom line in our discussion was that if he did not complete at least the minimum amount of work, I could not see how he could pass; but I would give him extra assignments to combat this "boredom" if he would complete the minimum work each day. For example, he had a rock collection he brought to class, and I allowed him to write (he *typed)* a report about it and presented it to the class. This motivated him to do his work and still be able to be in front of the class and entertain them.

At the end of the year, his dad shared with me that he himself had failed a grade and his son wasn't going to do that. I feel that somehow that particular fact added to this child's problem. In any case, it was a challenge to find the right "play," but giving Jim the opportunity to have this creative outlet with the class (what he wanted in the first place) when he met our performance standards (completing his assignments as did the other children — what I wanted in the first place) created a "win" all around at the bottom on the ninth!

The Tardy Slip

Setting: Last period, Senior English Class of thirty students.

Plot: The tardy bell has rung and several students are late. Their different personality styles are revealed in their actions.

Characters: Natalie, a beautiful cheerleader with curly, dark hair and deep dimples (an "I");

Anna, a girl who is dutiful and reliable, who plays by the rules (an "S");

Krystal, a big-boned, boyish looking, loud girl (a "D");

Pat, a good-looking athlete, potentially a problem who has been put "in charge" of filling out the Tardy List, placing it outside the door and returning to his desk at the front (a "C").

Natalie walks in, somehow managing to catch the attention of everyone, flashing her smile brightly all the way down the aisle to her seat. She says to Pat, "Ohhh, did the bell ring?"

Anna slips in quietly, looking a little embarrassed and feeling a little guilty. She clutches her books to her chest, looks down at the floor, and offers no excuse or comment as she slides into her desk as unobtrusively as possible.

Krystal squares her shoulders, stands in the middle of the aisle at the front of the room, thrusts her head out, shoves her fists into the pockets of her "roper's jeans" and challenges Pat: "I'm not tardy. I had to see the coach. The bell just rang!"

Pat does not look up, but dismisses her with a to-the-point comment: "Sounds like a personal problem to me." He finishes adding her name to the Tardy List, walks to the door, hangs up the slip, and finishes his tasks before sitting down in his assigned seat.

Class begins… as personality clashes have gotten us off to a great start!

English III

Personality styles have never been more evident that in this past school year, in my English III Class. At the conclusion of each semester, I used the final week before exams to help any student who wishes to pull up his grade by doing extra credit work. It is optional, and any student may work on an assignment of my choosing to help his average , whether he has an *A* average or an *F* average. I stress to the students that extra credit can only help a student's grade and that I would not allow the extra credit to lower his grade point average. *Boy, do the personalities come out!*

Our school's starting quarterback and starting pitcher is Johnny, whom I classify as a "D with C" personality. He began working on his extra credit assignment before I had finished my instructions. I knew he would ask for the instructions one more time because his "D" wasn't listening the first time they were given and because his "C" wanted to make sure he was getting credit for it. I have learned to wait for him to make his mistakes and find them on his own, rather than bringing them to his attention myself. He is not rude when I do, but he does get frustrated and agitated — mostly at himself. He is a good analytical thinker and had already calculated the value of the extra credit to get a *B+* before he began his work.

Lonny has to be a high "I." I must keep my "hind eyes" open to watch him. Within ten seconds of my back being turned, he shifts into high gear. Lonny is the boy who remembered as he was leaving home one morning that he had failed to put deodorant on. No big deal to him... so her grabbed it on the way out the door. He remembered to put it on in my class! Once, he laid his backpack down beside his truck when he came home from school in the afternoon. He did not discover the colony of fire ants that had moved in until he was in my class the next morning. Characteristically, he dumped them out on the floor of my classroom, causing panic among the other students. "Life With Lonny" would be an interesting soap opera! Needless to say, he could not find the time to do his extra credit work. He failed my class but did not seem too concerned. I am sure he will approach summer school as a way to meet new people and see new things.

Karen is one of the few high "S" students in my Junior English Class. She is exceptionally bright and a voracious reader. Karen seems to shrink two or three sizes when I call on students to answer questions in class. She was one of the few who did not need extra credit, but she was scared to ask me to look at her grades to see if she needed it. Her average was 97 going into the final exam and really did not need to raise it with extra credit.

Catherine, my "C," was a dream to teach. However, we teachers frequently remind her to relax. If I ever had the occasion to forget my notes for review, I would turn to Catherine. She takes notes better than any student I have ever taught and each night she enters them into her computer and prints them out. She has a daily planner book that goes with her everywhere and it is full of information from class assignments to friends' birthdays. Catherine was the Junior Class president this year, and as co-sponsor of the Junior-Senior Prom, I told her to plan it and give me some ideas. She organized the committees, ordered materials, watched over the finances and many other important things, and the prom was a tremendous success. *All I had to do was show up!* Catherine did not attempt any extra credit work in my class, nor did she need to. She finished the year with a 99 average and received my English Award. However, she would be more inclined to state that her average was 99.23, since she knows to the one-hundredth of a point what is was.

All of my students are different and special — Johnny, Lonny, Karen and Catherine are in many ways opposites in behavior, thought and personality. However, I love and respect each one of them simply for being themselves. *(Editor's Note: Amen!)*

Rule Number One

Setting: Sixth Grade Reading Class

The Sixth Grade teacher, Mrs. S (an "S" with some "C" characteristics) tells her class to get out their reading notebooks and pencils. This is the second six-week period of the school year. On the first day of school the compassionate, "S"-type teacher had explained (patiently and kindly!) that her students would need their reading notebooks in class *every* day of the school year. There would *never* be a day they would not need this notebook in class. Classroom Rule Number 1 related to the importance of bringing all necessary materials to class every day. This reading notebook would fall under Rule Number 1 — *are we clear on this?*

On being told to get out his reading notebook, Jim launches into a loud and complicated explanation of why he does not have his notebook with him, and that he knows for a fact that the other reading teacher does not require her students to bring their notebook every day. He wonders aloud why the other class gets to do more fun stuff. He lets his teacher know that her fellow teacher lets her class play games to learn and that they have lots of free time to do whatever they want. He wishes to himself that he could be in the other class.

Daryl jumps into the fray and tells Jim, "All you have to do is what the teacher says to do. She's only been telling us this for twelve weeks! Quit making excuses."

Connie leans over to Jim and quietly offers to give him some suggestions. She tells him that she finds it helpful to make a list of every book she will need for each class. She posts this list inside her locker door. She offers to help him make a list and will even organize his locker for him.

After class, Mrs. S calls Jim aside. She tells him she understands how much material he has to keep up with for all his classes. However, she is confident that such a bright student will be able to come prepared for her class every day.

Mrs. S catches Daryl after class to tell him how much she appreciates his input in the situation and the leadership he shows in the classroom. She kindly reminds him of Rule Number 2, which states that a student must be recognized before speaking.

That same day after school, Mrs. S asks Connie to come to her classroom. She praises Connie for her organizational skills and offers to let her help file papers in the classroom after school.

— — — — — Multiplication Bingo — — — —

Yes, this actually happened in my Third Grade Class. The names have been changed to protect the eight-year-olds...

Mrs. D (me, the teacher) says, "Class, today we are going to play a fun game called 'Multiplication Bingo.'"

Don, the high "D" student, jumps from his desk, snatches the bingo cards away from my hands and says, "Give me those! I'll pass them out right now!" He tosses them toward everyone's desk at fast as he can.

Biff, the high "I," is bouncing in his desk with a big smile on his face, saying, "Wow! This is great! This is going to be so much fun! Mrs. D, did you bring us candy to eat while we play?"

I reply, "Yes, Biff, I did. The candy is the prize you receive if you 'Bingo.'"

Salli, the high "S" student, sitting calmly in her desk says, "Mrs. D, you are *soooo* sweet to let us play a game. And thank you for bringing us candy. You are my favorite teacher!"

Claire, the high "C," after correcting Don on his improper placement of the bingo cards, says, "Mrs. D, I have never played this before, Will you call out answers and combinations, or just answers, or just combinations? How many dots must I have to 'Bingo'? And I noticed that there were several extra cards. Does that mean I can exchange my card for another one at the end of each game? And by the way, how many games are we going to play?"

Don interrupts: "Cut out the questions, Claire! Let's get on with it! I want that Watermelon Airhead candy I see over there!"

Salli calls me over to her desk and says, "Mrs. D, any flavor candy is fine with me, and if I 'Bingo,' will you bring it to me so I won't have to get up in front of everyone?"

Assuring her that I would, I begin the game after a careful, precise explanation a "C" teacher would give. The game progresses.

I hold up the number 20 and state it orally: "Yes, the number is twenty, class."

Claire says, "That could be 4X5 or 2X10. Am I not right? You do not have a 1X20, do you, because our times tables only went to the 12's?"

"Yes, Claire, you're correct."

Biff exudes, "Wow! We've just started and I'm already way ahead! This is great! We get to eat candy, play a game, and no work! Let's do this every day!"

Don is very tense, his hands gripping the sides of his desk, as he says, "This is a dumb game! You're not calling out any of my numbers! Let me mix up your cards for you so I can get some dots on my card, or I'm not playing anymore!"

Salli, very timidly and softly says, "Bingo!"

Don is angry. He says, "This is not fun. It's the most stupid game I've ever played! And I'm not playing it again." He throws his bingo card on the floor and gives Salli a mean look.

Claire asks, "Mrs. D, I need to ask a question. Did you check Salli's card with your master card to make certain she 'Bingo'd'? Are you positive she won? May I see her card and compare it to mine?"

Biff, waving his hand to get my attention, says, "If Salli didn't win, then I think I won! Can we play another game anyhow? This is the greatest day of my life!"

Salli thinks to herself, *Oh, no! Don is mad at me because I won instead of him. Biff believes he won, and Claire thinks I cheated. Probably the rest of the class feels the same way. I should have just kept quiet. It's all my fault.*

The "C" teacher is thinking to herself, *I planned this to be fun — what happened?*

Follow The Bouncing Ball

My DISC story comes from a computer programming assignment given to my Seniors this year. Each student was given a pre-scripted program of about 50 lines to enter in the computer. This should require the average student 20–25 minutes to type in and then another 10 minutes to correct any mistakes so it would "RUN" correctly. The end result was a simulation of a ball dropping from the top to the bottom of the monitor screen. The way each student approached the task reveals a great deal about his or her personality style.

The first personality I encountered was Presley, my big "D" in the class. I approached him about 10 minutes after the assignment was given. As usual, he was already up and running correctly, and he asked, "What's next? Is this all we have to do today?" Realizing that he would have 40 minutes to waste, I suggested that he jazz up the program by adding shadows or extra colors to the program. He responded, "What? The program runs just fine without extras. You didn't say anything about extras when you gave the assignment and I did everything perfect. I don't see the point in doing any more." I responded that he was absolutely correct. If he wanted an *average* grade, he could do what the average student would do and leave the program "as is." However, if he wanted a *perfect* grade of 100, he would jazz it up. Needless to say, he chose to jazz it up. In fact, he drove me crazy the rest of the class period by calling me to his computer every time he came up with something new — and being the perfect "D," he ended his program with a colorful flashing screen, proclaiming: "by Presley – The World's Greatest Programmer!"

The second computer I approached was "occupied" (not "used") by Samantha, a very high "I." Out of 50 program lines, she had five haphazardly types on the screen. Coming up from behind her, I realized that she was upset about something and I asked her about it. She responded hysterically, "I just can't believe he did that! There was absolutely no reason for it." Knowing it was a mistake (but needing to get her back on track) I asked *who* did *what*. Samantha whined, "Mr. H (the headmaster) made me throw away my clover bracelet, and it took me the entire lunch period to braid it. It was an absolute work of art. He is so unreasonable. I just *can't* believe he did that. He is the meanest person in the *whole* world!" I patted her on the back, calmed her down, and she began to get back on track by turning around to her computer. However, just as I began to walk away, she asked, "Mrs. P, where did you get those shoes? I just love them and have been looking for some just like them... I once had some brown shoes that were *sooo* comfortable..." I raised my "S" and lowered my "D" and "C," shrugged, and walked away.

At the next computer was Kaley, my "S" personality. As I approached, I observed her working with her head down. Once I was behind her, she stopped but did not respond. I asked her if she had any problems and she responded, "No, ma'am, everything is fine." A few minutes later, I noticed that she was getting an error message. Again I asked if she needed help and she answered again, "No, ma'am, I think I have it figured out. She never would admit a problem or call attention to herself by asking a question. I finally stood over her and quietly pointed out the error.

Finally, I noticed my "C" personality, TeeJay. Not only had he entered the program, but by the time I approached him he had altered it so the ball would bounce up *and* down on the screen. As I reached his desk, he began questioning: "Why is there a blank spot on the screen after the ball bounces? I figured the sine of the angle to change the ball's color and then determined that it should bounce at a rate of two times per second. But that blank spot should not be there. According to my calculations, the hole should fill when the ball begins moving upward." I tried to help him fill in the blank spot; however, I could tell he still was not happy when the bell rang for him to go to the next class. I didn't think much of his mood until he came back immediately after school with the program *written* and *graphed* on paper and began to discuss the blank spot. By the time he *finally* left at 4:30 that afternoon, not only had he filled the space on screen but he also had the ball bouncing around a curve in a tunnel as it changed colors.

Needless to say, I was "in a state" that day after Computer Class. Since that class followed lunchtime, I was convinced the cafeteria ladies had slipped something extra into my students' pocket-pizzas to make them all act so strange. Now I see that it wasn't the pizzas ...but their personalities that produced such different behaviors!

Drama Is Such High Drama

The time had come for what Miss C, the high "C" Literature teacher, had been dreading: the Drama unit. Unaware of the cause of her growing apprehension (she did not understand personality styles!), she worried that the orderly atmosphere of her classroom would be ruined by this drastic change in activity. However, she felt some of her students who weren't especially gifted in reading could "shine" in this situation. So, she mustered her subordinate (make that *dormant!*) "I" qualities to make an inspirational introduction to this study.

When Preston learned of the upcoming Drama curriculum, he went into high gear. This was a chance to use his "D" qualities! Of course, he would be the *director*— what better way to be dominant and demanding without being reprimanded! His diligent, determined efforts assured the class of a successful effort. Thank goodness no other strong "D's" were in the class to contest his dictatorial ways.

It became obvious that he group was blessed with several high "I's" when the actors' parts were assigned. As rehearsals began, it was apparent that their imaginative, enthusiastic personalities were well-suited to acting out their roles. They brought fun to the play and excitement to the audience, even when some failed to learn their parts and had to be prompted by the "S" behind the stage.

Speaking of "S" types, their steady support through this process was paramount to its success. Willing to be used wherever they were needed, they worked as artists, lighting specialists, program and costume designers, and in supporting actor roles. It didn't matter to them that their work was "behind the scenes." They preferred it that way! In fact, whenever a job became available that no one wanted to do, a submissive "S" would volunteer dutifully. Since they were dependable, practical and trustworthy, the "S's" were invaluable assets to the class project.

One "C" in this group was apparently its quota, and that was Miss C. She made it through and was able to retreat again from the spontaneity of the stage to the safety of the classics, with their predetermined characters and "everything put right" endings.

Our Book Fair

The Book Fair was over and it had been a huge success. All the parents had really enjoyed coming to school to see the books written, illustrated and published by the Second Graders. I was helping to straighten up the classroom. (I have always liked doing whatever I could to help my teachers.) I looked around at my classmates. I really hated for the school year to end.

I saw David, who was enjoying telling the principal that he was the reason the Book Fair had been so successful. I smiled and thought it really was true. The Book Fair had been David's idea. He had approached our teacher to see if it might be possible. She had given him some choices and that was all he had needed. He quickly formed committees of seven-year-olds and wouldn't let us quit for anything. He put Chad in charge of planning the refreshments and sending out the invitations. David thought Isabell would enjoy decorating the classroom and welcoming the guests when they arrived. I was really happy when David asked me to serve the good and be in charge of cleanup.

Chad's group did a great job. He made sure just the right food was served. In fact, he surveyed all the students to see which types of pizza and cookies they liked. He made sure there was plenty for everyone. His committee also did a fantastic job with the invitations. He had each student write down all the names of family members that should be invited before any invitations were made. As our teacher would say, "Chad didn't leave one stone unturned."

Isabell's group had lots of fun decorating our classroom. There were balloons and streamers at the windows. They even had a big "Welcome" sign on our door, with Isabell standing there to greet each guest by name!

My committee made sure everyone was served refreshments

after the "authors" shared their books. It was David's idea to call us authors. (You know, I guess we really were!)

It was a wonderful day. As I look back on that school year, I remember that it didn't begin with all of us working together. David used to make us angry because he was always telling us what to do. He never wanted to go by the rules. Isabell and Chad got into many disagreement. She would be talk-talk-talking while he was trying to do his work. I just wanted everyone to be happy, but I didn't know how to help.

In response to our problems, our teacher started reading to us from the Bible. One of her favorite chapters was Psalm 139, which says that we are all "fearfully and wonderfully made." She told us this meant we were each special and one-of-a-kind. While we would make lots of mistakes, we could learn to work together. Over the course of the school year, our class became a warm and safe place for a little girl named Susan — *me* — to be.

Now I am grown with a class of my own. I am still just a little bit shy, but I try to create that same wonderful atmosphere for my little **D**avids, **I**sabelles, **S**usans, and **C**hads today.

In The Can

The English teacher has just finished a study unit on *Beowulf*. She has assigned groups, each composed of four students, to select a work project from a list she distributes to all. The students have one week to complete their projects, and their personality styles will influence how they work on their projects.

Will (as in *Iron* Will) quickly scans the suggestions and decides, "We should do the video." He lists the fact that he has a video camera and equipment to edit the tape, and that he wants to get it "in the can" quickly.

Gabe (as in *Gabby* Gabe) jumps into the discussion, saying, "Yeah, let's do that! Besides, I've got the pond we need and the airplane hangar where we can shoot the Mead Hall. I'll get my mom to cook some food. Could I be Grendel? What do you think? I've got some good special effects — I want blood *all over me!*

Will says, "Shut up, Gabe — we'll get to that later! Let's get on with this plan..."

Barbara — you know, *Balance-Sheet* Barbara — says, "I will type out the script. This afternoon, I will check out the pond and the hangar to see if we can use them. We can schedule a meeting to rehearse tomorrow. Will, you will be good as Beowulf, and Gabe, you will be great as Grendel. I'll check the light and we'll make two tapes so we can choose the best scene to edit. Doreen, would you like to be my assistant?

Doreen the *Doormat* says, "Well, I guess I could help. I'll be happy to do what I can. I could go to the antique store and get costumes, but if you don't want me to do that, I won't. When do we want to do this, so I will have everything ready?"

Will speaks up and says, "I don't care when we do the taping as long as we are finished by Thursday!" Doreen says, "I'll be happy to help you, Barbara. Maybe I could call around and see if I can find a sword for Will. And I'll bake some cookies for our meeting tomorrow."

Gabe responds enthusiastically, "Oh boy! Cookies! I'll call my friends so we can have an army. It will be neat. Maybe you could get me some bones, Doreen, so we could pretend that I ate some folks! Then we could get someone to be Grendel's mother..."

Will shouts, "Shut up, Gabe! We don't need the whole school in this film. Let's just get this wrapped up."

Barbara says, "Okay, I'll do the script, plan the shooting time. Doreen will get the props and costumes. Gabe, you provide the location and we'll meet tomorrow afternoon to practice. Does everyone understand? Okay, we can do this. Gabe, I'll call you and remind you to be there. Does anyone have any questions?" (Will says, "Shut up, Gabe!")

= Goldilocks And The Three Hams =

Our First Graders are going to present their play, *Goldilocks and the Three Bears*. Under the spotlight of participation, we see their personality styles.

Julie says: "Can I be Goldilocks? I just love her. She's so pretty and sweet and I have blonde hair — just like her. But if somebody else wants to be her, that's okay. I could help her get her costume ready and help her memorize her part — and if she gets nervous, I'll make her feel better. So, it will be all right if you want me to do something else." (Her "S" has recovered to rescue her from *public* performance risked by a brief "I spasm"!)

Phil says: "I can be Papa Bear. I'm good at making bear noises, listen — Grrr-*rrr-rrrr*! We'll need to have a bear house and trees. The boys can make the house and the girls can make the trees. I'll draw a picture so they can see what to do. We need to get started!" (His "D" is going to find expression on the stage and behind the scenes, and he is already an expert six-year-old delegator!)

Sharon says: "Can I be Mama Bear? I love to cook and I can bring the porridge from home, already cooked. I could pretend to cook and then pour the porridge in the bowls. And I can bring bowls and spoons, too. I'd have to bring napkins — and wouldn't a tablecloth be good? Maybe we need glasses of milk on the table..." (Her "C" is busy making lists, and since the story is so familiar to her, she doesn't feel it is necessary to take a "wait and see " posture this time.)

Billy says: "I could be Baby Bear! I have a baby brother and we have so much fun together! I just love playing with him. When he's sleeping, Mama says I have to be quiet so I won't wake him up! But when he's awake, we play with blocks and sometimes we play in the sandbox — so I know about babies. I'd really like to act like Baby bear. I might want to be in the movies when I grow up. Did you see *Home Alone?* Wasn't that a great movie? Boy, this play is gonna be fun! Let's get started!" (Mentally, his "I" is already composing an acceptance speech for his award as the "Best Primary Student in the Role of a Forest Animal With Someone Asleep In His Bed!")

Just Desserts

It was the last week of school. A parent group had brought in a special lunch to be served to the teachers in the kitchen. More parents than usual were eating with their children "one last time" or "at least once" before school was out. Suzy Administrator started into the office when Roxy Teacher and Sparkle Secretary came up to her. Sparkle — for once *not* giggling — said, "I just want you to hear what Roxy has to say. It really makes me mad!"

Roxy quieted her class as it left the lunchroom and said, "he has done it all year and this is just the last straw! Mr. C comes every Wednesday to eat with his daughter, and he goes back into the kitchen to fix his baked potato where the teachers do, even though I have taken time to tape up those signs that say parents are not allowed back in the kitchen. He doesn't pay any attention. He's even taken his daughter back there. But today, we found him just filling up his plate with the teachers' special meal and he got the last piece of strawberry pie right before I was going to! Who does he think he is?"

"She's right," said Sparkle, "he's obnoxious!" Then, giggling and gesturing toward Roxy, she said, "Boy, that last piece of pie really got her!'

"All the teachers have seen it," Roxy said. "He needs to be told!"

"Okay, okay, relax," said Suzy Administrator. "I'll take care of it."

Mr. C was sitting at the end of the lunch table with his daughter, finishing off "his" strawberry pie. Suzy walked down and smiled and said, "Mr.. C, we're asking all of our parents not to go back in the kitchen when they come to lunch but just go through the line with their child. It just gets so crowded back there, we're trying to alleviate the crunch. Thanks for helping with this."

Mr. C looked up with an affronted expression. "Why, I was told at the first of the year that I could go back there and have done it all year. Why are you telling me now? I am embarrassed."

Suzy assured him there was no need for embarrassment. She knew he would want to help and hoped he would continue to come to lunch with his child.

"I am just shocked that you would come to me now. Why?"

Suzy explained that because there was a special lunch for teachers, it was more noticeable when others came back into the kitchen. Mr. C huffed that he had only taken a small spoonful of salad. Did she want him to pay extra for it!? Suzy smiled and said certainly not, please enjoy his lunch, and she left for an appointment. Later, she found a note to call Mr. C at his office. She also found that he had come up, almost tearfully, to his daughter's teacher, asking her if she didn't remember when the cafeteria lady had told him to go back into the kitchen; that he had been accused of doing something wrong.

Suzy decided in the interest of peace to apologize and just let him have his say. Mr. C had his say — for 15 minutes he made very clear how embarrassed he had been in front of his child, that he always set a good example and had been made to feel like a criminal. He also felt like a fool if teachers had been seeing him do something wrong fall year and he had not known it. Who had reported him anyway?

Suzy apologized again for her timing and thoughtlessness and assured him that no one thought he was a fool. (Liar Suzy!) She did say that there had been signs put up during the year. He ignored this and went on and on. Finally, Suzy said she had apologized and she wanted to know if he would accept her apology. He stiffly said yes he would, but he wanted her to go find the teachers who had "reported" him and explain to them how he was completely innocent. He ended the day calling his child's teacher and complaining to her how Suzy Administrator had misused him and insisted that the teacher find those teachers involved and explain his innocence to them.

And all because neither Suzy nor Roxy nor Sparkle — or anyone else on this highly educated staff — recognized the strong "C" personality. If they had, they would have either handled it very privately or ignored it until the beginning of the next year, making sure all parents understood they were not invited into the kitchen when eating lunch with their children. (Or, if Roxy ever becomes a principal, she can get the point across by *executing* the offending parent and the cafeteria lady under the flag pole!)

The Art of Understanding

I teach Art to 600 elementary students each week. Of course, I see their personality styles "in living color" every week.

A First Grade "D" boy came to Art Class for the first time and listened carefully to our rules about behavior in the art room. First Graders receive a little "warm fuzzy" each week if they are a good listener and a hard worker. After he heard our rules, he spoke out: "I don't want no fuzzball and I don't wanna draw!" I said, "All right, you may draw anything you want to draw, and you can color it or not. It is your decision and it's okay if you don't want a warm fuzzy." He talked out loud through the entire class time and waited at the end of the line when his class was leaving. He looked at me and said, "Why don't I get the fuzz ball? I thought I would get it!" We worked hard all year and I finally managed to find a happy, middle ground.

While they don't know what to call it, all my students know I am an "I" type personality myself. My "D's" relate to me, too. They all know I love to go to Walt Disney World and that I have been there 42 times. One day when the class was beginning a new project, one of my "I's" brought in a book on Disney, just to have a great discussion and some fun. I had to "raise my 'D'" and "lower my 'I'" after spending five minutes of class time having a spontaneous "Disney party."

I have one student in particular who really tries to help me all the time. She straightens my desk and picks up fallen materials off the floor. She is very shy and stays in the background. Of course, she is an "S" type, and I let her do things that help her feel useful. I thank her in front of the class and use the word "appreciate" a lot, letting them and her know that I notice how helpful she is.

One of my Fifth Graders is going to be a teacher or be involved with some field of organization. She asks questions about everything, from A to Z. She watches the time to let me know when it is time to put away their art materials. She develops a system of working on a project, then when she finishes it, she asks me what her grade is. She is, of course, a very task-oriented (not very people-oriented) "C" type child.

Chips Fall Where They May

In order to teach a certain math concept to my Kindergarten Class, I used chocolate chips. Each child needed nine chips for the lesson. Instead of counting out nine chips for each child, I gave each a small handful of chips. My directions were: Count out nine chips and put the extras in the middle of the table.

The "D" grabbed all the chips, ate a few, and then took his nine. Then he told everyone else what to do. The "I" child was so busy talking, he didn't even know he had chips. The "D" had to tell him what to do. The "S" arranged his nine chips and then checked to see if anybody needed any extras before he put his leftovers in the middle of the table.

After the lesson was finished, the children ate their chips. The "C" wanted to know "What happens to the extras in the middle of the table?" I told the children they could divide up the extras and eat them. One table had mostly "S" children. One "S" divided the extras with nobody grabbing. There were two left over — she decided she could eat them since she gave them out. Not one "S" complained! At another table, the "D" grabbed and ate all the extras before anybody could say anything. He said, "I got them first!" The "C" said, "I only got one and everybody else got two — that's not fair!" The "I" was still talking while somebody ate his extras (probably the "D")!

Give Them An Inch...

One beautiful Spring day, I was finishing up and reviewing a chapter for an Eighth Grade math test the next day. This was my last class to teach for the day. I finished my review about ten minutes before the bell rang. Mack, an "I" type student, asked, "Hey, Mrs. C, can we go out and sit in the bleachers for the rest of the class time? It's no nice outside." So being an easy "S" type, I said, "All right, but stay only on the bleachers."

By the time I got outside, two "D" type boys had made their way to the soft drink machine outside the building and were chugging down caffeine and bubble-water. I got very upset — my "S" was being taken advantage of, and my little "D" stood tall to protect my honor.

I told all the students to go back to the classroom, and I told the two boys to throw away their drinks. Many "C" and "S" students asked me to still let them sit outside, but I made all the students go back to the classroom. I gave the whole class a homework assignment when we returned.

Of course, everyone had a "way to go, guys" attitude about the two who had spoiled it for them. While peer pressure would have been more effective on an "I" or an "S" who had disobeyed, the idea that they had "blown" their leadership position gave the "D's" a moment's pause. Because I understand the motivations of the different personalities a little better, now I see what I need to do to "head off" this problem and avoid getting "ambushed" by personality styles again.

Kindergarten Klean-Up

On the first day of school, we always begin by teaching the manners that will be expected throughout the school year. By manners, we actually mean the rules of behavior that must be followed.

For some unexplainable reason, last year's Kindergarten class had an unusual amount of difficulty picking up their toys after their informal play time that was before class began each morning. No matter what approach I tried, cleanup time was often time-consuming and disastrous.

My "I" children usually spent the cleanup time wandering around the room, *looking* at the toys, sometimes stopping to *play* with a toy and then *putting it back* on the floor — but rarely did they start actually cleaning up unless my two high "D" students began their "assistant teacher routine."

These "D's" patrolled the room, re-telling everyone to pick up toys, and pointing out stray toys that needed to be put away or toys that had been picked up but put away in the wrong place. Any student not pulling his weight during cleanup time was sure to get a direct order or a "nudge" to speed things along.

My "S" students never needed to be told twice that it was cleanup time. Some played with an eye on the clock, but as a group they were the first to stop playing and start cleaning, and they never stopped until the room was spotless.

My "C's" were always sure to check the room after cleanup to verify that everything was in order. When these self-appointed inspectors were finished, they always came to my desk to tell me the room was clean and it was time to say the Pledge of Allegiance and start our day.

Blue Ribbons All Around

I feel God blessed me with a precious class this year! It was amazing to see how they supported and complemented one another. Now that I am learning to understand personality styles, it is so clear to me why this was true.

During our annual art contest, my First Graders' individuality really came out. Not only was this evident in their artwork (as you might expect), but also in their reactions after awards were presented. Faculty members judged the entries after school, and ribbons were affixed to the chosen pieces after the children had gone home. As the children arrived the next morning, many were eager to see if they had won a ribbon. Their pictures were displayed in the hallway outside our room, so they already knew whether or not they were prizewinners when they came into the room.

As soon as our class was assembled, I recognized our "winners" and we all congratulated them. (Understand that I was not a judge. I am an "S with C" and would have given every child an award, feeling they all deserved to "win.") I saw expressions of excitement, disappointment, sympathy and confusion.

Joey, our high "D," was the first to react: "Why didn't I get a ribbon? I worked hard on my pictures. They were all good and I should have won! What happened?"

Judith, our highest "S," came to the rescue as she said compassionately, "I think everyone is a winner, even if they didn't get a ribbon! The hallway is full of our beautiful pictures that we worked so hard on. I think we *are* all winners!"

Meanwhile, Ashleigh, a classic "I" type, was walking around to shake the hands of those who won ribbons and telling those who did not win that their pictures were very good and deserved to win also. She said, "The important thing is that we all had fun doing it. I can't wait for our next art contest!" When she had "covered the room," she returned to her desk, got out her art box and crafted a blue ribbon for every classmate!

Peter is a critical thinking "C" type, and it took him a while to respond. I could see that he was studying the situation and seemed both disappointed and confused. Finally he asked, "Why did they have to pick winners anyway? How many judges were there, and what exactly were they looking for? Just how many ribbons were given out? How many people did *not* get one? Did anyone win more than one ribbon? I worked hard to get my pictures just like I wanted them. Why didn't I win?"

Again, being an "S with C" blend, I responded predictably — winning isn't about ribbons and award. Winning is about putting your best into whatever you do. You all did that. You are *all* winners!" (I should have written Ward Cleaver's speeches for "Leave It To Beaver"!)

"Joey," I said, "you were so determined to get your pictures *done!* You worked hard and I *know* you did your best. Keep it up.

"Judith, I can tell you took your time on your pictures and you did your very best. Thank you for being so supportive of your classmates.

"Ashleigh, you were so creative with your artwork and it shows that you did your best. You are so thoughtful for making everyone a ribbon. We are all so happy you are in our class.

"Peter, I like how you thought through what you were going to do before you began your artwork. It shows that you worked hard and did your best. Thank you for being so thorough."

Because the award-winners are sent off to District judging, only the remaining pictures were left in the hall for everyone to see and enjoy. So I built this up as something very special — what an honor is was to be "on display." As the children prepared to go home that day, Ashleigh passed out her handmade blue ribbons and *everyone* went home a winner!

P.S. What I said to Ashleigh really was true — I was very happy to have her in my class. I also have her in my house. She not only went home as a winner that day, she goes home as *my daughter* every day!

Sweet Eyes

L et me set the stage for a school day as I begin my story. Between classes, I stood in the hall, eagerly awaiting the "sweet eyes" of my Eighth Graders arriving for seventh period American History.

Jeremy passed me on his way through the doorway and told me he had been waiting all day for seventh period. He was outgoing and impulsive, with a carefree and compassionate heart. I wondered if he would be this enthusiastic by the end of his Eighth Grade year. Yes, he was! Jeremy "lived" our lessons — his face showed many expressions and emotions; he was always full of fun and wanting to talk freely. I often reminded him to raise his hand. I allowed him to teach the part of our history lesson he liked best. He would become very excited and act out an explorer, a cowboy, a railroad worker, etc. — always making crazy paper hats to fit the character. He made history "live" for his classmates, with three other "I's" in the class to help him.

Darrin would pass me at the doorway each day, smile, and immediately begin asking me if I were going to allow Jeremy to act out part of the day's lesson. He believed we needed to "get on with it," and not let Jeremy slow us down. Darrin did well in group activities. He was the leader, assigning each student a specific part and reminding them that he was confident their group would be the winner in comparison to the other groups. Darrin worked very hard, enjoying any challenge of the unknown to earn extra credit.

Mandy sat across from Darrin. She was very reserved, sweet and easygoing. She reminded Darrin daily that Jeremy was okay, and to "please be patient with him — that's the way he learns." I was amazed at Mandy's innate "personality insights." She is a twin and very much an "S." In group activity, she smiled and would write all the information down, but she didn't want to get up in front of the class to present it. She often lingered after class to tell me she was sorry Darrin wasn't patient with Jeremy, which gave me an opportunity to thank her for her patience and understanding — reassuring her that God made us all and we must grow in acceptance of others. In Eighth Grade, I try to instill healthy tolerance. It is easy to present and implement these ideas through American History. The students will learn that freedom means responsibility as they grow *if* we teachers take the time to guide their unde rstanding.

When Jeremy, Darrin and Mandy are interacting, I know Aaron will correct them continually. Aaron will also ask me questions to make sure I am relating the lesson information accurately. In class, he is our idealist. In group work, he irritates others because he seems impossible to satisfy. He wants all the details presented perfectly and seems compulsive and critical. I would say to him, "Sweet Eyes, you need to remember we must have order in the classroom, and I know with your great imagination you will enjoy researching the questions we don't answer." Aaron always thought it would be more logical to do it his way. As he left class, he often reminded me that he appreciated my consistency and how he always knew what I expected in class time.

On the last day of school, I ask my students to answer three questions. Here are the questions and the answers supplied by my students according to their personality styles.

1. *What would help Mrs. B to be a better teacher?*
   D – Kick out the slow people.
   I – Don't lecture too much; lighten up.
   S – Nothing.
   C – Be more creative.

2. *What is your favorite class activity?*
   D – Being leader of a group.
   I – Group time.
   S – Anything.
   C – Doing time lines.

3. *How have you grown as a person this year?*
   D – Trying to take orders.
   I – Trying to be more self disciplined.
   S – Trying to become more bold.
   C – Trying to accept that people make mistakes.

Family Conflict

It was the Monday night before the ACT exams, which were to be given on Saturday morning as a first step toward college admission. A conflict was developing between the high "C" university professor and his high "I" soon-to-be high school Senior son.

After dinner, the professor was edging the grass at the curb of his front yard. Intent on getting the task completed, just right, before darkness fell, he was very focused as he aimed the edger carefully between the sod and the cement.

His son walked along side, a distraction who was explaining why he should be allowed to go camping with his friends for the night instead of preparing for the upcoming exam.

The "C" professor's conversation was full of facts, figures, and test preparation strategies. The "I" teen's conversation was about who would be there and how he didn't need to study until the night before the test.

Angry words were flying when the son sought out his mother's "S" style to support his side of the argument. True to her peace-keeping role, she explained both sides of the situation to the family members. Neither was eager to see the other's viewpoint .

Their older son, a "D," entered the scene. He listened to the issue and stated that his dad should just let his brother take the test on his own terms and handle whatever his results were. If he did not do well, he would learn that he should prepare for the next test date.

Four very different personality styles were asking *their own* questions while providing *their own* answers — each was speaking his own language and not hearing the others. The professor wanted to know *why* his son wasn't preparing intensely for the test. The son was concerned about *who* would be camping without him if he did not go. The mother wanted to know *how* she could make both of them happy. The older son wanted to know *what* the purpose was in making his brother study when he did not see the importance of the test to his future. *(Editor's Note: This is excellent insight!)*

The situation was finally resolved by compromise. The younger son was allowed to go camping if he came home early the following morning and worked one-on-one with a tutor. He got to camp with his friends and was relieved to be studying with someone who could help him focus. Working one-on-one for a short period was more appealing and productive than working alone night after night. The father was pleased that his son would spend some time reviewing before the ACT and knew more would be accomplished if the study were suited to his son's learning style. The mother was happy because they had stopped arguing and had begun listening to each other. The older son was eager to point out that many people are motivated by the *consequences* of their actions. If his younger brother truly wants to go to college with his friends, he will be eager to do well on his ACT.

In many homes, these kinds of conflicts escalate because parents do not understand their children's personality preferences and attitudes. And because children are not taught this information as a part of their "life skills" education in school, they do not understand themselves or others.

This episode had a happy resolution in *our* family because we have discovered our "DISC" design. In my class, I hope I can pass this key to relationships on to my students and their families.

By The Book

Being a high school librarian with an "S" personality, I do not have *classroom* stories to relate, but I would like to tell about some experiences I have had with *teachers* who have different personality styles. Of course, the issuing of a teaching certificate does not guarantee a balanced personality style, so I have seen some interesting displays of temperament types.

One procedure I ask teachers to follow in using library materials is to fill out a request form for video tapes, and to write their names on the calendar when reserving TV and video equipment.

The easiest teacher to work with in this regard is our Chemistry teacher. She is so organized, competent and "into" planning things out that she does her lesson plans by the month! Two weeks before she needs them, I will find her video request forms on my desk, in the chronological order in which she has planned to use them. If the program is an hour long, she will know exactly which segment she wants to use. She takes videos home to preview at night or over the weekend before showing them to her class. Her name is the first to go on when we "flip" to a new month on the calendar we use to reserve the television and VCR. She never keeps the tapes or TV longer than she needs them. This *lady* has a definite "C" type personality.

The junior high Social Studies teacher and baseball coach is just the opposite in his handling of materials. He never knows where the request forms are, so he does not fill them out. He waits until he is "tied up" in class and then sends a student to the library with a verbal request for a video tape. By the time the messenger gets to me, he often doesn't remember the title of the tape. Rather than looking in his handbook for resources, he has been known to request "anything on the Industrial Revolution." He is obviously an "I" type personality.

I have several English teachers who are very accommodating. They submit their written request forms with accompanying statements of this fashion: "If you could possibly get this for me, I would really appreciate it. If you can't, well, that's all right. I know how busy you are. I'll just send a student for it later. I really appreciate your doing this for me and I'm so sorry I interrupted your work." Of course, these are "S" type people.

Last but not least — especially in her own estimation — is our public relations person/art teacher. She comes on like a bulldozer! One of her jobs is to collect and cut out all mentions and photos about the school in our local newspapers. Since the library subscribed to all the area papers, guess who gets to be her "clipping service"? Being the "S" that I am, you know I don't really say no to this "D" that she is.

Another project she had was our school's major fund raising event. Most of her tickets and flyers were run on my office's copy machine. One day we had fallen behind, and she was in a turmoil. She had to go to the printer; she had a meeting with the fund raising committee; she had classes to teach — a typical "D" with so many irons in the fire at once. And her tongue is wired to some "I" slot in her brain! You have to see her in action to believe it — not only does she go 90 miles-per-hour into these projects, but so does her mouth! This sometimes gets her into trouble with people. She makes them mad by putting her mouth in motion before putting her brain in gear. But in typical "D" fashion, she never exhibits a minute of self-doubt.

With my "S" personality, I try my best to serve all of these behavioral styles. Sometimes it really is a challenge. As Dr. Rohm says, I am going to try to "raise my 'D'" (if I can find it) to get my teachers to follow the procedures I require for using materials in the library. After all, someone has to teach *them!*

――――――― Any Questions? ―――――

My Fifth Grade class was planning a field trip to Grand Gulf, Mississippi. As their teacher, I had given my students an overview of the day's activities.

"First we will board the chartered bus at 7:30 a.m., here at the school," I said. "You will need to pack a sack lunch and bring two drinks. We will put the drinks on ice in coolers."

I continued, "The trip to Grand Gulf will take approximately one and a half hours. We will tour the nuclear facility and have a guide to tell us how energy is made to run our electric lights and other electric things. Then we will be free to explore the Grand Gulf Museum, which is a 'hands on' museum."

"After the tour, we will board the buss to the military park," I plowed on. "There we will eat lunch, explore the park and the old cemetery, have a scavenger hunt, visit the museum and enjoy the day. Are there any questions?" (The fine print on their diploma says teachers *must* ask if there are any questions.)

Chet, sitting in the back of the room, piped up. Typical of the "I" type personality, Chet was too busy to gather all the information, but he did hear "fun" and "go." He asked loudly, "Can I sit by anyone I want? Can I bring my Walkman® and my Gameboy®? Can we sing on the bus?" His questions were whirling.

"Yes, Chet," I answered patiently. "We will work on all those details this week."

Another hand went up. It was Lisa, a high "C." She said, "Mrs. H, may I have a schedule. My mother needs one." (Knowing perfectly well that it was Lisa, not her mother, who needed the schedule!)

Gloria, by that time, was gathering her "Indians" around her. The "Chief" stated directly, "Laura and I will sit together!", motioning to Laura who nodded. "I will bring the sandwiches and Laura will bring the drinks and chips. Do you have to stay with the chaperone the entire time?"

"Yes, Gloria, but you will have the opportunity to choose where you want to go."

Laura was still nodding her head, as if agreeing to *whatever.*

Chet was back. "Can I take candy along and give it out on the bus?

The room became a *buzz....* I sat down and wondered if the administration would consider a *sub* for me to field trip day.

Espanol Escapades

Personality studies? Oh, yes, that always reminds me of certain students whose personalities are indelibly engraved in my memory. Have I ever told you about my sixth period Spanish II class?

First of all, it was huge. Why? When several student had to have their schedules changed, they needed to come to my sixth period class in order to make the rest of their schedules work. Although our school tries to maintain a low student-teacher ratio, we are also student-centered as we try to meet *their* needs. And "everyone knows how *accommodating* Señora M is..." ("Accommodating" is their word for "sucker" — the "S" is high on my graph!)

So as smaller classes became even smaller and this large class grew larger, I began to realize that we were in for a most unusual 50 minutes each day. Was it possible that so *many* highly kinetic, talkative pranksters could be in this *one* bunch?

But, oh, what I learned. Let's look at "Luis" — tall, blond, very bright, extremely sociable. He loved grand entrances, and everything was a crisis to him. Nearly every day he would come to class early and ask to leave — for water, to take medicine, to get his other notebook, to get his textbook, to talk to another teacher, to go to the bathroom... "It'll just take two minutes. I'll be back before the bell. You gotta let me go; it's an emergency!" The list was endless. One day, though, in the middle of class, he came rushing up to me, saying, "Señora, I need to get a Band-Aid®! I cut my finger! Look! See the blood!" Trying to lessen the interruption and get *Español* back on track before I lost it altogether, I glanced at his finger and said, "That certainly looks like red *ink* to me, but go ahead and get a Band-Aid." When he left, we discovered a broken red pen on the floor near his desk. I simply turned to the class and said, "In the presence of these witnesses, let me state that Luis has used up *all* his favors." Naturally, when he returned, proudly waving his Band-Aid'd "injury," we all laughed, and then I announced that he should not even *think* about asking me for anything the rest of the year. Being the strong "I" that he was, however, he tried a number of times to sneak one by me.

Can you believe that out of 30 (that's all the desks I had, so we cut off at 30), 12 were high "I's"? And six more were almost as strong, but they were usually overshadowed by the others!

The four "C's" probably felt that they had to make an appointment with me just to ask a question. In fact, "Miguel" often came by before class to clarify an assignment with me. This poor fellow had so many questions, and I felt sorry for him because he probably felt completely inhibited about asking anything in class with all those loud, party-loving folks. *Why didn't they want to work, too?*

We had a token "D" type, "Jorge," who provided controversy on a regular basis. One day he very deliberately (in a hostile takeover) monopolized a discussion by giving a very detailed and accurate accounting of the Mexican economy. You see, he read the Business/Financial section of the *Wall Street Journal* every day. A brilliant guy, he loved telling us — *me,* in particular — what he knew. Naturally, he saw no need to do those boring assignments I wanted him to do in class. So, he slept occasionally, probably just so he wouldn't have to hear me when I told him what to do. *Wake him up? Of course not!*

And then, there were the 7 "S's." On some days, it took a concentrated effort on my part to remember that those precious people were even in the room. But I was so very grateful for them! In fact, one day "Isabel," sitting quietly in the back of the room, motioned to me that some non-Spanish sounds were coming from a particular area near her. Bless her dear heart! I was able to squash a potentially thunderous uproar. She knew I needed help and she offered it — without anyone's seeing except me. The gratitude I expressed to her privately made her smile the biggest smile ever!

Personality styles? This group would be one we probably need to track for the next 20 years. My guess is that most of them will be rich and/or famous, and I just hope they remember the little ol' Spanish teacher who tried to be patient and give them room to grow.

Crackpot Comments

In Second Grade, the class studied a unit of Native American Indians. Through various activities, the children learned about several different tribes, their homes, their ways of life, and their clothing. The room mother and several other parents organized an Indian pow-wow for the unit's final activity.

The children were divided into groups to interact in Indian-related activities. One group was made up of the "basic four" personality styles. Laurel was a high "D" with great leadership qualities, but she was very domineering. Norm was the typical "class clown," an "I" with plenty of comical comments. Maureen was the sweet, loving "S" who was sentimental and sensitive. Lyle, very "C," was methodical, cautious, and a critical thinker.

This group's learning center activity involved each child in creating a clay pot, just as the Indians did, sitting in a circle on the floor with a lump of clay. Laurel tried to tell every child what to do and how to do it. Lyle sat off to the side, rubbing and molding his clay, over and over again to make his pot perfect. Laurel breached his space and, moving closer, tried to tell Lyle how to make his pot better. He ignored her for awhile before finally telling her to leave him alone and let him make his own pot. The teacher overheard the exchange and took Laurel aside, explaining that just as no one could push Laurel into doing something *she* didn't want to do, so *she* must realize that Lyle had his *own* ideas about making his pot. The teacher suggested that Laurel take her pottery and sit with Maureen. Then she told Lyle that he was a good example of self-reliance for others, but that he should try to be more gentle in his remarks when he does not want someone else's help.

Maureen was slower in working on her pot and was not certain how she wanted it to look. She made kind comments about Laurel's creative design. Laurel, in turn, suggested that Maureen might want to make a handle for her pot. Maureen did, and told Laurel it was a wonderful idea. As they completed their pottery projects, they showed their fine work to others.

Norm strolled by the girls and jokingly teased them about their pots. Other children overheard him and laughed out loud. Maureen was very embarrassed and her feelings were hurt. Laurel ran to tell the teacher, who took Norm aside and listened to his side of the story. Then she told him that he had to be careful how he used his wonderful sense of humor, or he could hurt people's feelings very easily. She asked how he could make Maureen feel better, and he apologized to Maureen, explaining that he did not mean to hurt her feelings. She accepted his apology readily and said it was okay. So, the teacher told Maureen that she was so compassionate and tenderhearted. It was good that she got along well with people, but she should also speak up the next time someone made fun of her or said unkind things.

Of course, the children's pots were as different as each creator. And in the process of putting them together, the children learned a little more about putting relationships together as well. *(Editor's Note: A fantastic grasp of DISC concepts!)*

Search And Re-Search

I have always had to adjust my style or approach for individual students, but until taking this course on personality styles and education, I did not realize what was really happening with them... and with me.

Each year, my Tenth Grade English Class writes a research paper. Being a high "C," I always explain in detail exactly what I want. Then I give each student written instructions, complete with examples, number of sources required, a dateline showing when different submission are due, literary subjects from which to choose, specific page numbers from the text, final paper due date, etc.

Mick could not wait for me to finish all of my teaching and instructions so he could start work on his paper. According to Mick, a high "D," he had "a grip on it." Of course, none of my suggested topics worked for him. He wanted to write on engineers, because that is what he wanted to be — he said he wanted to make *a lot* of money. After several days of "problems," I agreed that he could write about engineers as long as he narrowed the subject and followed some special guidelines. He started on his paper before the others but had trouble finishing before the deadline. After completing his research, he had found out what he wanted to know — and he was not quite as interested in finishing it for me. However, it was interesting and well-written.

On the other hand, Smitty, an "I," could not come to a definite decision about his subject. He thought every topic might be interesting to know about. So, when the date came to check the students' progress on their note cards, Smitty had *two partial sets* of notes — one for the original topic linked to the bibliography I had checked the previous week, and one for a new topic that had caught his interest while he was researching his original topic. Each time I checked his progress, he talked as fast as he could about unrelated things he had read while preparing for this paper. He finished his paper on time, but in making his deadline he ate only dry cereal from the box from Sunday breakfast until Monday noon. (He and his mother told me the same story!) His mother kept him on task during those final hours.

Brittany is not the best student I have ever had, but she has many good qualities, always helping others and showing concern for people — especially for me. She did not take long deciding about her research project. She met all of the deadlines but always asked questions to compensate for her lack of confidence in her skills. In fact, I went over the same issues with her a number of times. I did not expect her paper to be good, but I did think it would be better than what I read in its final form. Her organization of the information was terrible. I wrote all of the positive comments I could think of in her margins, but she was one of the few whose final grade was not good. When Brittany saw her grade, she burst into sobs, crying "real tears" so hard that she could not speak nor could she grasp anything I was trying to tell her. My "S" came up and I let her rework her paper — with my help — and I graded her again. Obviously, Brittany is an "S."

Morgan must be a "C" — all of her work is perfect. She did not want me to see her rough draft where she had erased, drawn lines, etc. She corrected everything on what was supposed to be her "rough" draft. And once she had finalized it, she handed me a computer-generated copy. I don't think she understood that the rough draft was for the purpose of correcting mistakes.

After completing this course, I am hopeful that I will deal better with *individual* students. Already, from simply *recognizing* their styles, I believe I'll be able to use appropriate phrases and actions to enhance their behavior, rather than provoke it to out-of-control reactions.

It All Adds Up

All right, class, today we are going to put some problems on the board. Who would like to volunteer? Great — Shari take #7, Sam take #10, Steve take #15, and Shana take #22."

Sam and Shari have gone to the white board. Shari practically raced to get there — that board has *markers!* Oh how Shari loves to see her name on the board in red, blue, yellow, and green! She will get around to working on the math problem in just a minute... Sam, on the other hand, has written *only* his answer. Again, I say to him, "Sam, write out the problem — show your work!" With his "I know more than you" attitude, he gives me only the answer, although I am quite sure his answer is correct.

Steve looks like he is having second thoughts about this as he takes his turn at the board. I will have to give him a little pep talk and perhaps get the class working on something else while he finishes.

And what has happened to Shana? Her hand is raised — she must have a question. "Shana," I ask, "do you need help?" She responds according to her methodical nature: "Well, I thought of several different ways to work this problem, and I'm not sure which one you would rather have, or maybe all of them? I was thinking the class might understand the first method more, but the second has a shortcut that really helps to lighten the workload. One of the examples in the book put in three more steps; that's why I have the third problem. Isn't is amazing that all three give the same answer? I just love the way math is so exact. If you want me to put all of these up, I can. Just whatever you prefer!"

"Shana," I replied, "I like the first one! That and an explanation should give the class all they need to know. Good job!"

"Hey... Shari! What number are you *supposed* to be doing...?"

Educational Pizza

Ron, a 12th Grade Trigonometry student, came into my room saying the same thing almost every day: "Mrs. H, we always *work* in here! Can we please have a party?" I love fun but I also have a serious side that hates to get off task, so I proposed that the class could have a party if they could relate it creatively to math. *I had caught their attention!*

Annette, a sweet but very logical girl, came up with the idea of a pizza party. Since we had been studying probability, she suggested we decide how many different combinations we could choose — from toppings of cheese, olives, sausage, pepperoni, Canadian bacon, mushroom, and onions. She had me hooked ...and hungry!

Molly, sitting in the last desk not wanting to be noticed, started to smile. I brought her into the project by asking if she would bring napkins. "Oh, yes," she said, "I'll bring the napkins and the paper cups and the paper plates and..."

"Hold on!" I said. "Others can help." I asked Justin to be the planning leader. He began delegating work to others, and before I knew it the party was organized.

This happened three years ago, and now I see how their personality styles caused each of these students to respond in a predictable manner. Ron was an "I," always wanting to party. Annette was a "C," who came up with the concept and details. Molly was an "S," offering to bring and to help. And Justin was a "D" with a preference for delegation and ability to get the students to do what he wanted.

Contract Time

The setting for this story is the teachers' lounge on the day that contracts for the following year are being handed out. Four teachers (David, Ingrid, Suzanne, and Casey) are sitting around the lounge break table when the principal walks in with contracts in hand.

David stands up immediately and reaches for his contract, never questioning that he was going to get one for next year. As he receives it, his only response is, "What kind of raise are we getting next year?" He does not open his envelope. Instead, he places it with his other papers, so he can look at it when it is convenient to him.

Then the principal gives Ingrid her contract, and her immediate response is, "Yes! I have income for the next 12 months! Let's all go to lunch!" She signs her contract on the spot for fear she might lay it down somewhere and forget to turn it in before the deadline.

Suzanne has spent every moment this morning worrying about whether or not she is going to be offered a contract. She has carefully evaluated every situation of the past year to determine if she acted properly in *all* situations. When the principal hands her a contract, she squelches her urge to hug him and says repeatedly, "How can I ever thank you. I will do a great job for you next year." She also signs her contract and returns it to the principal immediately, as if she fears he might change his mind.

Casey has been waiting very patiently for his envelope and studying the scene. As he takes his contract from the principal, he shows no emotion but asks, "When are these due back?" He does not intend to turn his in until deadline, so he can use the allotted time to read and reread its clauses.

Movers And Shakers

The scene is a Fourth Grade classroom. The characters are classmates Danny, Irma, Sally and Carl. The teacher announces to the class, "We will be changing out seating arrangements soon. I would like to hear your suggestions and ideas."

Danny responds: "I don't see why *I* can't choose where I want to sit. I know exactly where you should put me! I've already thought about this, and here is a list to show you the best spots for everyone. Friday afternoon is the best time for us to move these desks around."

Irma responds: "Yes! Finally! We could decide where everyone sits by playing a game. Everybody picks a number out of a box, then we go in that order to pick where we want to sit — wouldn't that be great? I'm ready to move. There are so many people in here I would like to sit near. By the way, about the lunch room, could we now mix in with other classes? You're so understanding and nice! Doesn't this sound awesome?"

Sally responds: "Thank you so much for moving us around. It's not that I'm unhappy right where I am, but I know a lot of people really want to move. As a matter of fact, I'll go wherever you need me to go if you don't want to leave me here. Danny asked me if I would swap with him if he doesn't like where you put him. That would be okay. By the way, wouldn't this be a great time to clean the floor? And we could clean the desk tops, too. I could bring some cleaning things from home."

Carl responds: "Don't you think placing these desks together in table form would be a good idea? Did you have a good reason for deciding to move us? With our 28 desks, we could put them in seven different groups with four in each group. This would make it much easier to collect and pass out papers. Also, wouldn't you like more freedom to move around the room? This way, you could be at four desks at one time. Don't you think graph paper would be a good way to set this up? Would you like these groups mixed, with boys and girls at each table? Actually, one table will need to have three boys and one girl because of uneven numbers. Sally wouldn't mind being at this table."

The teacher responds: "I'm so proud of the way you thought this through. This is what we are going to do: First of all, we will vote to decide whether we will move our desks into rows or tables. Carl has suggested tables because he thinks it would improve our classroom. We will use Irma's suggestion of drawing numbers to determine the order in which we will move. After we vote and draw numbers, Danny will explain how we will go about moving. We will do this as the last thing on Friday afternoon. Sally has a great suggestion that we take this opportunity to clean up the rest of our classroom, too!"

Tribal Warfare

The Second Grade was studying the different Native American Indian groups (Northwest, Southwest, Plains, Northeast and Southeast). At the end of the unit, the class was divided into five "tribes," with each being assigned to make a mural about one of these groups.

In putting the tribes together, I tried to include a variety of personality styles into each team. They received a sheet of manila paper on which to plan their mural, and I instructed each tribe to choose one person to do the actual drawing. After the murals were planned, each tribe received a stack of white paper on which to draw their mural, and then we would tape together the assembled layout of pages to create the full-size effect.

Martha, my high "D," did not handle the assignment very well. She was "bent out of shape" from the start since she was not chosen to sketch her tribe's mural ideas on the manila paper. She was very difficult to work with. The next day, when the children actually started drawing their mural sections from the plan, she tried to dominate the others by giving orders and taking over the project. When they resisted, she became angry and, at times, cruel.

Micah was one of my very high "I's." He will be Governor of our state one day — I think he is already campaigning! He was Mr. Enthusiastic about the project and got everyone in his tribe motivated. However, it wasn't long before I had to remind him gently to get back to the business at hand.

Ella was my type "S" child. She always did as she was instructed and enjoyed working on the mural with her tribe. She got along with everyone and always made room for someone else to work.

Nicky was my high "C" child, very gifted and intense in his work. Everything had to be perfect. He asked many questions and referenced the encyclopedia's illustrations.

Even though I was familiar with the DISC concept from hearing Dr. Rohm speak as a national teacher's workshop a year before, I could have handled Martha so much better if I had known then what I know now. It was a very difficult year for both of us. I am planning to tell her mother about the two books we read in our class this week (*Positive Personality Profiles,* by Dr. Rohm and *Different Children Different Needs,* by Charles F. Boyd, David Boehi and Dr. Rohm). Her mother is concerned and frustrated. I think it will help her to know that she has a "normal" high "D" child.

Thank you for a wonderful week. There is so much I have learned that can be put to such good use. (*Editor's Note: You're welcome!"*)

— — — Publishing Clearinghouse — — —

A s a way of reviewing all of the skills used in the process of writing, my class wrote original stories, which were "published" in actual blank books. They were truly keepsakes that a parent would cherish for a lifetime.

The project was announced at the beginning of the second six weeks, to be completed by the end of the school year. We discussed all of the elements of writing: brainstorming, choosing our topics, outlining, writing rough drafts, and proofreading. We discussed how the book would be put together and the parts of a book. As you can imagine, all of this was a long, drawn-out process. Not only was the child responsible for writing a book, but also for illustrating it. Instead of writing in our Journals on Fridays, we wrote in our books. I checked each student's progress weekly, as well as going over every skill.

Rusty was a high "D" with a good dose of "I." He attacked the project with a vengeance. His book was to be about traveling the world and meeting people in each country. He loved geography and could draw meticulous maps, so I thought the story was appropriate for his talents. Looking back, I can see that he chose to write about a lot of people because he has many "People Person" strengths. But he began to tire of the project in a few weeks. As a "D," he wanted to see the finished book, and the end was still weeks away. His papers became messier as time went on and he lost interest in the project. He finished, but it was not his best work. As he read his book to the class, he wanted everyone to make sure they saw his picture in the back.

Chuck was an "I with D" type blend, a likeable child who always had an answer for every question but didn't know how to raise his hand! He was slow to start the project because he was so busy trying to decide what his topic was going to be. He changed several times but finally decided he would write about a Mexican bandit he named "Enchilada Piñata." Because his "D" trait was task-oriented, he wanted his book to be the best. His drawings and script were both humorous and well written. I wish you could read his book — I "fell out" in the classroom as he read it to us one day. He said that the bandit's punishment was to go to a kids' party! Chuck loved reading his book to the class — he *performed* it! — and he loved hearing his classmates laugh.

Beth Marie was a sweet, mild-tempered "S." She always wanted to help me in the classroom. She wanted to know if she had the right answer to every question before she wrote the answer down. She had a hard time deciding what to write about, but she always brought each topic to me for my approval. After much discussion, she decided to write about her two younger brothers, and entitled it, *My Brothers, the Aliens.* She wrote that one day her brothers were picked up by a spaceship and identical robot dolls were left in their places. No one knew they were dolls except for Beth Marie. At the end she stated, "I always wanted to be an only child anyway." As she read her book to the class, Beth Marie looked around the room to make sure everyone liked what she had written.

Ari was a reserved, mild girl who always had perfect papers. She cried once when her daily grade was an 80. He work was always as neat as could be. She studied the ideas for her book for several days and finally decided to write about her father, a neurosurgeon. She told his life story, and I know he was very proud of her effort. Her work was so brilliant that it actually should be published. Each page had wonderful drawings, completely correct sentences, and the letters themselves looked as if a machine had printed them. As a matter of fact, Ari could have published her rough draft!

It was fun for me to go back and think about the personalities of each of my Third Grade students. After taking this course, I can see why they acted as they did. I feel I will do a much better job teaching next year if I put this information into practice. And by the way, if you think writing those books was a chore for the students, think what emotional turmoil it created for a "D with I" personality like mine. My "D" was frustrated when assignments weren't done on time, but the "I" in me always let my students have more time to complete each step.

Got It Covered

After doing several Creative Writing projects in our Third Grade classroom, I announced that each of my students would choose one favorite story and publish it in a hardback book cover. Students' reactions ranged from noisy pronouncements to excited delight to nervous anticipation to composed silence.

Wally, a "D," blurted out immediately, "All right! Mine will be the best book of all because I can write really cool stories and my drawings are great!"

After reminding Wally to raise his hand and work on his humility, I called on Todd, a high "I," who was waving his hand in the air furiously while his body wiggled in his desk and he grinned from ear to ear. "Yes, Todd," I asked.

"May we work in groups with our friends, please? And may we spread out around the room and talk while we work, please, please, please? Wow! This is going to be so much fun!"

Tiffany sat quietly and patiently in her desk, listening to

all that was going on around her and smiled sweetly when I walked over to her desk. Quietly I asked her, "Tiffany, what do you think about doing a hardback book?" She responded with, "Oh, I think it will be hard but I will try to do my best. I'm sorry I don't draw very well but I'll do the best I can. Would you like me to help you do anything? I might not be good at publishing a book, but I know I can help you... that is, if you want me to help."

During this entire scenario, Pam was already diligently writing out orderly notes and thoroughly analyzing all of her stories to choose the best one to publish as her book. I knew her selection would be carefully planned, perfectly copied and illustrated, with great care and detail. She probably would not like to "spread out" across the room as Todd suggested, but would prefer to work alone at her desk. I could count on it!

Tempera Tantrums

Art is not the only thing created in an Art Class. Situations among "artists" are also created due to the expression of their true, inner feelings. The Golden Rule of an Art Class is, "Don't mess with anybody's artwork, verbally or physically!"

One quiet October morning, the Fourth Graders were designing tempera paint faces on real pumpkins. Wendell, a high "C," questioned Nolan, a high "D," about the shape of his pumpkin's eyes. "Why did you paint them so small?" Before Nolan could answer, Sybil, a high "S," gently whispered to Wendell, "It's Nolan's art. Let him do it the way he wants to." Nolan became offended by Wendell's question and Sybil's attempt to defend him, and he responded by smashing his own pumpkin to the floor. What a short fuse!

Jerry, a high "I," yelled, "Food fight!" expecting to incite the class to rebellion. Nolan turned to Wendell and said sarcastically, "So, you think you could do better?" Jerry broke in, "No, Nolan, he didn't mean anything by it." And Sybil and Jerry slipped to the floor and began cleaning up the mess.

I am a high "S" myself, and did not care for the surprise outburst in my class. I escorted Nolan out of the art room and asked another student to get his classroom teacher. She escorted him to the principal's office to deal with the matter appropriately.

The "Remember Chair"

At the beginning of each new school year, we spend a great deal of time learning our K-4 Preschool Class rules. It is now easier for me to understand the reactions of my children after having been in Dr. Rohm's class on personality styles all week. The rule that draws the most reaction is: "Push your chair up to the table every time you leave your seat."

Lucy (I now know that she has a high "D" personality) did a quick check around the room. She could then report to me (and to any offenders) that they did not push in their chairs and will not go out to recess with the rest of the class. In the case of Trey (an "I" who does not even realize he has been sitting in a chair because for the most part he has been sprawled across the table talking to his neighbor!) Lucy demands that he push in his chair — and if he won't, *she will!*

Nancy has been scanning the classroom for chairs left out, also. As an "S" type, she tiptoes quietly across the room and pushed a chair up for a person who forgot.

Beckie, who is more a "C" type, wants to know why they must push in their chairs every time in the first place, because they will be returning to them off and on all day. In detail, I must explain to her that we wouldn't want anyone to trip and hurt themselves over a chair that has been left out, and it makes our room look nice to have the chairs pushed up.

To make a short story a little longer, Lucy spent time in the "Remember Chair" for being so bossy, Trey remained inside while the others went out (thinking he and Lucy would play inside!), Nancy tiptoed and lined up quietly, and Beckie was asking how much longer Lucy was going to have to sit in the "Remember Chair" and when Trey could come out to recess....

Sandy Science

One day, my Fourth Grade Class did a science experiment on soil erosion out on the playground. After we divided into groups and were heading outside, Evan (my high "S") asked, "Can I carry the pans outside?" Gary, (another "S") asked, "Can I bring the sand and water?"

After we all got outside, Luke (my high "I") was not paying attention or listening to directions. He was already pouring sand into a pan and wisecracking, "Look, Fort Walton Beach!" I told him it was great to show so much "get up and go," but next time, wait for directions.

Caleb (a "D") asked, "What are we going to do?" Whatever it was, he wanted to get on with it.

Jeri (my high "C") asked, "Why are we doing this? Why did we come outside? Why didn't we stay inside, where it is cool?" I told her those were good questions and gave her the factual reasons for doing this experiment. I also assured her we wouldn't be outside for too long.

Meanwhile, Luke made a mess trying to pour the sand back into the jug. He got distracted quickly and started talking to a friend.

I explained the procedures each group were to follow during the experiment. Jeri asked if she could pour the sand into the pan for her group.

Caleb asked, "What are *we* supposed to do since Luke *already* poured our sand into the pan?" I told him he could be the leader of his group and pick someone to pour the water into the pan slowly.

As the experiment progressed, Evan commented to me, "I like it when people work together and get along. I also like ideas that work and are easy to do."

When we had finished, the kids put their sand around a newly planted tree on the playground. As Caleb's group was pouring out its sand, he said, "That was a 'bogus' experiment! I *knew* that was going to happen."

I responded, "Caleb, I know you like to get results when you do things, and our experiments showed many excellent results that you had *not* known. You were a very good leader. You charge into new situations without fear."

All in all, I think our experiment was very productive and educational — and Caleb would have thought so, too, if he had known about "DISC"!

To The Playground!

It was time for the First Grade to go out to play on the first day of school. I told the class we were going downstairs to the playground. I began to explain that we would need to stay in line because we had to walk down the stars and be sure we went out the same door so we would not get lost.

David said, "I already know how to go to the playground because I go to church here,"

"That's great, David," I said, "but I still want you to stay in line with the class. I will have to stay at the front of the line, and since you know the right way to go, you stay at the end of the line and make sure nobody gets lost." That seemed to quiet him down and give him a job to perform.

Our line began to move. "Teacher, teacher!" I heard from behind me. I turned toward the commotion and saw two students scuffling and pushing. I stopped the line and walked back to them. "What's going on here?", I asked.

Caroline said, "Ivan told me I wasn't walking right. I know I am walking right because you told us to stay right behind the one in front of us. Ivan walked out and in and I followed, just like you told me to."

Ivan responded, "Gollllleeee, I was just playing a game. I didn't know you wanted a straight line."

The voice at the end of the line bellowed, "Everybody get in a straight line and let's get outside."

"Thank you, David," I said. We got down the stairs without incident.

As we approached the door leading to the playground, Susie said, "Teacher, teacher! They went that way!" Then she pointed to the front door leading to a heavily traveled street. My heart skipped a beat.

I stopped the line and told David to watch the children while I went to get my prodigals. I caught Ivan and his friend, "marched" them back to the line and proceeded to tell them (using my pointer finger!) that it was so dangerous not to follow directions. I reminded them that they could get lost or get hit by a car if they went out that side of the building. I really "laid down the law" on this first day of school.

Suddenly, I heard Susie choking and crying. Then she pulled on my blouse and I turned around to hug her and tell her I was not talking to her. She looked up at me, eyes afloat, and said, "I'll stay today, but I'm not coming back tomorrow."

Ivan and his friend just bounced back into line. David hollered, "Let's get outside and play!" Caroline said, "Everybody remember to stay in line." And Suzie just wiped her eyes and bowed her head.

"Ribbitt" Research

At the end of class one day, I announced that the following day would be what we had all been waiting for. The Seventh Graders were going to "cut up" their frogs!

The "I's" wanted to "cut up" right then — immediately. That was the only part of my announcement they heard. After making that correction, I asked if there were any questions.

"Yes, Irene?"

"Mrs. W, whose group am I in?"

"You'll find out tomorrow, Irene, and I will decide… Yes, Claire?"

"Mrs. W, what do we need to read to be ready for this assignment? Will there be a test? What do we need to bring to class? Will we have instructions?"

"Tomorrow, class, I will give out the instructions. You don't need to get ready for anything yet. I will explain everything tomorrow, but thank you for your questions."

"How long will this take?" asked David, without raising his hand.

"Please raise your hand next time, David. It will take about 25–30 minutes, and you will follow instructions... Sarah, you look like you have a question."

"Well, I was wondering is we would have to hurt the frogs. I don't think I could."

"The frogs have already been taken care of, Sarah. Don't worry, they won't feel a thing... Any more questions...? Okay, see you tomorrow."

The following day, the class came in excited. The "I's" wanted to know *whom* they were going to work with. The "S's" were still worried about the frogs. The "D's" just wanted to get started, and the "C's" wanted their instructions — *now!*

David, Irene, Sarah and Claire were grouped together. Instructions were passed out and students were told to read them over for several minutes. Then a diagram of the frog was placed on the overhead projector for all to see. I pointed out the organs to look for, and then sent the groups off to their "frog work."

David made the first cuts and got everybody off to a good start. Claire read the instructions aloud for the group and made sure they were followed. Irene kept wanting to visit the other groups to make sure they were having as much fun as she was. Sarah helped with the dissection by holding pins and wiping up messes. David and Claire kept telling Irene to stay put and pay attention.

David made sure the dissection was completed in 25 minutes. Claire made sure all the correct organs were identified by the whole group. Sarah cleaned up everything. Irene had a good time! Overall, it worked out well for everyone... except for the frogs!

What's Your Sign?

The teacher is ready to start her Seventh Grade Math Class. The lesson today is on adding integers. She begins with a review of the addition rules, and asks, "Class, who can tell me the addition rule for numbers with the same sign?"

Brandy, a "D," shouts out, "Add the numbers and get your answer." The teacher replies, "Brandy, please raise your hand before you answer." The girl demands, "Okay, but my answer's right, isn't it!" And the teacher answers, "Almost right."

Cary, an "I" student, jumps up and down with his hand up. "All right, Cary," the teacher says, "calm down and tell me what you think the answer is." He replies excitedly, "I think you should subtract the numbers — right?" The teacher says, "Well that's a good try, but we subtract the numbers when we have different signs and we are talking about same signs.

The teacher moves to Judith, a high "S," and asks her for the addition rule for same-sign numbers. "Julie, you've heard what Brandy and Cary had to say. What do you think the answer is? Take your time and think for a minute." Julie thinks quietly and answers almost as quietly, "I think you have to put the sign on your answer that the numbers have." The teacher responds, "Very good, Judith. That's exactly what you have to do."

Then the teacher goes to Ward, who is a high "C" type. "Ward, you've heard what Brandy, Cary, and Judith have said. What do you think?" Ward answers precisely, "Well, each of them answered parts of the rules correctly. But you asked for one addition rule regarding numbers with the same sign, so we have to put the correct parts together.

The complete answer is to add the numbers and put the same sign that the numbers have on the answer. For example +7 plus +2 equals +9, and -7 plus -2 equals -9."

"That's correct, Ward. Thank you all for your answers. I can tell that you have been looking at the rules I gave you to study. Now let's work some examples using this rule...."

In The Hive

Mastery of the multiplication tables is a major skill to be accomplished in the Third Grade. In order to spur my students toward this goal, I created a motivational device that we called, "In the Hive."

We made a large beehive out of brown craft paper and then the students created their own bees out of construction paper. All the bees were placed on a bulletin board "framing" the hive as we started this project.

Each Friday, we had a short multiplication quiz. Students completing all the problems correctly within the allotted time received a 100% grade and were allowed to move their bees into the hive. Once in the hive, the happy bees were there for good. The students could earn extra credit points for each consecutive 100 percent. Our class goal was a "beehive party" when everyone had made it into the hive.

After our first Friday quiz, the anxious and eager students waited for me to make the announcement. Tim, my highest "D," exclaimed, "Awesome! I *knew* I would get a hundred and be the first one in the hive! I am *so* smart!" I was amazed by his brazen boasting.

Lana, a "C," bombarded me with questions. Did she think *I*

didn't know *my* multiplication tables? "Mrs. O, are you sure you graded this right? Did you see this one? I thought for sure I had it right. How many did I miss? How many did I need to get right?"

The strongest "I" in our group, Sean, hollered out, "All right! I'm in the hive! When are we having the party?" He seemed to have no appreciation for the accomplishment itself.

Cindy, my sweetest little "S," was disappointed but resigned. "I missed eight!" she moaned. "I thought I studied hard, too! I can't believe I did that. It's all my fault. I'll have to study harder next week."

Looking back, I can see how much more effectively I could have handled each of those children's reactions if I had been aware of the DISC system. I would have been able to anticipate the children's reactions and could have responded more appropriately than simply affirming my "S" and shaking my head at the rest!

Personality Coaching

I am the boys' basketball coach at my school. My own personality style is high "S," with good amounts of "I" and "C." What is extremely low and "missing in the equation" is "D." This week, I encountered three different personalities on my team, to see what would happen if I used my new understanding of personalities. (The fourth encounter I will relate occurred several years ago.)

In the Spring, I had approached T.J. (an "S") about getting into weight training. He is probably the best player on our team, but he needs to become stronger and more imposing physically. I have noticed him spending more time in the weight room over his Summer vacation, so last night I caught up with him in the gym lobby during a practice break. "T.J.," I said, "I can tell you have gotten stronger. Because of your hard work, we will be a better basketball team. Thank you." As a result of my "appreciation" approach, he became the most energetic player on our team during the remainder of our practice session.

A high "I" named Eddie started for us last season, but I didn't feel he was very good defensively and stayed on him a lot. So, last night, in front of several players, I walked over to him and said, "Eddie, you have really improved your defense! It will make you a complete player!" This was the first time I have ever seen Eddie speechless. Because I praised him in front of people, he got public recognition and I knew he would "perform" for it again.

Randall is our point guard and played a lot last year. As the floor leader, he has to show some "D" traits. At practice, we had been working on focusing and drilling on running a secondary break. When the scrimmage started, Randall did not run the break the way we had been working on. He reverted to old habits and ended up throwing the ball away. Standard Operating Procedure in this instance is for the coach (me) to synthesize some "D" traits of my own and go crazy. The players froze in anticipation of my tirade. Instead, I walked calmly toward him and asked quietly, "Randall, what have we been working on?"

"Getting the ball to the wing…"

"And what did you just do?"

"Made the pass from the point…"

"And what was the result?"

"Turnover…"

I "patted" him on the rear end with my clipboard and walked away. I could hear the team whispering behind my back, "Has coach lost it?" Randall did not mess up that play again the rest of the practice because I had not shot down his floor leadership.

As mentioned, my "C" confrontation happened several years ago. We had missed several easy lay-ups in a game, and the next day in practice, players who missed a lay-up in drills had to run five "suicides." Benton was a perfectionist high "C." If he couldn't do it right, he didn't want to do it at all. So, he would not try his lay-up and he refused to run. I told him if he did not run he was off the team, and he left practice. Later that night, he called me to apologize. After running his suicides, making a team apology and a game suspension, I let him back on the team. Looking back, I see it would have been better for him if I had let him practice for awhile before setting up the "suicide" penalty. Also, I should have explained *why* it was so important to me that he and his teammates learn to make lay-ups.

I am looking forward to next winter, to see what personality skills I can use in myself and develop in my players under pressure. *(Editor's Note: How would you have liked to have a coach like this?)*

Who Wears Short-Shorts?

In our faculty meeting, the high school principal asked the faculty to be more aware of the dress code — especially the length of girls' shorts, as Spring had arrived and they were getting too short. His instruction was to send anyone not in compliance to the office.

The next day in my class, one girl wore shorts that were obviously too short, and I told her I thought they were. She was very embarrassed, and I thought she might cry. One of her friends spoke up. "I think mine are too short, too! Send me!" (She wanted to leave class at any cost.)

The student who was not in compliance is a very popular girl with a sterling reputation for always doing the right thing and never gets in trouble in *or* out of school. I didn't understand that other students had put her on an extremely high pedestal, and she had put herself on an even higher one, setting some very high expectations. Something as innocent as being sent to the office for wearing too short shorts absolutely devastated her.

Now, she felt everyone in school was talking about it... and she was right. Of course, by the time the news had begun to circulate, she had called her mother — a very young, cute, active, outgoing person. Within an hour, Mom and Daddy were at school to see me and the principal.

Our principal explained the steps that had been taken previously to warn all students about the dress code. He said that teachers had been asked to be aware of this. The parents' complaint was that their daughter had never done anything wrong before and was crushed because everyone in school knew she had done "something" to get into trouble. They insisted that they had more sense that to let her out of the house in clothing that was not decent. They decided that the fault was truly mine — I should have been more sensitive to the fact that she was a good girl who never got in trouble.

The next day, I talked with the girl and told her had *I known* how devastating it would have been for her, I never would have sent her to the office. I assumed falsely that she had the same attitudes (personality styles) as her friends. But while she is outgoing and friendly, she is also *very* sensitive and this was *not* an infraction worth being devastated over.

Now I understand that she is a very high "S," who more

than anything needs everyone's acceptance. Her parents were both "blessed" with a lot of "D" — the mother also had a lot of "I." The other girl in the story is an "I" who likes to be in the spotlight and cannot imagine why someone would *not* want to go to the office. The only "C" is our principal, who tried to make the parents realize that the school's rules apply regardless of a child's popularity or reputation.

The Trouble With Simone...

Simone, the high "D," never had anyone to work with among the other Third Graders. She was often too defiant in her attitudes to gain a helping hand from a friend. She had a high I.Q. and lots of potential, but she was a poor starter. Her behavior style drove people away because she was far too dominant and domineering in working with others.

Joy, the high "I," chose to work with lots of people. She worked quickly in order to have free talking time. Always smiling, she drew a crowd all the time. She spoke to Simone only to tell her she liked her vest.

Sherry, the high "S," was Simone's only friend. She is a peacemaker, voted Best Citizen in the Third Grade. You could always count on Sherry to include Simone in the conversation. Sherry is so sincere.

Lastly, there is Trisha, the high "C," a picky, technical, and calculating fireball. Simone drives Trisha crazy. She cannot tolerate any of Simone's actions —even the way Simone peels the paper off her crayons — and "tells her off" 15 times a day!

Of all my students, Simone is the greatest puzzle to me, and perhaps to herself. She never found her niche in our classroom. Her strong "D" behaviors caused classroom havoc every day!

---- Four Small Adjustments ----

T he school year started like most of the past twelve. I was anxious to meet my new students. Seventh Graders are fun to teach. This was such a new, exciting experience for them all — the first time to change classes each period, no teachers sitting with them at lunch, and of course, their very own locker! The first week ended, and I had to make some adjustment in my teaching style for four of my new students. I hoped these changes would have a lasting, positive affect on these four, while influencing the rest of the students. Here is what I did:

Derek was an outgoing, enthusiastic student who seems to challenge who was in charge of my room. After a few outbursts from him, I decided he needed to help me in the classroom by assuming extra duties and responsibilities. I put him in charge of taking attendance, filling out the absentee slip, and giving his classmates their homework assignments. His "D" personality style enabled him to enjoy and perform his job with gusto.

Noren was a very quiet girl who seemed to want to please us all. Whenever I needed to pass out books or supplied, I called on her to do the job. Because she was an "S," Noren thrived on helping others and these activities brought her in closer contact with her peers.

Foster seemed to be a very popular guy, but he seemed bored by my lecture/notetaking style of teaching. I decided to put him in charge of making up ten questions and answers for our Friday class. On that day, we divided into four teams, and the team that could answer a question would get two bonus points added to their lowest daily grade. Foster was our "game show emcee" and received four bonus points for all his work. He was an "I" personality style, and I chose him for this over a "C" because I wanted this to be fun for everyone and not so very technical.

Barry was an obvious "C" type, always asking why. He loved watching cable television's Discovery Channel and referred to it often. I asked him to video record two shows to present to the class, and asked him to make notes from his observation of these shows to discuss with us in a classroom forum.

The year progressed nicely after making these creative accommodations, and I believe each of these students and their classmates learned a lot.

On Their First Day

The first day of school is always an exciting time in the Kindergarten, filled with so much emotion. The five- and six-year-olds have been prepared for their first "school" experience by the various personality styles of their parents — and of course, they arrive with their own personality styles, too.

The high "D" child has his mind set on being in charge. He comes in with much self-confidence, and nothing seems to intimidate him — not even the teacher! He anticipates the challenge of his day enthusiastically, and he is ready to "do something" when he enters the door. He likes choices and challenging activities. He gets bored quickly with the routine of starting the school year. He may be one of the first discipline problems, as he likes confrontation. Since there will probably be one or two high "D's" (hopefully not more!) in a class of 20 children, it would seem beneficial for the teacher to plan ahead to meet the needs of this special little "leader."

The high "I" child comes to class ready for fun. He is excited and enthusiastic, ready to play with all his new friends. He can hardly wait to get into the toy center and asks immediately if he can go outside. The sitting and listening experiences are very difficult for him unless they are mixed with some "fun" activities. There will probably be about five or six of this personality style in a class of 20 children. It would be wise for a teacher to have a "special" play or talking time planned for these children. They love their teacher if she is fun, and they like to be hugged and give hugs. Since they like recognition, awards for good behavior and achievement are helpful.

The high "S" child comes into class calmly and appears easygoing. He is shy and reserved. He will slip into a seat close to someone he knows or near the teacher, if he feels secure there. Many times this child will try to take ownership of this seat for the entire year — or at least until he expands his comfort zone. Since there may be six to eight of these children in a class of 20, it is wise to tell these children their schedule for the day and what is expected of them. A picture schedule chart helps these preschoolers to feel secure. These children do not like to be called on or recognized until they feel comfortable, and they will give you the cue. They appreciate a quiet touch, and they enjoy familiar activities, such as coloring or completing a puzzle.

The high "C" child might have been "pulled" from his mother's neck. They may come in crying or very quiet. Often, they seem oblivious to their peers — they are not "social animals," and prefer to be left alone. The playground is probably not going to make this type of child happy at first. He may want to stay inside while others go out to play. Since there may be as many as four or five of these children in a class of 20, it is easy to have some interesting books available, and perhaps a table with a variety of objects that can be held, explored, and manipulated. This child will probably want to work and play alone initially. He likes the security of knowing what is expected of him and what the schedule is going to be. He likes the opportunity to ask questions when he feels comfortable doing it, and he likes quality answers to those questions.

It is certainly a challenge to plan for the needs of the various styles, but it is easier than playing "catch up" with them all day. It is a blessing to begin to get a handle on how to recognize their differences and to understand some of the expectations of the precious children who arrive on their first day of school. *(Editor's Note: The predicted number of personality styles in this story comes from research of approximate percentages in the general population: "D" is 5 to 10%, "I" is 25 to 30%, "S" is 30 to 35%, and "C" is 20 to 25%.)*

Speak Up

The first year I coached the senior high school Speech and Debate Team was a learning experience for me. I was told the class consisted of a group of select students who understood that they would be participating in a non-structured classroom setting, with a primary goal of competitive speaking.

Well, the first week was chaotic! I discovered this "select" group was chosen on the basis of having nowhere else to go during that period. Some students used the class as a study hall, some socialized, some never participated, and some seemed very confused. Since these students could compete in any number or combination of events, I knew I had to organize them and myself with some surefire methods.

First, I established four groups based on competition events: debate, original speaking, interpretation, and timekeeper. I explained that students would be divided into four groups and participate in that event's requirements for two weeks. I explained further that after each student rotated through all of the events, they would be allowed to choose events for competition.

I realized after a complete rotation that students chose events in which they felt most comfortable or confident. Based on this experiment, I can now help children find their best competitive event after a few days in class. Now, after this week, I know I grouped them according to personality styles. My best debaters seem to be "C's" because of their analytical and questioning nature. My best original speakers are "D's," because they express their ideas and opinions *all* of the time. My best interpretation event speakers are "I's," as they are actors and actresses at heart. I also understand that those kids who stay in class because they can help me behind the scenes (even though they have no desire for public exposure) are "S's."

I am confident that next year will be even more productive as I understand personality strengths and weaknesses. I am looking forward to working with each child in a more in-depth manner. This class offers an excellent opportunity for each child to develop his or her personality strengths — and to recognize personality weaknesses — since I require all to participate in every event area.

Life's A Stage

My Seventh and Eighth Grade English Literature classes read through plays as they act out the parts. I go over the roles, then tell the students to list three parts they would like to read, in order of preference. Whenever possible, I try to give each student his or her preference. It is interesting that students gravitate toward parts that fit their personality styles rather than their reading abilities. Sometimes, students who read well will choose small parts... *shy!* Students who don't read well may choose major roles. In making assignments, I try to accommodate these variables.

Students who want attention can get it through reading and acting out the story... or by *directing, narrating,* or *dressing up* for their roles, etc. Students who do not want attention can *take smaller roles,* or *dressing down* for their parts.

I not only try to involve everyone in a way that is comfortable for them, but I also try to stretch them whenever possible. Somtimes this requires small doses in the spotlight, or at other times, small doses in the background. Life requires each of us at times to lead something or to sit this one out. My students need a plan to believe *they can when necessary.* And if stretching isn't working, I change it. We all need to be flexible sometimes — even a "C" like me!

Three-Ring Classroom

What an exciting day it was for my First Grade Class. All of us were going to the circus for a field trip. Tyler, an "I," was beside himself. Sitting in his seat was impossible. His hand shot up. "Mrs. A," he exclaimed, "can you believe we are going to get to have fun all day?"

Wayne, a "D," held up his hand. "Mrs. A, let's go! I'm tired of waiting!"

Kathy, a "C," asked if we had enough time to get there. And Mary, my "S," assured her friends we would go soon and that there was plenty of time to get there. I gave Wayne the job of calling out names for the carpool.

We arrived on time for the circus, which made Kathy very happy, but she wanted to know what order we were going to sit in. I quickly arranged the children, making sure Tyler and Wayne sat by me. As we were being seated, Mary asked if she could sit next to me. She felt insecure with all the people around.

Everything was going great until Kathy started to the bathroom and fell on the steps. Tyler was too busy waving at everyone to even see what happened. Wayne was becoming bored — he was ready for the next act. Mary held Kathy's hand as we bandaged her knee (on a field trip, you carry *everything* in your purse!). Kathy wanted to know why they made the steps so large. They made her fall!

One of the main attractions of the circus was their inclusion of children from the audience in one or two of their acts. Clowns began to go through the crowd to pick children. They needed someone to assist the Master of Ceremonies. Guess who was picked? Wayne, my "D." I was so glad. He needed something to work at.

The clowns already new Tyler. He had stopped them each time he went to the bathroom! As he waved both hands, they picked him to be a clown. I've never seen him so happy. He almost forgot his name.

Mary hid behind me so they wouldn't pick her. Kathy was worried about whether we would have time to get back to school in time for afternoon carpool.

Well, Wayne made a wonderful Ringmaster. Tyler never stopped talking about how much fun he had being a clown. All in all, it was a wonderful day. Wayne got to be a leader, Tyler got to have fun and be the center of attention, Mary got to help a friend, and Kathy got to ask as many questions as she wanted to.

The Year Of The Trailer

T he "Year of the Trailer," as we call it, began last August. Due to rising enrollment, our Fifth Grade (the smallest class) was sentenced to a year in a lovely 12x60 foot trailer at the end of our building. My cohort, fellow teacher and great friend, Lorie and I (both "I's"), had long before decided to make this a fun adventure for both of our classes!

The extremely late arrival (five days before school opened!) of a "portable classroom" with no air conditioning and humid 98° weather squelched our enthusiasm somewhat. We were seriously behind schedule. One hot afternoon, we attempted to lift a 200-pound table into the trailer with no steps. My already stirred-up "D" traits went off the chart. You know that Enough + Enough = Enough? By this time, I'd had Enough^2! The only factor that saved me from full-time Wal-Mart employment was my steady friend whose "C" kicked in just in time. The Cavalry arrived (our "S" type board members) and provided everything we needed.

We did complete our rooms. Since the trailer was not really big enough for desks, tables were moved in and dividers made. Space was scarce, almost nonexistent! But hey, we are "I's"! We knew we could make this fun, exciting, and challenging for all concerned. We were finally ready.

All 26 students arrived on Monday morning. As they entered their new room (I used the term loosely), everyone was chatting. Parents were in awe that so many of us could actually fit in that one tiny space.

Lilly (a high "I") took one look and exclaimed, "Fantastic! There are people crammed everywhere! I love it — this year will be a blast! Fifth Grade, here I come!"

Larry (a "C") entered quietly and conducted an immediate

assessment. He muttered, "Where will I keep my books? Where will my lunch box go? I don't think my feet will reach the floor. Oh, gosh, I hope I'm not next to Lilly — she drives me nuts. What am I saying? *Everywhere* in here is next to Lilly! What would a tornado do to this piece of junk? We'd never be found. Oh, Mom, where are you? Is this trailer really legal? Can the school board do this to us? Mom, Mom, where are you?"

Lizzie (a real "D") plunged into the trailer, surveyed the situation and headed straight for the middle table, knocking down two other children in the process. Removing someone's books, she took over the table. "Hey, I like this! Cool, man! Those sissies have to be in the building. Just wait 'til I see them! Hey, you all sit down — you're in my way!"

Libbie (an "S") smiled quietly and said, "I think this will be okay. I guess it will. I hope it will be. I wish we could be back in the building, but this is okay. I know Mrs. C will be nice. Did I get your seat, Stephen? I'm so sorry. I'll move."

They all continued talking, laughing, settling in, and getting reacquainted. I thought what a wild week we'd had getting ready, then smiled to myself. *This is going to be some year...!*

Hey — did that trailer wall just move *in* a foot?

Reach For The Stars

My years teaching Kindergarten were fun and wonderful. I can remember how different children answered questions one day when we were in our Science

Center talking about and looking at a replica of the solar system.

I asked, "What are the names of the planets?" Before I could get the question completed and out of my mouth, Ben jumped up and recited the planets in order, with such boldness that I realized he could teach my class!

After that, I asked different children to name certain planets. I asked Alice about one planet, and after a slight pause, she responded, "Saturn..." Then, like taking the lid off, her questions hit: "Why does that planet have a 'circle' around it? Why are the planets in that order? Why don't they fall?" After trying to answer her questions, I pointed her to the *Childcraft Encyclopedia* and we moved on.

I asked Carlyn to name the planet furthest from the sun. Sweet Carlyn looked up and smiled and softly said, "I think... could it be... well, I'm not sure... is it maybe Plu----to?" After praising Carlyn and telling Ben to sit up straight and close his mouth, we continued. We finally concluded our Science Center visit with bright-eyed Maria suggesting that all the planets looked like a bunch of balloons!

A Legal Eagle

My oldest daughter's Kindergarten Class was participating in a program featuring a local entertainer and environmentalist. Paul had been singing various songs with the children and had paused to talk to the class for a few minutes. He asked them, "What is our country's national bird?"

Danny, a "D," was sitting on the front row, and jumped to fit feet to yell, "Eagle!"

Robby, an "I," was jumping up and down in the back row, waving his hands, so Paul allowed him to answer also. His answer was, "Big Bird!"

Sandra, with her calm, sweet "S" self, was sitting in the second row. She raised her hand shyly. Paul thought she was so cute that he couldn't resist calling on her, too. She replied, "I think... but I'm not positive... but I think it is the eagle."

"Very good," said Paul. "You are right."

Brenna, being a "C," raised her hand. She stood up, looked at Paul and said, "It is the bald eagle, to be exact." And she was!

Lock 'Em Up!

Every year, I take the Eighth Grade class to the Mississippi State Penitentiary in Parchman, Mississippi. As we tour the prison, we stop at several of the units that house inmates. This is a story about the trip we took this year.

At one of our stops, we had to get off the bus and walk through the gate of a minimum security housing unit. We walked into the building and through the cafeteria, where some of the inmates were eating; then crossed a courtyard where some inmates were playing basketball and lifting weights; and finally into a lobby area where we sat down to listen as two inmates gave their testimonies.

One inmate was a singer and an artist. He sang and then drew a picture of one of my students while the other inmate spoke.

This second inmate was rough and tough looking. He had tattoos up and down each arm. He told how he was a gang leader and used drugs. Both had been convicted of armed robbery. The singer/artist has eight more years to serve and the gang leader has 20 years left on his sentence.

Both men gave their testimony of how the found God after being in prison. They both seemed to feel sorry for what they had done.

When leaving the building, we walked by the inmates' cells and could see TVs, radios, books, cards, etc. The building was air conditioned. After leaving this building, there were mixed emotions and ideas about incarceration among my students.

The "S" students thought the two who spoke to us were nice and felt sorry for them. The "S's" were also very fearful when walking through the units.

The "C" students wanted to know about the inmates' daily schedule and thought they were given too many privileges in a prison with too many amenities. They thought that perhaps someone with a bad home life might commit a crime just to be in a prison as nice as this one, with free food.

The "I" students wanted to know how often the prisoners got to play basketball and lift weights, and asked what other forms of entertainment they had.

The "D" students thought the prisoners deserved anything and everything that might happen to them. They could not believe the inmates would be allowed to lift weights. They could get strong enough to beat up the guards and escape! The "D's" kept begging to go to the Maximum Security Unit, but the "S's" said, "No! Let's just get out of here!"

Hoop-la

Being a girls' basketball coach for the last 19 years has had its ups and downs. If you have never had the opportunity to coach teenage girls, you haven't experienced the true profession of coaching. Don't get me wrong — I really love coaching girls. It's just that it can be as difficult as it is rewarding.

At the risk of sounding chauvinistic, I never know what is on their minds. Some days they can come to practice and everything is just great, but on other days they can be a real pain in the neck to deal with. So many things seem to affect them. As a coach, I never know what my players have experienced prior to a practice session or a game. Things like test scores, a squabble with their best friends, misunderstandings with parents or teachers, a fight with a boyfriend — all of these and more can impact differing styles in different ways.

This is why it is so important to understand your players and their way of thinking. I have learned from experience that as their coach I can say certain things to some players and everything is fine, but I can say the same thing to others and they will just break down and cry. To me, if a coach can learn to deal with the feelings they experience, that coach can have a very successful career.

The occasion I want to tell you about was during our preparation for the overall State Basketball Championship tournament two years ago. It was the first time I had taken a team from my school that far. Although I had been in this situation before, it seemed like a whole new experience for me, and it was definitely a new experience for my players.

We had been on a roll the last three weeks on the season. Even though we lost one of our top players to a knee injury in the District tournament, we managed to win the consolation game in the State tournament, which brought us to this opportunity. One of my biggest concerns was how my kids were going to react. Well, after our first team meeting and our first practice, I knew they would handle themselves well. I firmly believe that you need a mixture of different types of kids and personalities on your team to be successful. So, let me tell you about one of the most rewarding experiences I have had with my teams.

During the team meeting, I said first, "Well, you have earned the right to be here; now what are you going to do about it?" I asked each of them to reveal their thoughts to the rest of the team. Two players, who were definitely team leaders, were the first to speak. They didn't say much — they didn't have to. Their "D" type comment was, "Coach, we are going to win." I sensed the desire and drive that these two generated within our team.

The next girl who spoke was just as sweet as she could be. I seldom had to correct her, and even though she did not possess the most ability on the team, she always did her best. She was the most steady player I had. In her "S" way she said, "Coach, don't worry. We have come this far and there is no way we are going to let you, the school, or the team down now."

A few more girls spoke, then one player made this "C" type remark that really made me feel good as their coach: "If we do what you have told us to do, play like we have been coached, and remember what our responsibilities are, we will always have a chance to win."

The last girl to speak had replaced my injured star and I could tell she had been dying to talk. With characteristic "I" insight, she said, "I have listened to everybody share their feelings and everybody has been so serious. Well, I just want everybody to remember this is what it is all about. You work so hard and so long to get this opportunity and now it's time to relax, have some fun and do the best we can. Who knows, if we like it, we might want to do it again. It's time to practice!"

You know you have a special group when kids can get

together, with so many different feelings, and seek one common goal. After the meeting, we had the best practice session of the year. We were focused, we realized our situation, and we all had fun in the attempt. We didn't win the overall State Championship, but we were runner-up. And working together, this had to be one of the greatest experiences of our lives.

The Shocking Band Trip

As band director in a K–12 school for five years, I have seen many things happen. My band averages 60 members each year and our trips are often very exciting. I distinctly remember one trip that proved to be embarrassing to me and to the school.

On one of our busses, several boys were sitting in the back, and one of the boys saw a Highway Patrolman behind them. One boy yelled to Tony (a "D"), "I dare you to 'flip him off'!" Sitting next to Tony was Robbie (an "I") who thought how much fun it would be to join his buddy — and the two of them delivered "half-of-a-peace-sign" gestures out the back window. The officer turned on his siren and lights immediately and pulled the bus over. He boarded the bus and took the two boys off onto the side of the road, where he scolded them extensively.

I was riding on the other bus and had gone on ahead with no knowledge of the incident. The second bus arrived 10 minutes after we reached our destination, and the driver found me and related what had happened. I got on the bus and asked my stepson, who is a big, trustworthy "S," and he told me what had happened. Being a high "D," I went ballistic.

Around the same time, our headmaster arrived. I told her

what had happened and she met with Tony and Robbie and the witnesses. She has a "D with C" type personality style, very logical and orderly, and remained patient and calm throughout the ordeal. She punished the boys through after-school detention and they apologized to the officer. She handled the situation in the best manner it could have been handled. (I know my high "D" personality, and I think I would have *first* killed those two and *then* kicked them out of the band!)

Several students commented on the event. The "I's" thought it was great, an adventure, while the "S's" were totally embarrassed. I'll never forget how angry I was but everything worked out and the episode "lives" as a graphic example to my students. As a result, we have not had any more serious problems on our band trips.

Granny's Green Hair

Grandparents' Day was coming on Friday. The children in Mrs. S's First Grade were making things to decorate the room and give to their visiting grandparents. Mrs. S passed out a coloring page picturing a grandmother and grandfather, and said, "Color these two figures as they really look in real life. If your granddaddy has gray hair, color your picture with gray hair. Do a neat job, and we'll put these up on the wall."

Bryan, a high "D," stared at his paper. Joanie, a fun-loving "I," waved her paper in the air. Missie, a sweet "S," got out her gray crayon. Mattie, a high "C" had already outlined her figures, added a belt to Grandma's dress, and put a hat on Grandpa's head.

The class worked excitedly for about five minutes, until Mattie raised her hand. "Bryan's Grandmother has *green* hair!" she reported. Mrs. S walked over to Bryan's desk and, sure enough, the lady definitely had bright green hair. After furnishing Bryan with another coloring page and further instructions, the coloring began again.

Pretty soon, Joanie began giggling loudly and pointing at Bryan's picture. Mrs. S walked calmly to his desk and was surprised to see *another* green-haired grandmother. She questioned Bryan and he only shrugged his shoulder. Missie was instructed to get him another sheet of paper. Mrs. S gave the directions more sternly this time and went back to her desk.

Joanie leaned over to Bryan and whispered, "Why don't you add a little *orange* this time?"

A hand went up in a short time, and it was revealed that Bryan's granny now had green *and* orange hair. This time, he was asked to come to Mrs. S's desk with his picture and a brown crayon. Reluctantly, Bryan colored over the green and orange hair. Finally, "granny" began to look more like her *real* self.

Form and Function

It is the first day of school in a Sixth Grade classroom. The teacher is instructing the students on how to "head" a piece of notebook paper for a Math assignment. Her formatting instructions are as follows: "Students, on the left side of the top line of your paper, write your first and last names. In the middle of the top line, please list the subject, which is Math. On the right of the top line, please write the date without abbreviating. Then skip a line. On the third line in the middle, please give the page number of the assignment and the numbers of the problems you are working." The teacher shows an example of a correctly-headed paper on an overhead projector while giving these instructions.

These thoughts pass through the minds of four Sixth Graders as they listen to the teacher's instructions.

Johnny: *This takes way too much time! Let's get on with this so I can finish the assignment and start working the problems. Why did the teacher take so long in going over how to head a paper? I know a better way to do this, anyway.*

Ann: *What did she say? I was watching that bird outside the window and didn't hear the instructions. Did the teacher say that those who headed their papers correctly would have extra play time today?*

Mary: *The teacher's instructions are very clear and her voice is pleasant. Also she is giving me enough time to complete her directions. Ann seems to be having some trouble with the instructions. I wonder if she needs my help...*

Jim: *Why do we have to head the paper this way? I guess it must help us to know which paper the teacher wants. I must try to use my very best handwriting and be sure to stay exactly on the top line and in the middle of the third line. I'll try not to make a single mistake on these problems.*

Of course, Johnny is a "D," who wants to get to the point, Ann is an "I," who is more easily distracted, Mary is an "S," who wants to help, and Jim is a "C" who wants to be correct.

Together Everyone Achieves More

This past year in my Sixth Grade Social Studies class, I did a number of different projects in groups and with partners.

We talked about working together both before and after the projects. It is my contention that the ability to work well in a group for a common end is a great need in today's world. I also believe that the various dynamics that go into this are, unfortunately, often learned simply by hard knocks and experience rather than these skills actually being taught and developed.

Many times groups are balanced, leaders chosen by the teacher, and the odds are stacked for a successful outcome. While this is fine for one objective, this is not often the way the real world works. I have enjoyed, and I think my students have benefited a lot from, different groupings and analyzing the results together.

One project that really dealt with personality types (although at the time I did not know it!) was a partner poster project. I assigned two students the task of creating a poster about a South American country. The only directions were that both partners had to work on it, the name of the country had to be on it, and all work had to be done in class, sharing school materials. These simple directions drove some people crazy!

I put two quiet young ladies together. One, I now know, had a lot of "C" characteristics, while the other was an "S." They worked well together, but Charlene ("C") nearly drove me crazy asking questions: "Can we draw a map? Do we print or write in cursive? How many facts need to be on it?" And then, as the poster began to develop: "How does this look? Should I put this here or at the bottom?" She spent as much time at my desk as with Sue, her partner. Each time, my response to her questions was, "Ask your partner, and you two decide together." Asking Sue ("S"), who was agreeable to most anything and simply wanted to get to work, only compounded Charlene's dilemma. The poster did get completed on time and was perfectly done. It was so neat that it looked professional.

Another team turned out to be two boys, one with lots of "I" traits and one who was a steady "S." They had a good social hour each day. It was a really fun project for them. I could tell where they were in the room by where most of the noise came from! The "I" checked out each group, visited and reported back to his "S" partner. He told the "S" what to do and then went roaming again. Only with my reminder that both parties must work on the poster did he alight long enough to color part of the map.

One of the most interesting combinations was two "D" boys. They spent the first three days discussing (arguing!) about what would be shown on the poster. Finally, they drew a line down the middle and each took a side. The continued to bicker about every little thing and how each thing looked. They were both really "bent out of shape" because they had to take turns sharing markers with some of the other students. I would not let them bring their own sets from home. This was just not fair. At the end of the time, these were the only two who did not complete their poster, but both could tell me immediately why and what they would do differently the next time. One thing they had forgotten was to put the name of the country on the poster... but then, whose side was it supposed to go on?

There were 11 other partner groups, each with their own "combinations," problems, and unique final products. It was a great learning week. Most wanted to do it again but some really wanted to pick their own partners the next time. We did do it again with new topics, but again, I picked the partners (new combinations to explore!).

Fight Of The Century

This incident is one I shall not forget for a long time. The students in this Geography Class are varied in ability as well as temperament. I did not know this until I had two students literally *fight* in my classroom — a girl and a boy! You must realize that I am a high "S," have been teaching for 20 years, and had never encountered such behavior until last year.

Supposedly, these two students were good friends. The young "gentleman" was a high "I," and the young "lady" was a high "D." The conflict had begun on Friday during lunch and had continued through the weekend. Little did I know on Monday that my fourth period classroom would become a boxing ring!

In one corner, Phillips, the high "I" just couldn't keep his thoughts and feelings to himself. In the other corner was my high "D," McIntire.

Phillips had stated that McIntire's boyfriend really didn't like her, wanted to break up, and just didn't know how to go about doing this. McIntire snapped back that this was a lie and told Phillips he had no idea what he was talking about.

Realize, also, that I had no idea what was taking place until I looked up and saw McIntire and Phillips nose-to-nose — that's when McIntire gave it her best, a right hook to Phillips' jaw! The *fight* had begun! Phillips grabbed McIntire, pinned her against the wall, and began saying something to her. I couldn't understand it because I was screaming for them to stop. Of course, this didn't work, but my instinct was to stop anything else from happening.

I had made my way to the back of the room and was able to separate them — or at least I thought I had. Their remarks to each other continued, and *Round Two* began.

Trying to talk, or yell, or scream, or any other action to stop this fight was useless. I was holding McIntire by the arm as tightly as possible while Phillips was holding the other arm. Finally, I realized I was in a situation that needed someone bigger and stronger than I to keep these two students from really hurting each other. I left the room just long enough to tell the basketball coach to get me some help. She did, and as I hurried back into the classroom, *Round Three* began.

One of my other young gentlemen came to my rescue. He grabbed Phillips in a "bear hug" and held him, then took him outside the classroom and talked to him until help arrived. Phillips was escorted to the office and he told what had happened.

In the meantime, I was talking with McIntire, trying to make sense out of what had just happened. She told me that no one called her bad names. (Phillips, she said, called her something but I did not see or hear it.) She stood her ground, she said, and no one ran over her! She was asked to go to the office where both students visited with our headmaster.

Before I was called to the office, the other students were still in shock and were wondering *What happened?* I was thinking the same thing.

The young man who helped pull Phillips away from McIntire was definitely an "S." Harris' *helpful* nature was what I needed. On the other hand, Willett, my high "C," was ready with all kinds of questions: "Mrs. K, what was that all about? I'll bet Phillips doesn't bother McIntire anymore. I can't believe this happened. What are you going to say to them? Are you mad at them? Will they be able to take their exams?"

"I don't know," I answered, "but I can tell you I am ready for this day to come to an end."

As I walked to the office for the meeting, I wondered if I could have prevented this from happening? It seems nowadays that people use their fists to solve many of their problems. I am not accustomed to this, and never wish to be. Needless to say, the fight ended with no one seriously hurt — just a few bruises and a sore jaw.

I taught McIntire this year in typing. We still talk about that day in Geography class. I did not have Phillips, but will have him this coming school year. And, by the way, Phillips and McIntire are still friends! They know now that each must make room for the other, that they must have their own space!

Thank you for a wonderful week of instruction and insight. This has been helpful to me, not only as a teacher, but also as a parent with three children, ages 9, 8 and 6.

Van Gogh Cut Off His Ear!

The first year teacher was excited about the school's first-time-ever Parents' Night. She decided her First Graders could make life-size models of themselves in paper, and color them to match what they were wearing. Then they could seat their "twins" at their desks for parents to see as they entered the classroom.

The day came for her students to begin the project. They were divided into teams of two and told to trace around each other's bodies on the paper laid out in the room. They began and each team was working steadily. Suddenly, as the teacher was walking around the room and checking the students' progress, she glanced down and screamed, putting her hands to her mouth! All 22 other children zoomed in and encircled one team.

Much to the teacher's surprise, she realized that "Determined D" had not only had his body traced, but had drawn his male body parts as well. Luckily for the teacher, the recess bell rang just after she screamed, and the children bolted for the door before they realized what had happened. And the teacher had time to compose herself, too, since she had playground duty.

During recess, "Determined D" and his partner, "Imaginative I" got together and decided to make his twin's "accessories" look like a zipper with pockets on each side. They also pulled sweet, helpful "Supportive S" into the project to do the coloring. Of course, after everyone had completed the project, "Correct C" asked, "Why did you draw all over the pockets? The pockets on your pants don't look like that!"

This story really happened. So, here are "Words of Wisdom" for the first year teacher:

1) Never scream in a classroom.

2) Never be shocked or surprised at what might happen!

Dino-Mite

Last year in my Second Grade class, I presented a project for the students to complete in a two-week time span. The project was to create a dinosaur (any one they chose) out of any materials they wanted to use. After I gave all the details for completing the project, I listened as my students discussed their plans with each other.

Douglas said he was going to pick a T-Rex because it was the biggest and meanest of all the dinosaurs. He went on to say it had the biggest teeth and could conquer all!

Buzz said he wanted to do them all! He said he could get his mom to make some homemade dough and maybe some cookies while she's at it, and set up a work spot in the kitchen and eat the cookies while making the dinosaur and play dino-music and just have a good old time!

Maureen had a difficult time deciding which one to choose. When listening to Douglas, she said it sounded great to make T-Rex, but then when she heard the other students talking about their different choices, she wanted to do those. Finally, she decided on a Triceratops but couldn't decide what to make it out of.

Ken was the first one to ask a question: "Why do we need to do this when everyone already knows what they look like? They are *dead!* Is this for a grade?" I replied, "Yes, this is for a grade, and I realize they are dead, but let's not forget they lived millions of years ago." Nick got a library book to make sure every detail was correct.

No Excuse!

As I start, my "S" wants to apologize for the length of this story, my "C" feels there are too many details to be brief — and my low "D" has gotten "fired up" again, because telling this story right is important! My story deals with an "I" type child, a "D" type parent, and me, a "C with S" Physical Education teacher (with a low "D").

The child is in my biggest First Grade Gym Class of 59 students. Fortunately, I have a lady who helps me with them. Some days, this helper is in charge and gives the children instructions. But other days, such as this one, she is like one of the kids, and I have to teach and motivate her.

This class has several very active "I" type children. We have 25 minutes for a class period, and 7 to 10 minutes of the time is spent in quieting the children, getting their attention, giving instructions and organizing them into relay race lines.

"Billy" came to me at the beginning of class to tell me he had sprained his ankle and his mother didn't want him to play. I reminded him that to be excused from P.E., students had to bring a note from a parent (for safety and liability reasons and to remind us at play time not to include them). He didn't have a note, but I saw he had an elastic wrap on his ankle, so I said, "Okay, but go back and sit in your exercise line." Before he left, I asked him how his mother knew it was sprained, and he said he went to the doctor.

I was a little in doubt of the severity of his injury since he didn't limp as he walked back to sit down. I also know that some "I" type children have a flair for the dramatic and that they like attention and sympathy when they are hurt even slightly. My tendency is not to "ooh and goo" over each bump or bruise because I don't have enough time to be one-on-one with a child for long periods. On some days, I would be nursing more than teaching!

I was under a lot of stress that week to get the Field Day relays taught — and adding to the stress, I had to change a relay at the last minute. I had to teach all the classes how to do the "Crab Walk" relay with only two days left before the contests. So I gave instructions and formed the children into relay lines. When 59 First Graders are yelling, screaming, and moving, it is very crazy and preoccupying! I glanced up to see Billy doing the relay and thought *Oh, no, he was to sit out — I forgot to tell him to sit out.*

Unfortunately, he didn't sit out after instructions, so he must not have understood that I wanted him to sit out the races. I hoped it wouldn't hurt him more and figured we wouldn't be doing any more activities. We were still trying to keep the rest of the group moving, so I was distracted and forgot to tell him to get out of line. Because I am not "auditory" sometimes, telling me something doesn't always stick. If he had given me a note, I would have remembered. We went on to another game and my helper and I both forgot about Billy, since he had joined in the relay and had played a little more. He probably "crab-walked" seven yards total and kicked a small rubber ball twice, but he never complained. I guess his excitement took over his discomfort and he wanted to play with the others.

That night, I got a call at home from his mother — she ate my lunch! She was a high "D" (with some "I" traits not far below her "D"). She told me that I had ignored her son and didn't believe him (his words)! I had been insensitive to his injury — *Why didn't I let him sit out?* I told her how he had approached me and what he told me about his injury. I told her our policy required an excuse note. She asked how he was expected to know this, and I explained that we reminded them very often in class and that it was included in the handbook, too. I said I didn't see why I should remind each child of the rule separately, every day.

Then I tried to explain that I made him sit down to make him feel comfortable with his friends, instead of sitting up front where he would be more isolated and uninvolved. He was going to feel left out when play began, so why make it worse? But rather than letting me explain, she continued to "sand blast" me. She was mad and wasn't going to listen to any rational explanations. I usually do well at calming parents, and at the end of a call both of us are happy and the problem is resolved. But this mom wanted to prove that she was right and I was wrong, that she knew how to teach and I did not. I wanted to justify myself, defend and protect my methods and actions for that day.

Finally, she said I wasn't listening to her and I told her she wasn't listening to me! The conversation ended with me apologizing for the *fourth* time, and I told her I would apologize to her son and explain my actions to him (maybe he would understand and listen better than she could!).

The next day, I received a written excuse note that kept him out of physical activities. In turn, I explained to him privately that I didn't get a note the day before, which would have helped me remember to keep him out of play. I apologized for making the mistake of not keeping him out, and how I sometimes forget when I get busy with instructions and organizing all the other boys and girls. I told him I cared about him and wouldn't want to hurt him or his feelings. I explained why I wanted him to sit with his friends instead of sitting up front and feeling lonely. I let him be my special helper during game time.

So, the problem was resolved between teacher and student (my "S" helped, along with his "I"). The issue with his mother was solved at some level because she got the message about sending the note. I don't think I have ever encountered such a strong "D" in my teaching career and it is the only time the "S" side of my own personality was unable to resolve a problem!

Learning And Loving

I have been teaching school for 14 years. Many children come to mind when I think back over those years as a Fourth Grade teacher. The "D's" and "I's" pop up first because they provide such wonderful "war stories."

On particular "D," named Marty, was especially driven to get things done so he could move on to something else (preferably tending to the teacher's business and everyone else's too!). I has a rule that no one could turn in an assignment until I had gone over the directions. As soon as the last word left my mouth, he turned in his papers! The amazing thing was that he always had every answer correct!

The "I" that comes to mind is Micah, whose business was keeping everyone entertained. Sometimes he said the cleverest things at just the right moment to crack everyone up (including me)! I found it hard to discipline him because he was just so likeable!

The "C" type I remember first was Josh, who was highly intelligent and made very good grades. I kept a journal of the questions he asked — many of them had no answer. When I turned the tables on him and let him find out the answers, he usually taught us all something.

The "S" types that come and go take a piece of your heart with them. I have had so many, such as Ginnie, who still needs and wants a hug each time I see her. Children like her can give you that shy smile that seems to say *You were special to me and I remember...*

There is no other profession where you can learn and love so much. I thank you for helping me to better understand myself, so that I can better understand my children.

The Test Of Time

I give my Second Grade students a timed "math facts" test about four times a week. It has 12 problems, and the children are allowed somewhere between one-and-a-half to two-and-a-half minutes to complete the test, depending on the difficulty of the problems. One morning I set the timer and work began on the test.

Davey (an "I") was in the front of the room talking with his neighbor when I said "Start." He watched to see when everyone else started. He gave a "thumbs up" signal to the little girl sitting across the room, and then he started the test about 20 seconds after everyone else. The first six problems were the "doubles" (4+4, 6+6, 8+8, etc.) and Davey breezed through them. He was so excited when he realized he knew the entire first row that it was all he could do to remain in his seat! And guess what? He never even finished that last row of problems!

As soon as the timer went off, Nathan (a "D") wanted to know if he was the first to finish, and he was sure he had all the answers correct. He could not understand why Davey hadn't finished — the problems were so simple!

Andrew (a "C") had looked over the problems and answered all the ones he was sure of first. He wanted to make sure he had all of them correct. Then time ran out before he finished. "Mrs. J," he asked, "are you sure you gave us the full two minutes to complete this test? According to my watch, it looks like we have six seconds left!"

Mrs. J (myself) is the highest "S" in the class! I answered, "Yes, Andrew, I allowed all of you the full two minutes according to my timer but you know, even if you didn't finish, we have another chance tomorrow to work some more problems, and maybe you and Davey will finish the test then. I won't even take grades on this test...." I could see peace settling in!

── Why Teachers Go "Buggy" ──

One of our very first "hands on" projects in Seventh Grade Science is collecting insects. I tell my students about this on the second day of school. Instructions are given to have their collection completed by the second week in October. I instruct them to "do in" their creepy-crawlies with alcohol, place them in a zip-lock bag, and store them in their freezer until it is time to put them in a shoe box and bring them to class. We do all of the classifications in class, so I will know that it is the student's project instead of Mama's. We write the insects' scientific and common names on pieces of paper I have cut into two-inch squares.

Every Wednesday, Thursday, and Friday before the Monday due date, I remind them about the deadline. I also tell them to remind each other any time they see each other over the weekend, as we *must* start on Monday and be through by Thursday. After all of this preparation when *The Day* arrives, most students enter my room with a shoe box under one arm.

Harry, a high "D," almost went into convulsions because he forgot to bring his insects. He was "outdone" with me because I wouldn't let him use the phone to call his mother. (We have a rule at our school that the phone is not used by students for "forgotten things," but only for emergencies.) He sat at the table with Julie, the high "C," and spent *D-Day* pleading with her for the book and looking in it to find insects he remembered as being in his collection. He wrote down the book, page number and scientific name so his whole day wouldn't be wasted. And the end of class, he had his required number classified — and he didn't even have his insects! Of course, I cautioned him to be very sure to check everything the next day — and he did because he was very determined to get an A. Harry was a dominant, demanding, determined, decisive, doer, diligent, and defiant, strong-willed, productive and competitive young man.

Annie, my high "I," was so excited to see everyone's collection and to tell them which insects they had in common with her. She squealed loudly when they found an occasional insect that wasn't completely dead before bring frozen and therefore "returned to life." I quieted her down several times to give instructions and reminded her that she wouldn't get much work done if she walked around. The students enjoy sitting together at two-seat lab tables. Only one reference book is available at each table, and Annie loved looking up her friends' insects in her book. At the end of the first day, her personal classification list was only one or two insects instead of the expected minimum of five. Annie was an interested, imaginative, impressionable, impulsive, illogical, talkative, outgoing, enthusiastic and excited young lady.

Tabitha, a high "S," never got to use the book at her table because she sat next to an "I" who helped everyone else identify insects. I had to make her partner let her use the book. She looked up one insect and then someone asked to borrow her book, and she gave it to them! When all the other students called my name for help or got up from their seats to come to me with their questions, Tabitha sat quietly with her hand up, waiting for me to notice her. Needless to say, she didn't get very far with her identifications on the first day, either. Tabitha was a steady, supportive, stable, sweet, shy, sentimental, calm, easygoing, diplomatic, cooperative, softhearted young lady.

Janet, a high "C," came with her insects in perfect, stacked order. Everything was so neat. She did not use zip-lock bags (too large, wasted space), but had tiny hardware parts bags from her grandfather's John Deere dealership. She had attached stick-on labels and used my magnifying glass to examine each specimen closely. She had a hard time deciding between two similar insect illustrations in the book and had me approve her decision before she wrote it down. She had difficulty finishing because she wanted to check all the reference books to make sure she had chosen the correct scientific name. Janet was a competent, cautious, correct, consistent, conscientious, analytical, perfectionist, orderly, questioning young lady.

I can see all of this so clearly now! I knew at the time that I had to watch out for Tabitha, make Janet not ask me if every answer was correct, keep Annie in her seat and working, and keep Harry from having a nervous breakdown! I didn't know *why* I had to do this, but just that I did.

Finding The Solution

The place is a Seventh Grade Math classroom. The assignment is to put last night's homework problems on the board.

Before the teacher can give any further instructions, Duke (the "D") announces that he wants to do the first problem — and before the teacher can agree, he is already out of his desk and on his way. Because he wrote only the *answers* in his notebook (he sees no reason to copy the *problem),* he takes his book with him. He *copies* the *problem* and writes his *answer.* That's all — why show your work to verify his answer? Why check it when you know it's right? When he finishes, he remains at the board and directs the other students. The teacher asks him to sit down, and with a look of disgust he says, "They're too slow. I was trying to help."

Amber is an "I." When she hears "We're going to the board," she can't wait! It means she will be up in front of the whole class. As she goes, she stumbles over someone's purse, causing everyone to laugh. She writes the equation on the board and answers it correctly. When she is finished, she sees the opportunity to show off her artistic abilities. She decorates her problem with flowers and balloons, and adds *Have A Nice Day* and *Math Is Awesome!* When asked to sit down, she begs the teacher for another problem, which would mean more "art work" and more time in front of her audience.

Benni is an "S" who sits quietly in her desk. When the teacher asks if she would like to go to the board, Benni answers with a sweet, quiet, "Yes, ma'am." She copies the problem exactly as she has been instructed. Each step is carefully written on the board, just as the teacher showed them the day before. As she works, Duke breaks his chalk and asks her if he could use her long piece of chalk. Of course, she gives it to him and then uses a "nub" of chalk to complete her own work. When she is finished, she sits down immediately and continues to check her homework answers with those on the board.

Marilyn is a "C" who works her board problem step-by-step. Halfway through, she turns to the teacher and asks, "I *did* have number *four...?*" Affirmed, she finishes the problem, careful not to leave out a step. Off to the side, she checks her problem two different ways just to be sure. She asks a student in the front row if he has the same answer. When she returns to her seat, she works the problem again to see if she will get the same answer.

Four students, four different personalities, four solutions!

Be A Sport

It had been a normal day at school until two small boys were brought to my office for fighting. The teacher also provided two witnesses to the incident.

As I asked the Second Graders about the problem, Zane (our "D") spoke up first. He declared that the fault was with Jamie — it was *his* game and Jamie just messed it up with his changes! Jamie always wanted to change the game, and since Zane had organized the game, he should make the rules! (It seemed a matter of justice crying out in the streets!)

Jamie (our "I") had a simpler version — he just wanted to have fun! He thought running the bases backwards in a baseball game would make everybody laugh! He also thought "no strike-outs" would cause everyone to like the game more. After all, more people hitting, more runs scored — everyone would like his new rules.

It was easy to see where the problem arose. However, the witnesses still needed to tell what they had seen. Stefan (our "S") was first and was reluctant to take sides. He did not want to make either boy angry with him or get them in trouble. He actually tried to make peace between them before the fight started outside. According to Stefan, the disagreement over the rules moved to harsh words and then to shoving before Mrs. A stopped them. As he concluded his testimony, Stefan reassured both boys that he was sorry and hoped they could all remain friends.

Now it was Corey's turn to report on the problem. He wasn't really sure why he was there. After all, he wasn't playing at all, but sitting near first base trying to finish his spelling words. Zane interrupted boldly: "Corey's here because he knows *everything!*" Corey (our "C") continued by questioning the logic of getting upset over a silly game. He was careful to give exact details about every move and statement made. His primary concern was that this whole incident cost him valuable study time.

In the end, the boys were willing to work things out. Using a suggestion from Stefan, Zane and Jamie were assigned to be teammates for all recess games for one week.

----- Gimme A B-R-E-A-K! -----

I have been a First Grade teacher for more than 20 years. I am also the Cheerleader sponsor, a nonpaying, nerve-racking yet satisfying job that I worked at for over 16 years. Most times, these teenage girls will cause more problems during the 10 or 11 weeks of football season that a First Grade class can conjure up in an entire school year! So, from some of these situations dealing with cheerleaders, I'd like to blossom this tale.

The Varsity Cheerleading Squad always practices four days each week from the opening of school through football season. Each girl reads and signs a "cheerleader contract" at the end of the previous school year when she was elected a cheerleader. Either one or both parents must also sign this contract, making the rules, regulations and demerit system known and understood by all. One of the main rules is that Cheerleading takes priority over all extracurricular activities. Any cheerleader missing two practice sessions during the week must sit out the pep rally that week; should she miss three practices, she must miss both the pep rally and the game. However, during both activities, she must dress in cheerleader attire and sit with the sponsor.

Keri missed two practices in a week. On Monday, she went to her after-school job to work extra hours, in order not to miss any of the upcoming pregame activities. On Tuesday, she missed her second practice, being "the only person" in town who had a car to take Bev to pick up her dress for Friday's activities — oh, did I mention that this "just happened" to be Homecoming Week, one of the biggest high school occasions of the year!?

The squad had 10 members, three of which were Seniors. These three had been cheerleaders since Seventh Grade. All of the girls, including Keri (a Sophomore), had planned and practiced for weeks getting ready for a "Senior Grand Finale Pep Rally." One of the Senior cheerleaders was a "climber" and did all sorts of stunts. For this pep rally, they all planned for her to do a single-based, elevated extension, throw-into-a-basket toss. And who was the base for this stunt? That's right — Keri!

So, here's the question: Do you follow and stick to the rules, making Keri miss the pep rally, leaving the girls without the chance to perform after they had worked so hard? Or do you let them make the decision to postpone her suspension for a week? Here are four of the cheerleaders' ideas:

Donna the "D" — Make her miss the pep rally. She knew the rules before she broke them. Let her find out what her irresponsibility did for the squad. And she should have to miss the game, too!

Irene the "I" — She probably didn't think about Mrs. L or the squad saying anything because they had already practiced everything. It is Homecoming Week, and nobody would want Bev not to get her dress. Maybe she will think ahead next time.

Sonya the "S" — Well, I don't know what Mrs. L should do. I know she doesn't want the Seniors to miss working these stunts into their last Homecoming pep rally, but I'm afraid Keri will be upset and hurt if we vote for her to miss the rally. I'm really just not quite sure what Mrs. L or we should do, but whatever everybody else decides to do is okay with me.

Clarissa the "C" — She should have made her plans to take Bev after practice. She should have asked her boss about making up some extra hours after practice time or on Saturday, since she works at a grocery store. She knew the rules up front. She should not have put Mrs. L or us in this situation. She needs to take her punishment, missing one pep rally and getting two demerits.

Donna took over their discussion — Keri did wrong. She knows it. She knows she's got to suffer the consequences. But we all should not have to suffer because of her. So, if Mrs. L agrees, Keri will cheer at the pep rally and the game this week, but next week, she will practice every day, miss the pep rally and the game *and* get *three* demerits (one for added aggravation!), which will put her under probation for two weeks — if she gets another demerit for any broken rule, she's off the team!

That Old, Gray-Headed...!

Steve McGill was the chairman of the Physical Education Department in a large urban high school. Mr. McGill's organizational skills, management skills, and structure allowed him not only to supervise effectively, but also to teach three classes. Fourth period Physical Education had 28 students on the roll. Among the students was Clay Smitherman. Clay was a carefree, fun loving, talkative individual who did not always follow Mr. McGill's instructions in the explicit fashion that was desired.

On the Monday before Thanksgiving holidays were to begin, Clay in a restless, devious mood — and with some degree of spontaneity — kicked the volleyball being used in a teaching unit onto the top of the gymnasium. Mr. McGill, quite disturbed by Clay's thoughtlessness and lack of self-discipline, reprimanded him firmly. Clay responded under his breath, muttering to himself, "...that old, gray-headed @#&*+#@!!"

Mr. McGill overheard the remark and immediately called to Clay, telling him to "Come here!" Clay refused, seeming to ignore the request. At that point, Mr. McGill did not wait further for Clay to respond, but walked quickly toward him. Upon reaching him, he grabbed him by the shoulders, shook him, and thrust him against the concrete gym wall, telling him he had better get his act together because there was no room for "punks" like him in his class or at the school.

The next morning, Mr. and Mrs. Smitherman, Clay's parents, called Mr. Barton, the high school principal, indicating that they would soon be on their way to the school and wished to see him immediately concerning the inhumane treatment afforded their son by Mr. McGill. Promptly at 8:30, Mr. and Mrs. Smitherman entered Mr. Barton's outer office. Mrs. Smitherman, appearing to be very intense and calculating, marches past the secretary and directly into Mr. Barton's office, with Mr. Smitherman trailing passively. Mrs. Smitherman (a "D") quickly got to the point, explaining how their precious son, Clay, had been physically accosted, manhandled and abused. She then demanded the immediate dismissal of Mr. McGill, stating that he was unfit to have contact with young people and that the school should not have an employee of this type.

Mr. Smitherman (an "S"), who had been quiet to this point, calmly addressed his wife and said, "Honey, let's trust the school to sort this out. I have confidence in them and fully support Mr. Barton. I have faith that there will be a satisfactory resolution of this matter."

Mr. Barton (a "C") then responded in a careful and calm manner, telling them that he must first speak with Mr. McGill to gain a complete understanding of the circumstances. He assured Mr. and Mrs. Smitherman that he would explore and examine the issue with a high degree of seriousness and analytical thought, promising that a spirit of fairness would prevail.

Result: Mr. McGill (a "D") and Clay Smitherman (an "I") met with Mr. Barton to discuss the incident, both separately and together. Proper apologies were exchanged. Clay was disciplined for using profanity and for showing disrespect toward his teacher, Mr. McGill. Mr. McGill was reprimanded privately for his loss of control and physical confrontation with a student.

And yes, with only a touch of gentility added to appease a Southerner's need for civility, this event really did happen!

POSITIVE PERSONALITY PROFILES

This is Dr. Rohm's introductory book on personality styles. Filled with anecdotes, practical examples and motivational techniques for parents, teachers and counselors. Complete explanations for the "Four Behavior Style" theories — and a biblical rationale answering, "Is D-I-S-C Scriptural?" (Appx 200 pp.)

DIFFERENT CHILDREN, DIFFERENT NEEDS

Dr. Rohm collaborated with Charles F. Boyd and David Boehi. This book's theme is "the Art of Adjustable Parenting" — how to discover each child's motivations and tailor your parenting style to meet each child's needs. (Appx 220 pp.)

Price $10.00

ORDERING BY PHONE

Fax a photocopy of this page with the items you want to order circled. Include your name, address, telephone number, credit card number, name on the card, and the expiration date. Or call us directly to give us this information. Fax (770) 509-1484. Or telephone (770) 509-7113. *(All orders please include 10% for shipping. Georgia residents must add 5% sales tax.)*

COMPLETE VIDEO SEMINAR

Dr. Rohm presents "Understanding Yourself and Others" with energy and excitement — this video album is like attending a fun, fast-paced, complete, 3-hour seminar again and again! You receive *two video tapes, six cassette tapes* (the seminar sound track) for use in your car, plus *four FUNbooks* (which Dr. Rohm and the studio audience work with), *one Case Studies* booklet, and *four Self-Scoring Profile Assessments!* Ideal for small group study — additional supplies are available. (VHS only.) *A $95 value!*

Price $79.00

BREAKING THROUGH THE WALLS That Hinder Communication

Dr. Rohm's 3-hour Seminar sound track on audio cassettes! Includes "Introduction to the Model of Human Behavior," the "D," "I," "S," and "C" types, and "Understanding Personality Blends." Great stories supplement the technical material — now includes a pocket-size *Funbook* so you can follow along. (3-tape album.)

Price $20.00

ORDERING BY MAIL

Our mailing address is P.O. Box 28592, Atlanta GA 30358-0592. *Please mail a copy of this form with your check or credit card information.*

WISDOM FOR THE AGES

32 half-hour sessions — a studio-recorded cassette tape study of the Book of Proverbs. Learn how this ancient wisdom is more up-to-date than CNN, packed with success principles we all need to practice. Dr. Rohm's personal favorite. (16 tape album with 68-page *Study Guide*.)

Price **$79.00**

ADULT PERSONALITY PROFILE ASSESSMENT

Complete this *Personality Insights™ Profile Assessment* in just 15 minutes — then read through additional pages of insightful information to discover your own "keys" to success. Includes complete explanations of personality styles and blends, to help you discover why and how to function best in your environment — and how to succeed when working with other styles. Complete with everything you need to understand your style: charts, graphs, explanations, goal-setting, team building motivation and management ideas. (Appx. 56 pp.)

Complete Kit Price ... $15.00
Additional Assessments $10.00

"GET REAL!" Teen Profile Assessment

A very practical tool to help teenagers understand themselves! In addition to the *Get Real!* book, we include a *Self-Scoring Profile Assessment* that can be completed in about 15 minutes and an audio cassette by Dr. Rohm. *Get Real!* shows how to chart your own profile graphs and explains what they mean, and includes occupational suggestions, communication tips, information on learning styles, keys for motivation, and goal-setting ideas. Written in simple language, appropriate for middle school and high school. (Appx 64 pages.)

Complete Kit Price ... $15.00
Additional Assessments $10.00

ALL ABOUT BOTS™ – ALL ABOUT YOU! Child Profile Assessment

Elementary school age children look at stories and "coloring book" pictures of these four robot friends, then choose which of the BOTS™ they feel most and least like. Also has graph explanations for parents, with encouragement tips, learning styles, communication and motivation keys. Gender- and ethnic-neutral, for kindergarten through elementary school. Cassette tape reads stories in a "neutral voice." (Appx 48 pp.)

Complete Kit Price ... $15.00
Additional Assessments $10.00

About the Author

Dr. Robert A. Rohm is the president of Personality Insights, Inc., in Atlanta, GA. He has spoken to audiences in nearly every conceivable situation: schools, businesses, churches, weddings, funerals, children's groups, nursing homes, cruise ships, beaches, hospitals, college campuses, conventions, and others! He has traveled across America, Canada and Europe speaking, teaching and training people how to develop better relationships.

Dr. Rohm has served with Dr. Charles Stanley at First Baptist Church of Atlanta as Minister of Adult Education. Before moving to Atlanta, he was Associate Pastor of First Baptist Church, Dallas, TX, with Senior Pastor Dr. W. A. Criswell. He worked with Zig Ziglar's "Auditorium Class," and over 500 families in the church were under his care. In the field of education, he has been a classroom teacher, school administrator, and supervisor of curriculum development.

Dr. Rohm is a graduate of Dallas Theological Seminary, where he was named to the National Deans' List while earning his Th.M. degree. He received his Ph.D. in Higher Education Administration and Counseling from the University of North Texas. He is a recipient of the National Jaycees' "Outstanding Young Men in America" award, and has been listed in *Who's Who in the South and Southwest*. He is a member of the American Association of Christian Counselors.

Dr. Rohm is also a certified human behavior consultant, teaching parents specific ways to understand and motivate their children, and teaching adults ways to improve communication skills in marriage, work and dating relationships. He has been a keynote speaker at banquets, seminars and workshops across America. His unique blend of humor, stories and illustrations makes him a popular speaker with young and old alike.